STAR CRAFT Magazine
Aleuti Francesca

Primary Sources For The Study Of the UFO Phenomena

SAUCERIAN PUBLISHER
Original Sources in Ufology

ISBN: **978-1-955087-29-2**

2022, Saucerian Publisher

Al rights reserved. No part of this publication maybe reproduced, translate, store in a retrieval system, or transmitted in any form or by any means, electronic, mechanical, photocopying, recording or otherwise, without prior written permision from the publisher.

PROLOGUE

It is generally a good idea to return to the classics in any genre. This also goes for UFO literature. Rereading a book, or reviewing old documents after ten or twenty years is a rewarding experience. You will discover new data and ideas you didn´t notice before. The reason, of course, is that you are, in many ways, not the same person reading the book the second or third time. Hopefully you have advanced in knowledge, experience, intellectual and spiritual discernment. A good starting point is to reread the contactee classics material in order to understand the deeper mystery involved in what happened during that era.

StarCraft was the official publication of Aleuti Francesca's Solar Light Retreat Center. This collection of magazines were recovered from the property of the now defunct Solar Light Center founded by Tele-thought contactee Aleuti Francesca. The Center was around for about forty years and closed in 2008. The Center was established in 1966 in the foothills of southern Oregon, 20 miles outside of Medford. Francesca (known initially as Marianne Francis; she changed her name legally in 1975) became interested in UFOs in 1947 in London, England, where she was born and grew up. In 1954, she moved with her American husband, Kenneth Kellar, to Santa Barbara, California, where she also studied Hatha Yoga with Indra Devi and Baala Krishna. Telepathic and highly sensitive all her life, her sensitivity increased as she and Kenneth Kellar conducted experiments with Light Beam apparatus to contact otherworldly beings. This publication is a primary source of information for any serious devout ufologist. This title has the following issues:

Vol.1(No.3&4) FALL & WINTER 1966; Vol.2 (No.2 & 3)SUMMER/FALL 1967; Vol. 3. SUMMER 1968;Vol.3 FALL/WINTER 1968; Vol 4. (No.1) SPRING 1969; VoL. 4 (No. 2 & 3) SUMMER/FALL 1969; Vol. 4 (No. 4) WINTER 1969; Vol. 5 (No. 1) SPRING 1970; Vol 5 (No. 2 & 3) FALL/WINTER 1970; Vol. 11 (Nos. 1,2,3) SPRING/SUMMER 1977 &1978.

This book is a facsimile reproduction of the original printed text in shades of gray. Because this material is culturally important, we have made it available as part of our commitment to protect, preserve and promote knowledge in the world. This book has been formatted from their original version for publication. **IMPORTANT, although we have attempted to maintain the integrity of the issues accurately, the present reproduction could have missing and blurred pages poor pictures due to the age of the original scanned copy.** Because this material is culturally important, we have made it available as part of our commitment to protect, preserve and promote knowledge in the world.

Editor
Saucerian Publisher

STARCRAFT

SOLAR LIGHT CENTER

Vol. 1, No. 3&4　　　　　　　　　　　　　　　　FALL & WINTER 1966

STARCRAFT ------------ FALL & WINTER, 1966

CONTENTS

EDITORIAL	3
THE PHOENIX - A Poem by Marianne Francis	6
LIGHT AND DARKNESS - By Orlon, a Space Brother	7
FLYING SAUCERS BECOME RESPECTABLE - By K. M. Kellar	10
CHANGES IN CELLULAR STRUCTURE - By ARKON, a Space Brother	11
SCIENCE DEPARTMENT: ETHERIC MATTER — By K. M. Kellar	13
THE GROUNDING OF LIGHT CONSCIOUSNESS - By CLYTRON	17
WORLD CHANGES - By Rev. Lysa Waring	19
THE COMING UPHEAVALS - By ZENTLA of Mars	21
CLEANSING OF SELF - By Marianne Francis	23
CENTER NEWS & TRAVELS - By Marianne Francis	26
ANNOUNCEMENTS & PUBLICATIONS	28

* * * * * * * * * * *

COMPLIMENTARY COPIES

It is our policy to give out Complimentary copies of STARCRAFT to interested newcomers. If you have friends who you believe might be interested, please send us their names and addresses and we will send them their first copy free. If they should then wish to continue receiving STARCRAFT, they should subscribe.

* * * * * * * * * * *

Director & Editor - - - - - - - - - Marianne Francis, Dr.Sp.Sc.
Science Director & Business Manager - - Kenneth M. Kellar, B.A.

Published quarterly by SOLAR LIGHT CENTER
a non-profit corporation.

COPYRIGHT reserved - - - - - Write for permission to reprint.

ADDRESS ALL CORRESPONDENCE TO:
SOLAR LIGHT CENTER
Rt. 2, Box 572-J   (formerly Box 572-C)
Central Point, Ore.
97501

EDITORIAL - by Marianne Francis, Dr.Sp.Sc.

As I write this editorial we stand on the verge of 1967, perhaps a year of great destiny to the peoples of this planet. Why do I believe this? I believe it because so many signs point to a winding-up of affairs as they now stand in our so-called civilization. The signs are everywhere apparent in the crumbling, rotting structure of society, the wholesale decline in ethical values, the escalation of war, and a desperate search for escape mechanisms which affects the masses. We also have the fact that China is close to producing an H-Bomb and has every intention of using it. History also teaches that every scientific method of wholesale murder has sooner or later been used in war by all who possessed it.

Yet, there are other signs also, signs of a very different kind: signs which point to another alternative, not so much a winding-up as a new beginning.

Now it has seldom if ever been true that the mass mind has been in the fore-front of progress. A few individuals, gifted with vision, have always seen beyond their time and their civilization. These men and women have guided the thoughts and destinies of peoples from time immemorial. Now, however, the time has come, not for a cultural, political, or social revolution, but for a revolutionary process pertaining to Mankind's soul or spiritual nature. The world's ills will NOT be cured by a new political system, a new religion, or a different standard of morality.

Centuries of wars, upheavals, revolutions, changing politics, and changing religions have not brought Peace or Harmony to planet Earth. One ill has merely been exchanged for another and the sickness has become deeper and more nearly terminal. Why is this so? There is a saying: "First things first". Man is first and foremost an eternal soul or being created of God. His ills spring from a disregard of this salient fact. Until Man, as a species, seeks understanding of his eternal nature or intrinsic being, how may he understand his world or his brother? Least of all, how may he understand Cosmic Law?

The religions of this planet which attempt to deal with Man and his God, are largely ineffective because they interpret God through the eyes of mortal Man. Jealous gods, racial gods, tribal gods, gods to whom prayers are addressed in battles, gods of fertility, gods of vengence: These gods abound throughout history. Yes, you may say: But these gods are not the God of our present religions. - - - Are they not? Have not Christians prayed to their god for defeat of the enemy? Have not Catholics a jealous god who disapproves of all other religions as false? Does not one narrow Christian sect deplore all others and feel that their religion alone is a gateway to heaven?? Allah favors Holy Wars waged in his name and Muslims think of Christians as infidels! Christians take part in pograms against Jews and Negros in the South are often treated as second class citizens by the orthodox Christians, and so on ad infinitum!

Avatars and beings of Light, whose inspired, divine revelations brought some measure of Truth to Earth, are crucified in one form or another. After a time, though their names are revered, a corrupt priesthood usurps their truths, waters down their divine inspirations and renders the adherents priest-dependent. Salvation is achieved b propitiating not a Diety, but a dogma. The masses throughout the planet pay lip service to their religions, but their deeds are those of primitive Man!

Annihilation of all civilization stands high on the list of possibilities as we enter 1967! The outlook for humanity would, indeed, be grim were it not for those other signs which I mentioned at the beginning of this article. What are these other signs? They are signs of a revolutionary process taking place in spiritual affairs:- a restoration or establishment of a DIRECT LINK WITH THE DIVINE!

First of these signs has been the coming of the Space People in their Starcraft (UFO's) travelling from other planets and from other dimensions to help Earth at its time of Change.

Second has been the tremendous increase in mystical experiences which individuals are having throughout the world. Spiritual and psychic healing (including etheric surgery) are also manifesting in various countries and, incidentally, will present the entrenched medical monopolies with their greatest challenge to date!

Third, Science itself, in its more recent developments, is extending its observations into unseen realms and into areas beyond the fiv known senses of Man.

Perhaps most important of all, a being of Light, a "Christlike archetypal figure" is being seen in seemingly solid form in different parts of the world. This being first appeared to an ordinary real estate agent Richard Grave, in England in 1961. The being pointed to a picture of angels announcing the coming of Christ and said: "I AM HE", apparently meaning "I am Christ". The story of this apparition is told in the Monographs listed below.* This being has apeared to Richard Grave more than six thousand times. It is, however the content of what "He" has said which concerns us now:

"Time is of little consequence now. As night approaches, day may never come. Instead, the Light will pour forth from my Father House."

"Have no thought towards the seeming confusion of others around you. - ALL is in MY Universal Plan.--- No man can know the DAY or HOUR when MY great Universal Revelation will be enacted, however,

(*The Weeping Angel Prediction, and Prophecy '67, from)
(FUTURA PRESS, 5949 Gregory Ave., Los Angeles, Cal.90038)

I must repeat: BY THE FIRST SECOND OF THE FIRST HOUR OF CHRISTMAS MORNING 1967, I WILL HAVE REVEALED BYSELF TO THE UNIVERSE through the medium of NUCLEAR EVOLUTION. This is my PLAN which is absolute."

"A major world conflict will herald the last stage of the Universal Progress. In the meantime, general world conditions will show evidence of a leading up to the introduction of a NUCLEAR DEVICE that will bring about the final human level episode. The major conflict I speak of will be between nations and it will be MOST SUDDEN!"

"A human press-button device will be used and, simultaneously with the pressing of the button, INSTEAD OF DISASTER, the UNIVERSAL REVELATION WILL OCCUR!"

* * * * * * * * * * * *

These are a few of the statements made by this being. If "He" is who "He" appears to be, these statements are the key to the major events of this year of 1967. Before 12 months elapse, we will know the answer!

In recent communications received from the "Brothers" here at the Solar Light Center, mention has frequently been made of the "division of the wheat from the chaff". We are told that time has speeded up, the Law of Cause and Effect has speeded up. Indications are given of a "New Heaven and a New Earth" fast approaching. All this correlates with the possibility of a sudden termination of third-dimensional existence as we know it. Please note: I said AS WE KNOW IT, not a termination of life, not a prophecy of doom, but a CHANGE of dimension!

I have given considerable thought to the wealth of material reaching us from many sources, all indicating one imminent CHANGE or another. Some sources of prophecy indicate wide-spread devastation of the Earth. Other sources speak only of a Golden Age of Light. Again it would seem that provision has been made for a wide-spread evacuation of the planet by Spacecraft, thus removing many of the Earth's peoples to huge floating cities in Space and, perhaps, to neighboring planets.

It would appear that these sources all conflict as to what the future will bring. But, in reality, do they conflict? After much thought and analysis I have come to the following conclusions:

Extreme emphasis is being given by the "Brothers" to the urgent need for attunement with highest levels of consciousness: the god-within, or god-consciousness. They state that the level of consciousness will determine where the individual will stand at the time of the greater CHANGE. Does this not suggest that all prophecies for the future could be true and these individuals are merely tuning in to differing levels or dimensions of planet Earth in the years ahead. If there is to be a change through the medium of NUCLEAR EVOLUTION, could it not be that a 4th-dimensional Earth will become the abiding place of the evolved peoples? At this same time, the slowly decaying shell of the 3rd-dimensional Earth, torn by war and cataclysms, possibly bombarded by asteroids such as Icarus, would continue to house all peoples weighed down with negativity and gross materialism. For, "As ye sow (in consciousness and deed) so shall ye reap."

Where does this leave the people removed by Spacecraft? Perhaps, they will be returned to the New Earth after a period of re-conditioning. It may be that, freed of the 3rd-dimensional Earth's gravitational field, these people will rise rapidly in consciousness and become of 4th-etheric composition in their cellular structure. Whereas, prior to the Change, this one last effort was beyond them, yet intrinsically they were "wheat" and not "chaff".

However, it is obvious that the Spacecraft will evacuate only those people who are aspiring to Light consciousness, people who feel Love and not hate, people who know within themselves at some level of being that God is in His heaven and all is right with the world! - appearances not-withstanding!

Is 1967 the Year of Destiny? I feel that it may be, however, whether it be 1967, 1968, or even as late as 1975, TIME, it would seem, IS SHORT, and changes are upon us!

As I have said before, you are _not_ pawns in a game played on a giant chessboard; _you are gods in essence_! Each individual upon this planet has freewill to decide his or her own destiny. No matter how negative a person is, they can, if they wish, change their reality to that of a CREATIVE BEING OF LIGHT. The choice is an individual one and "_no man maketh thy choice for thee_"!

WHAT WILL BE YOUR CHOICE IN 1967 ???

* * * * * * * * * * * * * * * *

THE PHOENIX

O golden bird of strange antiquity,
Famed embodiment of the Sun god Ra:
Arisen from ash to immortality,
Consumed and yet reborn of sacred fire.
The poet, (a phoenix bird of rarer hue)
Consumed in suffering for a blinded Earth,
In time must burn away all dross by truth
Arising from a point of inner worth.
Ah! must this world of Men a phoenix prove,
Destroying by a freely chosen act;
Reducing all to ashes for some proof
Of immortality, beyond the actors?
Shall Man yet heed the poets truer vision?
The phoenix bird alighted not by fission.

— by Marianne Francis

LIGHT and DARKNESS

(A lecture given by **Orlon**, A Space Brother)

Our brothers, our sisters of the Earth planet, I, Orlon, speaking from the craft as spokesman for many, greet you upon this occasion with much joy at your presence here tonight. We are your brothers, your sisters from Space, as you term it, though Space is a much varied term which covers many, many forms of existence and many areas of unlimited activity in far-reaching realms of the One Creator's creation.

I speak with you on the subject of Light and Darkness, for upon the Earth planet you concern yourselves much with that which is of Light, or that which is of Darkness or what you may term evil, negative. Whatever the terminology you employ, it is that which is the opposite of Light. Since Light encompasses all of the Creator's Universe, that which you of the Earth planet term Dark or Darkness, is merely the shadow or reflection from that which is Light. Since the shadow is not the reality, you have that which is illusion. If the people of Earth would recognize that those things which they term evil, negative, of darkness, are merely an illusion or shadow, imperfectly perceived, of the reality which is Light, then would they understand that all things are of the Creator's creation. Only as illusion is held in the mind of the beholder do they shield themselves from a greater Light than that which they then know or understand.

The soul of man upon the planet Earth is a strange being; it is a being contorted through many incarnations, through many facets of existence upon a planet, itself that is vibrating on a frequency of dissonance or disharmony with the Cosmic Laws of the All-Knowing One. It is a planet which has wandered far in consciousness of its life-wave from the Light of the One Creator, due to the many, many centuries and ages and ages, and ages, of misdirected energies; For the energy which is Light, directed through the consciousness of all life, manifests in many aspects. It manifests in accord with Cosmic Laws, with the laws of the All-Knowing One, the One Creator, when it manifests in accord with that which is <u>creative</u> and not destructive. But when a life-wave upon a planet plunges deep into illusion and delusion and strays far from understanding of laws Cosmic in nature and perceives only with Earthman consciousness, then much which you call darkness, evil, decadence, results. This again is only what you term the other side of the coin. This again is the reverse of Light and the shadows thrown by its brilliance. It is a shadow; it is not reality! Again I make this point.

My channel, and perhaps many of you, perceive at this time upon your world, much which partakes of the nature of decadence, of degeneracy, and we ourselves would be the last to deny this as a fact. But in the delusion and illusion of this degeneracy, this decadence, this twisting and warping of that which was originally creative in intent is the pattern of these days and these times. Through this period all beings must pass, and through this period and <u>beyond</u> it exists the One Light, the

One Creative Intent of the All-Knowing One. The children of Planet Earth, being also His children, must return in consciousness to the Laws which are Cosmic to bring about realization of the Oneness and the Unity of all Creation.

Darkness and Light: It is said by many of your Ancients that one cannot exist without the other, for does not Light always throw a shadow? At least in your understanding, on your planet and in your world, does not Light always throw a shadow? Yet, in realms and existence beyond the understanding of 3rd dimensional Earthman, lies that which is an effulgent Light, a Light, which perceived, throws no shadows, a Light within which dwells only creative energy: A Light within which many of those whom you think of as "beings from other planets" exist and perform their existence in accord with things Cosmic.

Earthman has lived too long with a concept of Darkness and Light, of evil and good, and sees only one as an alternative to the other. May we suggest that it is not necessary to have two extreme opposites: That at the point of contact with the One Reality of all Light, at the point of conscious attunement with the Creator, there ceases to be two opposing opposites. There ceases to be anything but ONE unified undiverse, Creative Energy!

Earthman would do well to acquaint himself with the concept of unity within his own being, within his existence, within his world; for truly if he does not, his world will break into many pieces, for only the consciousness of the inhabitants of any planet bring about the conditions upon that planet. We have stated this truth many times to your peoples, but it seems that it is a concept too simple for them to grasp in its entirety. Only in the unified oneness of all creation of the One Being may that be found which presents itself as Light.

Among your warring "tribes", though they may be called nations, for they act as the tribes of many centuries of primitive beings, warring with each other in thought, warring with each other in action, warring with each other in all that in which they should be unified. In these many diverse activities upon your planet, is that which breeds destruction, is that which brings about the many wars which have spread throughout your surface and torn your planet with discords, with turmoil and with turbulence. Mankind upon planet Earth has reached an impasse and if he cannot bring himself into conscious attunement with the Laws of One Creator, with the unified consciousness of All Being, then he must, indeed, vanish from the surface of the planet. Thus comes about that which your Holy Works speak of as "the division of the sheep and the goats", and thus comes about the division of all peoples as to whether they align themselves with things of the One Light or with those things which are of destruction. It is a choice all must reach upon your Planet at this time, at this period, at this ending of an Age. It is a choice that your peoples face now, and we who observe you from other planets, who are your brothers in Light, who seek at all times to reach you with love, with understanding, with so much that we would give from the depths of our beings, freely unto your peoples, we say to you: This choice, our brothers, is for you to make upon your planet. If you align yourselves with the things which are of reality, of Cosmic Law, of the One Creator, you align yourselves with creative ongoing intent. If you align yourselves with that which is destructive, you become at one with a tearing down process which is taking place even at this time. Only you, our brothers, our sisters of Earth, can make the choice. We observe you; we come in our craft; we speak to you; we give to you of our knowledge in many ways, through many channels, but we cannot force upon you that which is not our right to force. We can only wait for those who perceive the One Light, who perceive that they are as one with us, to reach upwards to us in consciousness. We meet with these, we speak with these, we reach in consciousness to these. Our hearts and our minds are as one and there is no division, for division is part of the lack of unity within Earthman's consciousness.

A choice is fast approaching upon your planet: A choice which must be made by all mankind; and soon our craft will be seen in many numbers in your skies in various localities, for the <u>time of manifestation</u> of our presence with you is fast approaching! This time we know that many upon your surface stand with us to bring about an Age which you term one of Golden Light, an Age, shall we say, of Reason, at last, in Earthman's consciousness: An Age wherein he ceases to tear himself or his brother into small pieces and scatter the remains upon the surface of his small planet; wherein he ceases to tear the bowels of the earth and thunder through the skies, and pollute the atmosphere. It will be an Age where Reason and Understanding shall take precedence, and Mankind shall seek not in humility, not in arrogance, but in LOVE, to <u>understand</u>, to widen his horizons, to know of those things which lie beyond his present knowledge.

Light and Darkness: there is only **Light!** There is only the One Creative effulgent Flame. For there is no choice other than life or death, eternal, immortal, undying life on planets, on systems, in galaxies farflung unto the furthest reaches of a universe of a myriad, myriad stars!

My speech with you has, I find, filled me with much emotion upon this occasion, for I perceive many things in my vantage point above your planet which your peoples do not yet perceive. Changes come fast now and also is the coming of the Great Avatar upon your planet in the Light of the New Age. Before His coming, many changes shall have taken place upon your surface and we ourselves will mingle freely with you. Therefore, do not cut yourselves off from us, or think of us as far distant, for not only do we sail your skies, but we reach you at many times of your day, of your night, when your thoughts turn to us in search of a greater oneness. Only as you shut us out, in consciousness, are we absent from you, for truly, my brothers, we are one. In the Light of Our Radiant One, I leave you, yet am with you in consciousness.

                Adonai vassu, my brothers.

(By Telethought transmission, 29 May 66. Channel: Marianne Francis)

FLYING SAUCERS BECOME RESPECTABLE

The Air Force announced in October, 1966, that a "thorough investigation of UFO's will be conducted at the University of Colorado by a team of distinguished scientists, headed by Dr. Edward Condon".

With this announcement, Flying Saucers became "respectable". After a long delay of over 18 years, finally UFO's (Flying Saucers) have been accepted as a serious subject for scientific investigation!

The results of this official announcement have been far-reaching. Much publicity is now being given to Saucers in the news, over radio and Television programs, and even in the more respectable magazines. Suddenly UFO's are being featured seriously in an unprecedented manner. Authoritative articles have recently appeared in such magazines as Look, Reader's Digest, Life, Science, Saturday Evening Post, and Science and Mechanics. A series of articles on UFO's by Lloyd Mallan is currently being featured in Science & Mechanics magazine. These articles include a "Complete Directory of UFO's" and feature the "Unexplained Sightings from Project Bluebook".

A very interesting article entitled "Are Flying Saucers Real" by Dr. J. Allen Hynek is featured in the December 17th, 1966, issue of Saturday Evening Post. Dr. Hynek, now chairman of Northwestern University's Astronomy Department, has spent nearly two decades studying UFO reports, serving as consultant on UFO's for the Air Force. Of the 10,147 UFO reports studied under Project Bluebook, Dr. Hynek is especially interested in the 600 odd cases still unidentified! He suggested that UFO's deserved a much closer study than was being given them, especially in view of the fact that sightings occur throughout the planet.

With a scientists conservative analysis, Dr. Hynek puts forth four possible explanations of UFO including the possibility that Saucers may actually be Spacecraft from other planets. He also appears quite open--minded on this possibility, in view of the tremendous scientific and technological progress Earth-man has made in the past 100 years. The conquest of Space appears just around the corner for us, hence it is entirely feasible that much older civilizations on other planets would already have achieved Space travel centuries ago.

Various UFO phenomena have been reported long before the advent of the airplane. In fact, centuries ago strange aeriel phenomena occurred, indicating the likelihood that Space Visitors were visiting Earth then. Perhaps they have been observing our civilization since its infancy! Who knows! In the book, "Flying Saucers have Landed" by D. Leslie and Adamski, numerous sightings are recorded which took place in the 17th and 18th centuries and earlier. Some researchers claim that the WHEELS seen by Ezekiel and the STAR of Bethlehem were Spacecraft!

A more thorough investigation of UFO's is highly desirable, especially since sightings have increased in the past three years. We are delighted that steps have been taken to put UFO research on a sound basis with scientific authorities.

CHANGES IN CELLULAR STRUCTURE

(A Lecture by ARKON, a Space Brother)

I come from 4th density level to speak, to communicate certain instruction to you at this time, relevant to the changes which are taking place in the structure of cellular matter or tissue. My information relates to the previous data given on density level transition. My name is Arkon, and I communicate while the opportunity presents itself to me.

All cellular rates of vibration are in process of change: change meaning the raising or lowering of vibration. The individual alone is the determining factor as to which alternative takes place. Consciousness determines the raising or lowering of vibratory rate in cellular structure. Not only are the cells of humans on planet Earth being affected, but all cellular tissue is likewise affected, not in the individualized sense as humans, by consciousness, but by the incoming vibratory fields of energies flowing in from the Cosmos now.

A conflicting picture presents itself due to the fact that radiation fallout upon your planet has reached a degree capable of affecting most forms of life from the organic to the inorganic. Only those capable of individualized consciousness, such as the human life-wave on planet Earth, are capable of determining their own destiny at this time, as all other effects will be of an arbitrary nature.

The incoming Cosmic Energies are bringing increased vibratory fields of Light. The radiation is bringing destruction of cellular structures through a slowly degenerative process. A point has been reached wherein a more rapid change will manifest itself on the planet in accord with other detailed information given through this and many other qualified channels. You are already, I understand, acquainted with the nature of the change which is taking place. I merely come upon this occasion to add my voice and my authority to those who have spoken. I would, in the nature of friendly advice, give to you the facts as they now stand:

ALL NEGATIVE THOUGHT, ALL NEGATIVE ACTIONS WILL PRESENT NEGATIVE EFFECTS IN A MUCH SHORTER PERIOD OF TIME THAN HAS BEEN PREVIOUSLY OBSERVED. In other words, the Law of CAUSE and EFFECT has been speeded up!!!

Therefore, it would be suggested by ourselves that those who prepare themselves for transition into 4th density level of being make an unprecedented effort to attune, AT ALL TIMES, with GOD-CONSCIOUS CREATIVE ENDEAVOR.

The Law which I speak of, the Law of CAUSE and EFFECT, is absolute, and its effects to be observed will be, to say the very least, startling, in the near future on your planet!!

The Law which I speak of, the Law of CAUSE and EFFECT, is absolute, and its effects to be observed will be, to say the very least, startling, in the near future on your planet!!!

Each determines his own destiny. The <u>time of the GREAT CHALLENGE is upon you</u>! The time for discarding of falsities of Earth origin is upon you. Attunement with intuitive levels of being leads directly to the god-within, to creative levels of consciousness releasing energies here-to-fore untapped! The utilizing of these energies for the purpose of transition to higher levels of being will be a necessity, for much degeneration will occur upon the 3rd density level of planet Earth, as the changes come rapidly upon it.

Consider the words of your Holy Works which speak of a New Heaven and a New Earth. Consider the sloughing off of a shell of your own self as comparable with the sloughing off of the shell of the planet itself. Reduced levels of choice only present themselves to individuals who choose a negative approach. The god-consciousness offers an ever-expanding freeing of the innate being of all children of Light

My purpose is merely to acquaint you, and though I find I should not have used the word "instructions" but rather "friendly advice", I couch my advice in terms of utmost seriousness, for time is short and children of the Earth planet who do not have the advantage we have of viewing things from an off-the-planet perspective are apt to overestimate the period of time which remains in which to make choices.

We speak of <u>children</u> of Earth, for truly, my brothers, my sisters, all are as children in the eyes of a civilization many, many thousands of years in advance of the present one on this planet. This is not meant in any sense to be derogatory but is said with love and understanding.

I, Arkon, relate these things to you that you may know and may not underestimate the decisions which each upon this planet must make

May Light from the One Source be with you.

* * * * * * * * *

Channel: Marianne Francis

(Received through Telethought transmission, 3 January, 1967)

* * * * * * * * * *

"ENERGY FOLLOWS WHERE CONSCIOUSNESS IS DIRECTED. DO NOT DIRECT CONSCIOUSNESS INTO LEVELS WHERE ENERGY IS ABSORBED BY NEGATIVE INTELLIGENCES, WORKING UNDER THEIR OWN DIRECTIVES FOR THEIR OWN PURPOSES."

-- "The Brothers"

SCIENCE DEPARTMENT   K.M.Kellar, BA, Editor

ETHERIC MATTER

The nature of etheric matter (or "luminiferous ether") has long been a subject of interest and debate. The famous Michelson-Morley experiment of several decades ago seemed to prove the absence of any "ether drift" and, hence, of ether itself. Subsequently, little work in this field has been done by physicist in recent years although many questions are still unresolved. However, much research on the nature of chemical and etheric matter has been done by Occult investigators over a forty year period which sheds much light on it.

Two famous Theosophists, Annie Besant and C.W. Leadbeater, compiled an interesting book entitled "Occult Chemistry" first published in 1908 and revised in 1951. This book contains the results of a comprehensive study of the basic structure of the chemical elements and of etheric matter as observed by clairvoyant means. This research technique has a great advantage over that used in Modern Physics in that matter can be observed <u>directly</u> and in its <u>normal state</u>. In fact, certain isotopes were discovered and put on record long before they were re-discovered by orthodox scientists.

The techniques of Modern Physics are in sharp contrast to those of clairvoyant researchers in that great stresses are put upon the matter under observation. High-velocity particle accelerators or atom smashers are used to bombard atoms with protons, deuterons, or with heavier particles. The trajectories of the resulting products are then studied to obtain <u>indirectly</u> the nature of the target material. Huge expensive and elaborate equipment is required, in fact, today the magnitude of a country's scientific achievement is gauged by the size and number of its particle accelerators!

In contrast, the trained clairvoyant needs no scientific equipment. He uses a rare form of projected sense-perception resulting from the development of the <u>third eye</u> (Ajna Chakra) which is associated with the pineal gland. This special ability enables the observer to magnify sub-atomic particles so they can be observed at an optimum size and in full detail. Also, by exerting will power, the particles can be observed in slow motion or in the rest state. This latter ability makes this technique especially valuable as a tool. It is unfortunate that such techniques are not yet accepted as valid by orthodox science even though accurate predictions of isotopes were made prior to their discovery by scientists!

The research conducted by Besant and Leadbeater covered all the known chemical elements in addition to the <u>etheric atoms</u>. Many of the chemical <u>compounds</u> were also studied and the nature of valence bonds which hold atoms together in their compounds. The nature of the Periodic Table is clarified by showing the similarities within each of the <u>eight families</u> of Chemical Elements. The increasing in complexity as the atoms of greater mass are studied is clearly shown.

In this introductory article, only a brief description of etheric type atoms will be presented. First, consider the nature of etheric planes associated with Earth. The Etheric World or "plane" is really a sphere being concentric with planet Earth and consisting of four types of etheric matter. The first Ether (E1) is the lightest and least complex. The second, third and fourth Ethers are of increasing density and complexity. The so-called Physical Plane is made up of solids, liquids, and gases together with these four Ethers.

The "ultimate physical atom", both of etheric and physical matter, is a complex heart-shaped vortex of force, the ANU, which is illustrated in Figure 1.

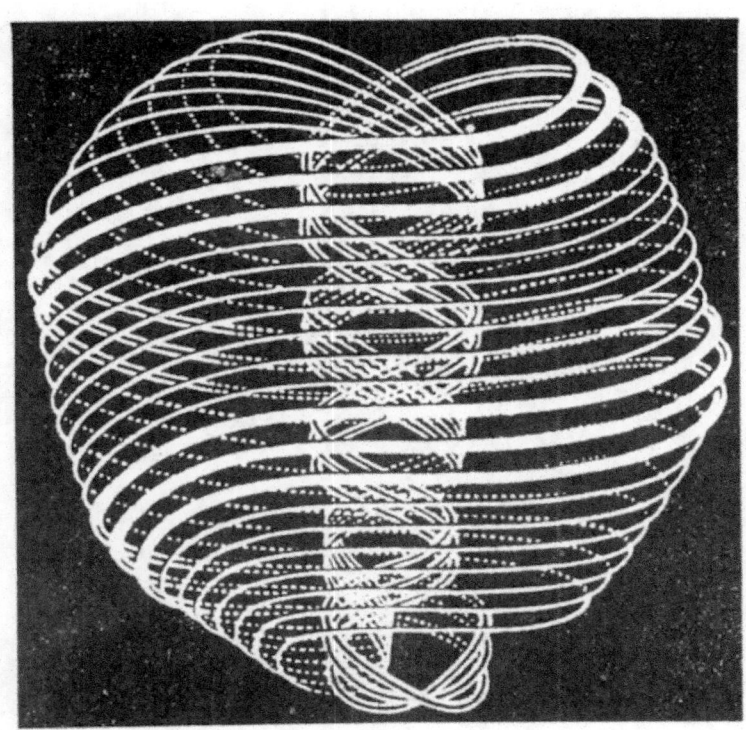

Figure 1

POSITIVE ANU

The ten spiral "Whorls" or loops rotate rapidly. Three whorls are thicker than the other seven. Negative ANU spiral in the reverse direction.

These basic building blocks, the ANU, are of two types: positive or negative depending upon their direction of rotation. The heart-shape of the ANU is formed by the force field surrounding the <u>ten spiral loops</u> or "<u>whorls</u>" which make up the ANU. In the positive type ANU as shown (fig. 1), force pours in from fourth-dimensional space (Astral Plane) passing through the ANU and into the physical world of three dimensions. In negative ANU the force is reversed, passing from physical plane to the fourth dimensional state. The Whorls form intermeshed spirals each having $2\frac{1}{2}$ turns on the outer part of the Anu going from top to bottom, then spiralling upward through the center to its origin. Three of the ten Whorls are thicker and brighter than the other seven.

The seven finer whorls respond to various stimuli from heat, light, sound, etc. and have their own resonant frequency, corresponding to the seven colors in the spectrum. The ten whorls themselves are made up of a series of finer spirals — spirals within spirals to the 7th order. The ANU has three distinct types of motion normally:

(1) The ANU spins on its axis like a top.

(2) The axis of rotation precesses like a wobbling top.

(3) The ANU pulses like a heart, regularly expanding and contracting.

Positive and Negative ANU have their whorls spiralling in opposite directions. The Negative type is a mirror image of the Positive Anu. The normal motions of ANU are incessant, even when other motions are superimposed on them from external forces such as electric, magnetic, light, heat, sound, and the like.

The simplest type of Etheric Matter, that of the first sub-plane (E1) is composed of single ANU of both types, positive and negative.

The next most complex Etheric matter is that on the E2 sub-plane. These atoms are composed of from two to seven ANU in varying configurations. Types of E2 atoms are illustrated in Figure 2.

TYPES OF E2 MATTER

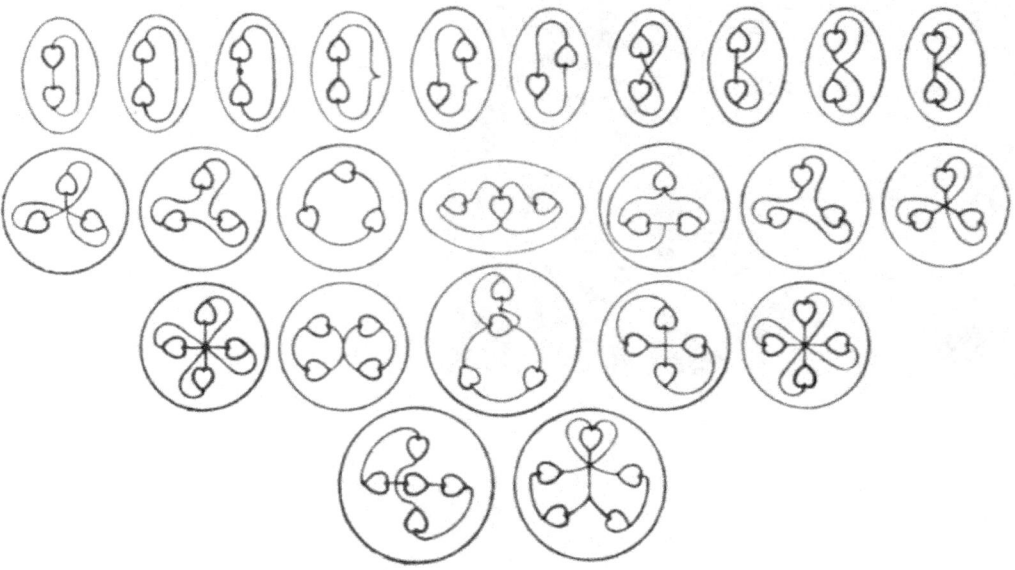

Figure 2

The ANU are represented by a simple heart-shape in the illustration with the force flow represented by connecting lines. The atoms are shown in a two-dimensional plane, however, a three-dimensional view would be more representative.

The force usually flows through the ANU by entering at the top of the ANU and out at the bottom. In some cases, however, the force is observed to "well up" outside the ANU and this is represented by a dot in the illustrations. Polarity of ANU is indicated generally by the direction in which the heart-shaped ANU points. Positive ANU are often shown pointing outward while negative types point inward.

The polarity of the resulting "etheric molecule" depends upon the net positive or negative surplus and on the internal arrangement of ANU. The force field surrounding the rotating groups of ANU creates an apparent cell-wall which is spherical or ovoid as indicated. This cell-wall presumably is made up of finer "Astral" matter.

Matter of the third Etheric sub-plane (E3) is similar to that of the E2 level. In some cases the atoms have the same number of ANU, however, E3 Atoms usually have the larger number of ANU. The clairvoyant observer can distinguish these types by the manner in which they break up. The E2 type always breaks up into single ANU while the E3 atoms break into groups of two or more ANU. E3 atoms are shown in Figure 3.

TYPES OF E3 MATTER

Figure 3

There is much yet to be learned about the internal forces in atoms. The chemical elements as well as Etheric matter all are built up from various combinations of ANU, the number being proportional to the Atomic Weight. Deuterium, for example, has twice the ANU as in Hydrogen and exactly twice the Atomic Weight. Carbon (At.Wt.12) has 12 X 18 or 216 ANU. The nature and composition of the heavier atoms will be discussed in a future article. Occult observation of the chemical elements has verified the Periodic Table and thrown much light on valence bonds between atoms combined in molecules. (To be continued).

THE GROUNDING OF LIGHT CONSCIOUSNESS

(A Lecture by CLYTRON)

I am Clytron and would speak with thee this night upon the grounding of Light Consciousness. Consider well, children of the Light planet, wherein Light dwells that ye may ground the energies of Light in consciousness. For if these energies be not grounded in consciousness, then how may they be grounded through the elements of your bodies? And if they be not grounded through the elements of your bodies, then surely are ye NOT filled with Light essence.

In consciousness of being Light alone is perceived, the Light which is eternally the reality of the inner being, of the inmost one, the Creator. Many children of the Earth plane stumble in darkness, for they know not wherein Light is found nor its resting place within their beings. Yet, if that Light be but grounded in consciousness, it must surely enfill the being to every limit or extension of that being's bodies. And this Light so stayed, so grounded, illuminates and transcends and transmutes not only that being, but all beings who come within the compass of that radiance. Light is energy, highest energy, highest frequency, highest potential. Light is outpouring of energy from realms beyond the physical, from levels of consciousness, directed by beings of pure Light, of pure transcendence, of pure illumination.

It is long since I spoke with thee and my travels have taken me far into the leagues of Space, into the worlds of other Kingdoms, of other realms of the One Creator. Now have I returned unto this one who is my channel for this planet, to speak to thee of the transcendent illuminating qualities of Light projections and of the need to attune with these that ye also may transcend, may become illuminated beings.

As the darkness gathers around thee, as the confusions deepen, as the beings upon this planet Earth rush in confusions of their own making, so must ye rise above these things, so must ye become lighter in composition, in structure of body through illumination of mind, of soul, of being. As those who are heavier in density sink into the morass of Men's makings, into the mud and the mire and the darkness of the planet's decadence, so must ye RISE, so must ye become at one with all things of higher consciousness, in order to make the change, when that change comes in frequency. For changes, children of Earth, cannot longer be delayed: CHANGE MUST COME. Changes stand at the threshold of a new dawn and a New Age of Light. Change is the order of the day and beings who aspire to Light and consciousness of other realms must attune, must rise, must loose themselves from the chains of old concepts of decay and death.

Thy teachers have been many upon this planet but few have there been who have listened and even thy teachers have taught of things of which they had small knowledge save those who came from highest realms. of Light. The confusions of Men's minds are confusions brought into being by the battle for supremacy among victors who seek for mortal spoils, for mortal glories, for things of little value. The teachers who came from Light realms spoke of Love and of Light, of simplicity of being, of the pathways of service and sought not glories nor crowns for their heads, nor baubles of no accounting.

When the battle for Men's minds is over, it will be found that they who sought from the heart and from the soul found Truth and a pathway of Light. They who sought through purely mental processes or through sensation-seeking or through the elements of physical matter alone, found pathways of delusion and, like lost children, strayed from the Source of All Being.

In thy seekings, oh children of the Earth Planet, seek in simplicity, seek from the heart, seek with love, with compassion, with service to thy brothers and sisters upon the path, and higher beings will reach thee in consciousness and will become at one with thy minds. But seek not with the mind alone, for it has been said: "The mind betrays the real". The mind of Man upon this planet has dwelt in strange byways and has followed pursuits through many long centuries which have led into confusion of the inner being. Through centuries and through lives, many have followed these pathways of falsehood and illusion. Many have sought in rigid doctrines and dogmas for those things which are of the Creator and have found them not, for they are not so found. They are found in simplicity, in Love, in Light, and in Service.

The teachers upon planet Earth who have taught of those things which were false shall most surely reap of these falsehoods, shall most surely walk pathways of their own confusions. Yet, the children of Light shall walk past these things into a new dawn, into a new Light, into a new understanding of the oneness of all created life, of the harmony of being, and of the interlacing of all things created of God in all the Galaxies of Light, unto the furthest reaches of the Universe of One Creator. Even so shall they find! Even so walk thee, children of the Earth planet, that thy strivings be not in vain, that thy heart-aches pass from thee, that thy oneness become apparent and those things for which thou hast longed, for which thou has prayed for which thou hast long, long endured, shall become as one with thee, in the days of Light before thee.

I speak with thee now in consciousness of thy beings, even as long before I spoke with a gathering upon the Earth planet, knowing of turmoil and tumult upon the outer scene, yet spoke we thus in a small inner chamber, yet spoke we thus of peace and tranquility.

Let your inner Lights so shine that they become as a lantern unto the children of Men that they illumine the pathways of darkness which many walk. Let your Love so endure that it reaches forth and soothes the hurts of many. Let your service so manifest before thee that many are attracted to the pathway which ye walk in serenity and purpose of being.

I, who call myself Clytron upon the Earth planet, have spoken and will speak with thee again and our meeting of minds shall be e'en closer than before.

May Light shine upon thy pathways. May the galaxies of God spread before thee and may thy beings hold consciousness only of Light.

(By Telethought transmission, 11 Oct. 66. Channel: Marianne Francis)

* * * * * * * *

WORLD CHANGES   by Rev. Lysa Waring

Our Earth seems to be in a constant state of upheaval in these latter times as predicted so thoroughly by many sources including the Bible. It is not only the bible student or psychic who is aware of this. Our news sources have evidentally been given the word to play down the upheavals, just as they do with UFO reports. The items listed below represent only just a few of the actual happenings that I have been able to glean from one or two sources. It reminds me of an old adage that is so true, that if you see a mouse in your house, you know that you have seven that you cannot see. For each one of the reports, it might be staggering to know how many are unreported, or reported only once and then hushed up. The one thing we are sure of, however, is that our world is in turmoil, the handwriting is on the wall. Is it possible that all these world predictions might be true?

RECENT UPHEAVALS

8/12 Mt. Awu near Jakarta, Celebes erupts, kills 28; 40,000 homeless.
8/15 Earthquake in New Delhi, India.
8/18 Earthquake in Varto, Turkey; thousands killed.
8/28 Earthquake in Tokyo, Japan.
8/30 Earthquakes (Richter 6) in Anchorage, Alaska.
9/2 Earthquake (Richter 5) in Anchorage, Alaska.
9/2 Earth tremor, thousands flee, 80 miles SW of Athens, Greece.
9/4 Earthquake, Bagota, Columbia. Damage and loss of life.
9/11 Mt. Etna in Sicili erupts.
9/12 Earthquake (Richter 6.5) Nevada & Calif. Roads blocked, power off.
9/26 Violent storm in Japan. 193 people killed.
9/29 Hurricane in Cuba. Thousands killed and thousands homeless.
10/1 Floods and Cyclones in Pakistan. 5000 killed.
10/2 Intense earthquake in Trinidad, Colorado.
10/2 Violent storm, East Coast USA, 19 dead. Worst in recent history.
10/3 Floods in Italy kill and make thousands homeless.
10/4 Earthquake in Italy.
10/5 Hurricane in Yucatan.
10/7 Earthquake in Anchorage, Alaska.
10/8 Earthquake, (Richter 3.7) in Tokyo, Japan.
10/8 Klyuckevsky erupts in E. Russia; blows 2000' hole in side.
10/9 Floods in Algeria; 82 killed.
10/12 Torrential rains in Central Japan; 2 killed, 8 injured.
10/13 Earthquake in Central Japan.
10/15 Floods in Saigon; 70,000 made homeless.
10/15 Tornado in Iowa; 6 killed, hundreds homeless.
10/17 Earthquake in Peru; 120 killed, 3000 homeless; tidal waves.

May Light shine upon thy pathways. May the galaxies of God spread before thee and may thy beings hold consciousness only of Light.

(By Telethought transmission, 11 Oct. 66. Channel: Marianne Francis)

* * * * * * * * *

WORLD CHANGES   by Rev. Lysa Waring

Our Earth seems to be in a constant state of upheaval in these latter times as predicted so thoroughly by many sources including the Bible. It is not only the bible student or psychic who is aware of this. Our news sources have evidently been given the word to play down the upheavals, just as they do with UFO reports. The items listed below represent only just a few of the actual happenings that I have been able to glean from one or two sources. It reminds me of an old adage that is so true, that if you see a mouse in your house, you know that you have seven that you cannot see. For each one of the reports, it might be staggering to know how many are unreported, or reported only once and then hushed up. The one thing we are sure of, however, is that our world is in turmoil, the handwriting is on the wall. Is it possible that all these world predictions might be true?

RECENT UPHEAVALS

8/12 Mt.Awu near Jakarta, Celebes erupts, kills 28; 40,000 homeless.
8/15 Earthquake in New Delhi, India.
8/18 Earthquake in Varto, Turkey; thousands killed.
8/28 Earthquake in Tokyo, Japan.
8/30 Earthquakes (Richter 6) in Anchorage, Alaska.
9/2 Earthquake (Richter 5) in Anchorage, Alaska.
9/2 Earth tremor, thousands flee, 80 miles SW of Athens, Greece.
9/4 Earthquake, Bagota, Columbia. Damage and loss of life.
9/11 Mt. Etna in Sicili erupts.
9/12 Earthquake (Richter 6.5) Nevada & Calif. Roads blocked, power off.
9/26 Violent storm in Japan. 193 people killed.
9/29 Hurricane in Cuba. Thousands killed and thousands homeless.
10/1 Floods and Cyclones in Pakistan. 5000 killed.
10/2 Intense earthquake in Trinidad, Colorado.
10/2 Violent storm, East Coast USA, 19 dead. Worst in recent history.
10/3 Floods in Italy kill and make thousands homeless.
10/4 Earthquake in Italy.
10/5 Hurricane in Yucatan.
10/7 Earthquake in Anchorage, Alaska.
10/8 Earthquake, (Richter 3.7) in Tokyo, Japan.
10/8 Klyuckevsky erupts in E. Russia; blows 2000' hole in side.
10/9 Floods in Algeria; 82 killed.
10/12 Torrential rains in Central Japan; 2 killed, 8 injured.
10/13 Earthquake in Central Japan.
10/15 Floods in Saigon; 70,000 made homeless.
10/15 Tornado in Iowa; 6 killed, hundreds homeless.
10/17 Earthquake in Peru; 120 killed, 3000 homeless; tidal waves.

10/18 Two earth tremors in Bogata, Columbia.
10/20 Tornado in Seaside, Oregon.
10/21 Earthquake in Belen, Argentina.
10/21 Mudslides in Wales bury homes and school with 254 children.
10/26 Worst floods in history hit Brittany, Redon, France.
10/30 Rain in Japan carries 300 times normal radioactivity.
10/31 Earthquake in Seattle and Japan.
11/5 Blizzards in the Alps; 11 dead, thousands isolated.
11/5 Floods in Panama; 8 dead, hundreds homeless.
11/10 Rolling earth tremor in Argentina.
11/11 Tornado in Alabama.
11/17 More flooding and gales in Italy.
11/23 Monsoons flood Malaya.
11/23 Floods in Rome, Italy.
11/23 Severe Earthquake in Denver, Colorado.
11/24 Smog in New York reaches emergency danger level.
11/25 Bubonic (black) plague reported spreading thru Asia.
11/25 Avalanches and floods in N. Italy.
11/26 Cholera epidemic in Canton, China.
11/28 Snow paralyses Great Lakes area.
12/1 Freezing weather in Mexico City.
12/1 Hurricane winds in Valdez, Alaska.
12/2 Severe blizzards in New York.
12/2 More flooding in Italy.
12/4 Earthquake in Tashkent, USSR.
12/7 Floods and wind damage in Central and Southern Calif.
12/10 Earthquake (Richter 6/5) in Central America.
12/10 Flooding continues in Calif.
12/13 Flooding in Oregon and Washington states.
12/14 Strong earthquake in Tokyo (3.5 on scale of 7).
12/16 Earthquake (Richter 5) in Anchorage, Alaska.
12/18 Floods in Vancouver Island, B.C.
12/19 Floods in Scotland.
12/21 Plague in Himalayan village, India; 8 people die.
12/23 Earthquake (Richter 6.5) in New Guina.
12/24 Earth tremor, Everette, Wash.
12/26 Earthquake north of Tokyo, Japan.
12/28 Earthquake (9) in Chili.
12/29 Earthquake (5) in Chili.
12/29 Blizzards & floods in Eastern US.
12/31 Earthquakes in New Hebrides Islands (7.7 on scale of 12).

It would be very well at this time to note the striking coincidence (?) of time between the recent atomic tests and the tremendous reaction of earthquakes around the world. In the last weeks of December, there were three atomic tests, followed almost immediately by remarkable earthquake activity around the world!! It should be obvious to mankind what the consequences will be if he continues to experiment with these forces and perhaps loose them in total war!!! "There shall be wars and rumors of war...and EARTHQUAKES in divers places".

THE COMING UPHEAVALS

(A Communication received from ZENTLA, a Space Brother)

I bring my salutations to each one of you. I speak with you from my craft stationed many miles above the surface of your planet. I speak as what you would term Commander of a Fleet of Spacecraft, activated at this time for the specific purpose of cleansing your planetary confines of certain of the radiation released by the most recent tests conducted in your atmosphere.

My peoples are well aware of the dangers which planet Earth is incurring at this period of time by the releasing of further radiation fallout within the atmosphere of your planet. Shortly, due to these radiations, the structural changes deep within the core of your planet are about to rip asunder certain strata layers beneath your Pacific ocean. This in turn will bring about an eruption of volcanic lava to the surface of these areas and will affect many, many of your peoples!

Our mission at this time is to render whatever aid is possible and to nullify as far as is now possible the effects of these conditions within your atmosphere and within the bowels of your planet. I speak with you upon this occasion in order to communicate these facts for your attention and to verify certain material reaching you from other sources. It is with much sadness in my heart that I observe the further insanities of your peoples at this period of time.

Little time now remains in which we may nullify effects arising from causes. When this time elapses, as it must shortly do, we can only then stand by to assist your people who carry within their souls or beings the Light of Our Radiant One and who are what may be termed the innocent Children of Light.

Consider the time which remains as time to be used in preparing yourselves for the coming natural upheavals, insofar as these may be termed natural. The processes of inner attunement of that which some of you have felt impelled to take, the cleansing of the body of toxins, are necessary steps for each one to undertake in this time which remains. The purpose is that as the body, as the consciousness, are freed of the toxins, of the dross of long endured conditions, the cellular tissue may more easily vibrate to an increased frequency and may rise and become lightened, and you may become more one-pointed in attunement with the incoming energies of the Cosmos.

Relatively little time now remains before vast changes must occur upon the planet Earth: <u>changes so vast as to stagger the imagination</u> of peoples who walk the streets of your planet. I, who speak with you, speak at this time through direct transmission of mental attunement, or telethought transmission. I will upon future occasions communicate with you. My craft are of Martian origin. I, myself, am from that planet, and my name may be known to you as Zentla. My attunement with this instrument is new, but I find my purpose well served.

A withdrawal from all contaminating influences is well advised, since now comes the division of the wheat from the chaff on the planet Earth. We use the words of your biblical prophecies. Avoidance of contaminating elements of thought, spirit, of body, of emotion, are a necessary part of the cleansing of each individual for the coming greater cleansing of a planetary nature. Unity of action, dispersion of Light and Love energies are integral parts of the patterns of coming events. Re-distribution of Light lines throughout the planet and the cutting away of weak or semi-effective conductors is also part of the plan.

Fortify yourselves, my brothers, my sisters of the Earth planet, with the thought that a New Age surely dawns in your dispensation, a new being. My peoples observe closely until the time appointed for their coming in the now near future.

I disconnect from transmission. May the One Light be yours.
Zentla, Commander of Fleet, Martian Craft 12.

* * * * * * * * * * * * * * *

Channel: Marianne Francis

(Received by Telethought transmission, 5 Nov. 66)

PROJECTS & DONATIONS

As we stand at the threshold of 1967, we would like to draw your attention to the need for expanding the facilities here at the Center. Several projects listed in the Spring issue have been accomplished:

(1) An electric pump has kindly been donated by generous friends.
(2) A '61 Oldsmobile replaced the old '57 Dodge Wagon.
(3) A strategically placed lot adjoining the Center is being purchased.
(4) Two much-needed windows were installed at the Center.

PROJECTS REMAINING TO BE DONE

1. Science lab/workshop to be constructed and equipped.

2. Studio/Retreat needed (so Miss Francis may work undisturbed).

3. Garage with storage space and extra bedroom to be built.

4. A deep well is needed to supply extra water during the dry season.

5. An acre lot between Workshop and Center remains to be purchased.

6. Utility center with rest rooms, shower, etc. needed for guests.

7. The electric typewriter (now on rental) should be purchased.

8. Filing and storage equipment is needed for books, magazines, etc.

9. Further landscaping and garden work is planned for the Spring.

10. The Center needs interior decorating, new paint, furniture, etc.

CLEANSING OF SELF

PART I   —Marianne Francis, Dr.Sp.Sc.

Reference is made in the Zentla transmission of the need for an individual cleansing for all who aspire to attunement with the coming greater cleansing of planetary nature. Material reaching us here from the Brothers now frequently stresses this inner cleansing as a necessity for the children of Light.

The levels of being at which all function are Spirit, Mind, Emotions and Body. In this first article I will take one aspect, the material or body aspect: the physical, 3rd-dimensional part of Man.

This body should be the <u>temple</u> of the living soul. Any student of the related fields of Flying Saucers, Metaphysics, Esotericism, Mysticism, etc. who regards the body as "unclean", of "little importance", or "sin-ridden" is <u>sick</u> and unbalanced in their own being. Know that a balanced being, an advanced being on other planets, regards his "body" with respect, treats it with intelligence, feeds it with life-giving elements, clothes it in grace and charm, and uses it with love to express the outpourings of his soul.

To some degree or another, nearly all beings on this planet are unbalanced or unwise in their treatment of the physical vehicle (body) they possess. Consequently, toxic matter is accumulated, bad habits are built in over the years, improper fuel is supplied to the body, and impure air is breathed. Toxins are retained, causing disease or lack of ease within the tissues.

Despite adequate sources of natural food, many individuals in the world are under-nourished. Millions suffer from mineral and vitamin deficiencies in countries where an over-abundance of "foodless" food is found on super-market shelves.

Contaminating elements of thought and emotion: fear, greed, malice, hatred, jealousy, resentment, self-pity, and pettiness, create additional toxins in an improperly nourished body and the result is constant ill health. Individuals who think of themselves as so spiritual and speak frequently of spiritual realities, yet suffer from one physical ill after another, are out of balance with their High Self and with the Laws of Nature.

Conversely, one who seeks understanding of their inner being must at some time or other undergo a period of cleansing wherein they eliminate from their system accumulated toxins, drugs, and waste matter. During this time a strong reaction will occur and much mucus and toxin will be expelled from the system, quite possibly in the form of heavy colds, flu, and even pneumonia or other fevers.

Natural methods of healing teach that drugs cure nothing, they merely suppress a condition which later erupts in another form with another label attached to it. A healthy body, housing a healthy mind and emotions, resists disease and is NATURALLY IMMUNE to all germs.

We are now in a period when a healthy body, a healthy strong mind, and loving, normal emotions, directed by a rapidly evolving soul, will be a necessity. Thus, starting in this article, the physical methods of cleansing will be given. Six methods of CLEANSING recommended by this writer are listed below:

(1) Fasting (water only).

(2) Cleansing with juices (vegetable & fruit).

(3) Hatha Yoga: Cleansing Breath.

(4) Vegetarian diet: raw foods, natural organic foods.

(5) Changed diet: wholesome, life-giving foods, not food-less food.

(6) Water cleansing: steam and sauna baths, enemas, colonics, and cleansing of pores by friction rubs, air and sun baths.

1. FASTING

The first method is by far the quickest for wholesale cleansing and may be undertaken with a minimum of effort: only <u>will power</u> is required A fast not exceeding 36 hours is suggested as a preliminary. If a long er fast is then attempted within a matter of weeks, qualified advice should be sought. If many drugs, medicines, or harmful chemicals (ingested from sprayed fruits and vegetables) have been accumulated in the body over a period of years (including penicillin, anti-biotics, cortizone, codeine, and even aspirin, etc.) do NOT, I repeat, do NOT undertake a long fast until you have attempted many short ones and cleansed your system with pure foods, juices and water. The reason for this is that drugs and chemicals are stored in the tissues <u>for years</u> and are only released into the system again when fasting. Too many of these released at <u>one time</u> can literally poison an individual.

Extra rest, peaceful conditions and a good supply of distilled water with a little lemon juice and honey added are the other ingredients needed for a successful fast. Expect the release of toxins from the system, possible headaches or dizziness, and heaviness of body, -- but remember: IT IS ALL WORTH WHILE. A new you, a more youthful, vital YOU will emerge, a <u>New Age YOU</u>!

2. CLEANSING WITH JUICES

This method may be undertaken instead of the distilled water fast. Otherwise, juices may be taken every day between meals as a start towards cleansing and rebuilding the body. Juices spoken of here are not the canned or frozen type but preferably should be freshly extracted with a juicer wherever possible. Bottled grape, apple, or other juices which contain no added sugar or preservatives are permissable but less effective.

3. HATHA YOGA

This is a system of very ancient exercises (Asanas) coupled with a specific type of breathing -- Yoga breathing. These Asanas assist in removing impurities and obstructions from the body. Further to this, the Asanas "tend to normalise the functions of the entire organism, to regulate the involuntary processes of respiration, circulation, digestion, elimination, metabolism, etc., and to affect the working of all the glands and organs as well as the nervous system and the mind".

Yoga influences Man physically, mentally, morally, and spiritually. A sense of awakening is experienced and all the capacities are heightened. In Yoga, "relaxation is taught as an art, breathing as a science, and mental control of the body as a means of harmonizing body, mind, and spirit". Yogis regard the human body as a temple of the Living Spirit and believe it should be brought to the highest stage of perfection. A freeing of the higher self or soul is thus achieved. The higher aspects of Man are then able to become at one with inflowing Cosmic energies.

(To be continued in the next issue)

NOTE: All persons wishing to undertake fasts, juice cleansing, or a drastic change of diet are advised to check with a qualified Naturopath, Chiropractor, Herbalist, or known expert on fasting. Cases vary greatly with individuals and no responsibility can be accepted by the Solar Light Center for individuals who do not seek qualified help in this New Age field of Health.

REFERENCES:

THE MIRACLE OF FASTING, - Paul C. Bragg, PhT
RATIONAL FASTING, - Prof. A. Ehret
RAW VEGETABLE JUICES, - N. W. Walker, Dr.Sc.
FOREVER YOUNG, FOREVER HEALTHY, - Indra Devi

* * * * * * * * * * * * * * * * * * *

SHAKLEE PRODUCTS

BASIC H is a concentrated ORGANIC CLEANSER for use in washing dishes, floors, automobiles, and general household cleaning. It does not harm the skin and is non-poisonous. It is especially good for washing DDT and other harmful sprays from salad vegetables. This is only one of the health products developed by Dr. Shaklee who produces a full line of Vitamins and health cosmetics. Please write us for information if you are interested as we are authorized distributors of Shaklee Products.

CENTER NEWS AND TRAVELS

As the heat of Summer ended, Sept. brought a lecture trip to Portland. A new group has formed there headed by Lars and Patricia Wiklund. The first meeting held at Park Haviland Hotel was attended by over 270 people. Don Hamrick, late of Syndyne Corp. shared the speaker's platform with me. Further monthly meetings are being planned by this group.

October came in cool and delightful. By mid-month I was on my way to Santa Cruz to rendezvous with Dr. Dan Fry and wife, Tahalita. From there we continued on to Los Angeles where I was the guest of Gabriel and Helen Green while I lectured for the Aetherius Society. A quick trip to Santa Barbara followed where I lectured for an Understanding Unit. Many dear friends were visited, if only briefly, and with a nostalgic feeling I drove south again to rejoin Dr. & Mrs. Fry. Back in L.A. I attended a press conference for Dr. Fry from which I learned a great deal.

Giant Rock was next on our itinerary and my hostess, Teska, of White Star Center. The pure air of the desert brought a cleansing from the smoke and smog of L.A. resulting in my having a streaming nose and chills. Hence I registered little at the Convention except that most of the regular speakers whom I had heard were there. Teska and I sat and talked into the wee small hours, since that was the only time to converse undisturbed!

By the second day of the Convention, Dr. Fry's schedule demanded we leave at 3:00 p.m. for Santa Cruz where we stayed at Mrs. Fry's delightful little house on a river bank. This proved restful and I undertook a short fast to offset the effects of the smoke and smog allergy. I had planned a lazy week preceeding the Berkeley Convention, however, it became a round of unexpected visits. Two days were spent with charming Roland and Muriel West in their beautiful home and, of course, talking Flying Saucers with them and their very delightful daughter. It was a lovely interlude filled with memories of warm people, a beautiful house and garden which, I must admit, I would have loved to transport to this Center!

The end of the week found me in San Mateo looking for my dear Elaine and the City of Light headquarters. After some searching, I found Elaine and husband Lile with son Danny and ended up spending all that evening and night with them. (Sleeping bags for unexpected guests are a must in the movement

The Berkeley Understanding Convention that last weekend in October was extremely well-attended. It featured such delightful and well-informed speakers as Gayne Myers, Dr. Paul Wherritt, Gina Cerminara, Riley Craab, Dr. Dan Fry, Gabriel Green, Nelson Decker, and others. It was unfortunate, however that the organizer, Mrs. Angela Kilsby, found it impossible to allot some free lecture time to visiting lecturers present including Maj. Wayne Aho and Lenora Croft, Wayne Guthrie, Hal Wilcox, Rev. Violet Gilbert and myself. A further mistake in policy was the witholding of <u>empty</u> book tables from the above mentioned lecturers. However, we understand this policy was not attributable to Understanding but only the organizer's personal preferences. This flaw in an otherwise well-organized Convention is not expected to be repeated in the 1967 Convention.

A brief but enjoyable visit with Gayne and Roberta Myers of the Solar Cross group, at their home in Auburn, followed the Convention. Greatly respected and sought after as a speaker, Gayne is a dear and warm friend to me linked from other lives and other lands in our search for Truth. Having analysed the current trends, speakers and experiences since last we met, we parted, well satisfied that "something big is imminent", and we are but waiting in the wings for the curtain call on the real show of the ages!

Returning to the Center the next day, I found mountains of magazines (or so it seemed) ready to address and mail out: the delayed Summer issue of STARCRAFT! Kenneth was patiently stapling and addressing some 800 copies and continued to re-address many which came back due to many change of address. My goodness, how some of you move about in one year! Please be sure we have your new address if you should move.

The Fall rains set in during November in earnest, and little could be accomplished outside. Two interesting guest sessions were channelled and several new people visited us here at the Center. Thanksgiving week-end saw us driving up to Major Aho's social get-together at Eatonville, Wash. with Ray and Jeanne Greaves. Our hosts in nearby Puyallup were, as always, our dear friends and New Age workers, Peg and John Carpenter. Much fellowship was shared that weekend, and Wayne Aho and I discovered we had received identical information from "upstairs" some few weeks previously.

Back once more at the Center, life moved along though now the pace had slowed considerably. A weekly class in Hatha Yoga was taught in cooperation with Karen Phillips at the local YMCA. This proved quite enjoyable and another series is planned for January to March. Our students discovered that a sore throat really can be cured with a Yoga asana and it's cheaper that way, too!

Christmas came and went quietly except for the project of getting out the Newsletter. The mountain continued to be wet, but unlike last year, was not covered with two feet of snow for several weeks! This news would not be complete without mentioning the invaluable services of Margaret Hadley, my volunteer part-time secretary. Those who have received neatly typed letters may thank Margaret, too! Many thanks also go to Lysa Waring, another valuable volunteer helper here on the mountain. With her help all the back-log of channelled material has been typed and the tape recordings transcribed.

Donations made by some generous individuals have allowed both Kenneth Kellar and myself to stay on the mountain this winter and work full-time on Center projects. Otherwise, it would have been difficult to get the magazine published. Further donations will be needed from others who can contribute in order to carry out the work projects listed elsewhere. Also, volunteer work is needed and will be greatly appreciated. How about a "working vacation" in fresh mountain air during the Spring? It is beautiful here then, green and cool with masses of wildflowers. If you can come, please be sure to let us know well in advance.

As I close, it is January and still little snow. We are hoping for an early Spring so that the landscaping, building and painting projects can be resumed.

- Marianne Francis

* * * * * * * * * * * * * * * * *

"FROM WORLDS AFAR"

The record (LLP) of MOLLIE THOMPSON's Space Ballads is now available in the USA. Send $3.98 to: Michigan ESP Research Associates, P.O. Box 28, East Lansing, Mich. 48823. Please mention STARCRAFT.

ANNOUNCEMENTS

<u>GUEST CHANNELLING SESSIONS</u>: At the SOLAR LIGHT CENTER.

The next two Guest Sessions will be held at 8:00 p.m. on Saturday March 25th and April 29th, 1966. Normally they are on the last Saturday of each month unless Miss Francis is on a lecture tour then. Interested New Age students are invited to attend.

<u>LECTURE PUBLICATIONS</u>:

We expect to have the following two lectures printed in the next few weeks: "Men from Space and Prophecies of Earth Changes" and "Starcraft Contact". We ask that those who have requested or ordered these lectures please be patient yet a little while.

HAVE YOU CHANGED ADDRESS?

If you have moved, please let us know your new address as soon as possible, as third class mail is not forwarded. Some STARCRAFT have been returned and mailed out again two or three times. Since postage rates are threatening to rise, we find this an increasing expense, especially as we send out many complimentary copies of each issue.

PUBLICATIONS OF THE SOLAR LIGHT CENTER

Lectures by Marianne Francis:
 God-Man or Animal-Man - - - 1.00   The New Dimension & New Age- - 1.00*
 Men from Space & Prophecies 1.00* Starcraft Contact - - - - - - 1.00*
        (*These items are not yet reprinted.)

<u>Channelled material</u> from Space Brothers:
 From Whence Cometh the Light - .30   Lords of the Sirius Sun - - - .20
 Message from Galactic Tribunal .30   Know Ye Are Gods - Clytron) - .30
 Love Suffers Much & is Kind- - .30   False Images and Truth - - - .30
 Children of the Sanctuaries- - .20   New Age Vistas - - - - - - - .30
 The Light Wanderers - - - - - .20   Love is an Energy - - - - - - .20
 Clytron Speaks of Light - - - .20

<u>Aleuti Scripts</u> (Superconscious communication) - - - - - - - - - - - .60

<u>SUBSCRIPTION & ORDER FORM</u>   (Please print)

Name_____ Address_____

_____   _____

Please enter my subscription to STARCRAFT magazine for _____ issues.
  (Subscription: $2.00 per year or 4 issues; 50¢ per single issue.)
Please send publications listed. Enclosed please find $_____

This <u>double</u> issue: $1.00 each.   Enclosed please find $_____
Send to: SOLAR LIGHT CENTER, Rt.2, Box 572-J, Central Point, Ore.97501

STARCRAFT

Vol.2, No. 2 & 3   SOLAR LIGHT CENTER   SUMMER/FALL 1967

STARCRAFT

CONTENTS - SUMMER & FALL - 1967

EDITORIAL: COUNTDOWN-THREE MONTHS?	3
A PROPHECY FOR 1967	7
STABILIZATION MEASURES - ORLON	8
SIMULTANEOUS UFO SIGHTINGS	10
SCIENCE DEPT. - OCCULT CHEMISTRY AND THE PERIODIC TABLE	11
A CHALLENGE TO YOUNG PEOPLE - by SPACE BROTHERS	15
A SPACE MAN'S PRAYER - KORTON of MARS	17
CRAFT XY7 CONTACT	18
PROPHECY OF THE MESSIAH	21
COMING CHANGES IN MATTER AND TIME - ORLON	22
CENTER NEWS AND TRAVELS	26
ANNOUNCEMENTS AND PUBLICATIONS	28

* * * * * * * * * * * * * * * * * * * *

Director & Editor - - - - - - Marianne Francis, Dr. Sp. Sc.
Science Director & Business Manager - - Kenneth M. Kellar, B.A.

Published quarterly by SOLAR LIGHT CENTER
a non-profit corporation.

COPYRIGHT reserved - - - - Write for permission to reprint.

Please remember to give your ZIP Code and correct address when writing.

ADDRESS ALL CORRESPONDENCE TO:
SOLAR LIGHT CENTER
Rt. 2, Box 572-J
Central Point, Ore. 97501

EDITORIAL —MARIANNE FRANCIS

COUNTDOWN: THREE MONTHS?

We are now entering the Fall as I write this editorial. Three months of 1967 remain, three months that may prove to be highly crucial for this planet and its peoples.

The Summer has come and gone, weather records have been broken in many areas, race riots have reached a new crescendo, and all indications point to an escalated war in Viet-nam resulting in World War III.

In our Spring issue, we enclosed a loose-leaf pamphlet entitled: "We Come In Peace" received here at the Center by Tele-thought beam on June 3rd. Our readers will note that stress was laid on the fact that "a tremendous unleashing of violence in third-dimensional form" was being brought into being. Further stress was laid on the fact that "the midnight hour approaches for CHANGE" upon this planet.

I would refer you, our readers, once more to my editorial in the Fall/Winter '66 issue of STARCRAFT wherein I asked "Is 1967 the Year of Destiny?". While dates have ever proved difficult to predict, it would seem many reliable sources indicate a termination of third-dimensional existence AS WE KNOW IT, before this year ends. Since my editorial of '66, and since the receival of "We Come in Peace", several new sources of information have opened to me. These sources are channels I regard as valid ones. Information coming from these sources correlates to a high degree with the statements made by the Space Brothers we contact here and with the Universal Link material, regarding the imminence of change and the Second Coming.

Turbulence is everywhere and tremendous instability is manifesting in individuals as a whole. Many, many Light Centers and their personnel have been beset with difficulties, and attacks from negative factions have increased. All sensitive persons to whom I have talked this past Summer have been aware of tremendous pressures and many have literally had to struggle daily to remain stable and integrated.

Were we aware of this or were we not? Were we not warned constantly by the Space Brothers that this time would come and these pressures would bear down? The need for inner stability and balance has been emphasized again and again in Tele-thought communications received from "The Brothers" this last year. A preparation in consciousness for the coming events and changes has been given and we hope our readers have followed these suggestions. In brief, it is suggested that all serious students of Life gather their inner forces and marshal these in poise and tranquility to await the <u>Coming</u> of the <u>Christ Presence</u> and the Great Changes. Forces of dissension and materialism scream on all sides. Unstable individuals, both within and without the Space and esoteric groups run hither and thither, torn by their own inner conflicts. These people tear down spiritual realities, attack the reputations of those who carry enlightenment to the masses, and spread their own malaise and infection of soul to all whom they can reach. Though these sick souls may need compassion, it is foolish for workers assisting the Space and Hierarchal programs to allow such to obstruct or distract them. Energy is drawn from Light workers when their prolonged attention is turned on these sick souls and their antics.

Vital energies must be conserved by Light workers themselves for their own poise and the needs of the work itself, hence, it becomes of paramount importance that all destructive and highly unstable individuals be virtually ignored. Remember, it was said, "Evil contains within itself the seeds of its own destruction". All individuals in any walk of life who live by destructive motivations and actions will find soon that this statement holds truth. "He who lives by the sword will die by the sword" and he who lives by destructive impulses will die by these same energies.

It seems necessary at this time to examine the Space movement as a whole and analyse the motivations of the various groups, clubs, and organizations. We find the "scientific" groups who search for pieces of "hardware", sightings of craft, and lately, "Space monsters", in order to assure themselves that they <u>are</u> hard-headed scientific investigators. These people and organizations deplore what they term the mystics, cultists, and psychics whom they feel clutter up the "Saucer" field and cause confusion and derision in the scientific ranks. These people look on all contactees as "nuts", harmless or otherwise, and cut themselves off from any link with such "undesirables". This is scientific??? Particularly do they deplore <u>spiritual</u> matters being linked with the coming of the Saucers.

Then we have those who regard certain <u>physical</u> contacts as valid but deride all telepathic contacts, channels or information as "psychic" or mystical and thereby, invalid. Orthon, a Space man, has this to say: "One thing which we want to make clear to all is that the mental contacts we have been discussing are definitely NOT what your people call "psychic" or "spiritualistic", but direct messages from one mind to another. We call this mental telepathy, a unified state of consciousness between two points, the sender and the receiver, and it is the method of communication most commonly used on our planets, especially on planet Venus. Messages can be conveyed between individuals on our planet, from our planet to our Space Craft whereever they may be, and from planet to planet. Space or 'distance' as you call it is no barrier". This is quoted from Inside the Space Ships, by George Adamski.

On the reverse side we find many psychic and pseudo-esoteric groups receiving "astral" contacts masquerading as Space people. Beyond this are the occultists who also speak deridingly of physical contacts with humanoids from other planets in this system as invalid and not in accord with their particular school of thought.

Very few of these people are seeing more than one facet of the whole picture. Yet, each group believes its own facet to be a whole. The picture is one of dissension and confusion which must cause much genuine bewilderment and concern to the Space beings who are visiting this planet at this crucial time and attempting to bring aid and enlightenment.

Let us state very definitely that Space people coming from the Solar and Galactic Confederations have utilised many types of contact. These include contact by physical meetings, radio, telephone, telepathy, tensor beam, mental impressions, and inspiration. On occasion they may also have chosen psychic means of contact (trance mediums, automatic writing, clairvoyance and the like). I believe, however, that these psychic means have only been used when a need to contact an individual existed and all other means of contact were unavailable.

Much evidence among genuine contactees (whether these be physical or telepathic contactees) points to the fact that the majority of Space beings visiting this planet are evolved humanoid types of life. They are evolved and balanced in that they see life as a whole, they live within a framework of Cosmic and Galactic Law, and they ARE well aware of SPIRITUAL REALITIES. The more evolved Space beings may be representatives of the Saturn Tribunal or Solar Confederation. Their knowledge of life in all its manifestations far transcends Earthman's comprehension.

If the materialistic scientist cannot accept the reality of life on other spheres, planets, or higher dimensions, it is only evidence of his limited comprehension, his imbalance and compartmentised existence. His understanding is limited to what he can learn through his five physical senses. He cannot understand or accept higher truths until by spiritual growth the extrasensory perceptions are opened up and a greater understanding gained through an inner perception or intuition. Evolved Space beings have this higher perception and awareness which gives them knowledge of Cosmic Truth. Hence, they view Earthman's religions as limited, being based on man-made Church dogma often lacking in true spiritual understanding. They speak from a knowledge of Universal Science and Universal Law, of the Cosmic Christ and of the Creator, the All-Knowing One. They speak of evolvement of consciousness and frequencies of Light. If these thoughts and con-concepts are unacceptable to the so-called scientific or materialist groups on Earth, what matter?? They have all eternity (off this planet, I may add) to rectify their errors, enlarge their knowledge, and free themselves from their limitations.

Merely because we dwell on a materialistic planet, where science is divorced from spiritual Laws and realities, does not compel us to apologise for Space people or contactees who ARE aware of these and seek to teach the masses of truths at many levels of being.

I suggest that "psychologically minded" investigators and Saucer groups who dismiss all contactee claims with evolved Space men and women as false, yet embrace with avidity Space "monster" contacts, take a serious look into the dark recesses of their own minds and souls. Likewise, it is suggested that groups purporting to do serious research in this field, cease branding as "psychic" all who receive genuine telepathic contacts.

The Solar Light Center is NOT a psychic organisation, it does not publish material received psychically, neither are its channels contacted psychically. This does not imply we disapprove of the psychic field of investigation. We merely regard it as another field of activity and not our own. Any serious student of occult sciences is well aware that psychics, by and large, contact the ASTRAL plane of existence. This is NOT our work. We are, therefore, not a "psychic Saucer research magazine" as one small newsletter from Michigan, in ignorance of facts, described us.

In order to finally clarify this point, the following facts are given: Telepathy (tele-thought) communication is the normal and natural means of communication used by the Space people to communicate among themselves. This is also the means by which they contact many channels on the Earth. Tele-thought communication is the means by which material for publication in STARCRAFT is received. I do NOT use psychic means. I do NOT hear voices, see visions, go into trances, or "imagine" communications. Regular times are set up for "contact" when I make my mind passive, establish contact, and receive, through pure telepathy or telethought beam mechanism, a communication. As this enters my consciousness, I then speak it verbatim into a microphone and it is recorded on tape. This is then transcribed and published as given, except for necessary punctuation.

On several occasions Starcraft (or Saucers if the term is preferred) have been observed over our Center and also in areas where I lectured <u>after</u> I had been impressed that they would put in an appearance. Several people have been with me on these occasions and verified that I had telepathic impressions with immediate subsequent sightings. This, I think, should effectively dispose of the odd question sometimes asked by the layman: "Miss Francis, do you think all this could come from your subconscious mind or a psychic realm?" In answer I can only say, if this is so, I have an almighty powerful subconscious that manifests as a large, physical Starcraft from time to time!!!

Let us reason together and realise life as a whole consists of many levels of existence from the physical third-dimensional to the etheric (<u>rarefied physical matter</u>) and on up to levels of pure spirit. Many beings at many levels are aware of and concerned about the coming FREQUENCY CHANGE and the COMING of the COSMIC CHRIST and the SECOND COMING. Enlightened Space people are our elder brothers and sisters and their contribution at this time is invaluable. Let us have peace and tolerance among the Space groups, the scientists, and the laymen that more knowledge may be gained.

This year, 1967, rolls on, and if the lessons of peace and brotherly love are not learnt, events themselves will force drastic reappraisal by many people on the surface of planet Earth!

* * * * * * * * *

PROPHECY FOR 1967 GIVEN IN 1923

Received by Marguerite Walker of Medford, Oregon, in 1923:

> "THOU SHALT SEE THE END OF MAN'S CYCLE AS HE
> LIVES TODAY, IN THE YEAR OF 1967"

As these words were spoken into my consciousness, I saw a blackboard with a circle three-quarters drawn on it. As I watched, a piece of chalk finished drawing the circle and wrote 1967.

This was given to me when I was 16 years old, just after I had gone through a very hard testing period.

—Marguerite Walker

Quoted from a Reader:

"It was with great pleasure and deep inner satisfaction that I received and read four of your wonderful publications. Your work is of the greatest benefit to mankind, and you and your staff are to be highly complimented for your diligent effort.... — J.B.

STABILIZATION MEASURES
(A lecture by Orlon)

We come this evening and communicate with you upon this occasion. Our transmission is, of necessity, somewhat impeded due to the atmospheric conditions prevalent upon this section of the surface of your planet. The inclemencies and extremes of your weather are only in the nature of that which we have previously prophecied (if we may use this word) to you as due to make their appearance at this time. The changes in climate which are taking place in these areas are due to the acceleration in the polar shift and to the degree of axial unbalance already manifesting in the planet.

Now, we do not ourselves anticipate an abrupt axial slippage at this present time. There is, none-the-less, great danger of temperature conditions radically deteriorating to extremes unheard of in the annuals of your records. Further than this, the outbreaks of violence, both within your cities and within your nations, will also accelerate due to the increasing frequencies now flowing in and the degree of unbalance manifesting among your peoples.

We, without doubt, consider the condition upon your planet at this period within the emergency range of what you might term a "red alert" condition, and are taking all measures possible from our vantage point to bring about stabilizing agents as far as is now possible within the limits of Cosmic Law, such law dealing with non-interference in the internal affairs of a planet. However, planet Earth is now on the verge of such tremendous change that if this is not offset by the stabilizing forces, it will become magnetically unbalanced to the degree of an axial flip and resultant effect on the magnetic balance of nearby planets, such as Venus and Mars. Thus, we are bringing into play stabilizing agents on the outer perimeters of your stratospheric layer and will continue to do so. Also, many of our peoples are being withdrawn from the surface of your planet and those who remain will do so only for a short period of time until evacuation procedures can be carried out among those of your peoples qualified to leave.

Much disruption of the atmospheric layers of the planet is due to take place in any case as the approach of the comet or asteroid becomes obvious, the one particular asteroid which your astronomers have spoken of called Icarus. However, in the months preceding this, a great deal of abnormalities will manifest within the magnetic field of the planet and electrical storms of much ferocity may be expected.

Within yourselves, our brothers, our sisters, already much has been given you as to the necessity for stabilization in order that you may remain as poised as possible at this time. However, we would stress that all who are working with the Light Centers and the Sanctuary areas throughout the planet in any way, shape, or form, are requested to do their utmost within their own pattern of being to stabilize such areas against the onslaught of the greater violence of thought forms and against the negative patterns of the masses who do not understand of the nature of these changes.

Those who work consciously in conscious attunement with the Light energies and with ourselves at this time are relatively but a handful upon the surface of your planet compared to your many millions who walk its surface. Therefore, that which is requested of them is in the nature of a herculean task, and we are aware that demands have been put upon many such as would not have been the case under altered circumstances of greater time or a greater degree of harmony within your peoples themselves. Such being the case, it is necessary for all true Light bearers to exchange that which is the nature of energy, of Light, of Love, of Understanding, in order to assist each other and each Center at this time of great stress and strain upon the few.

We, ourselves, are doing all that which is possible and permitted to us, and since emergency conditions are in being at this time and will continue to be, we cannot render certain aid which would have been the case on a more personalized basis had there been greater time, and concerns of personalized nature are somewhat to be sacrificed for the greater good of the planetary concern as a whole.

You as individuals can only do that which each one feels within his own being possible to render in service to the One Light, the All-Knowing One, Our Creator. For all service of a true nature is done with this motivation. All service is of service to the One Light, and those of you who work with us join us in this venture, do not serve us but serve the One Light, do not serve any upon this planet, but serve the One Light. Our Radiant One in His infinite wisdom has decreed through the Laws which we have followed and understood for many milleniums of our existence, that certain changes take place as certain periods of time end, and it is by our understanding of the nature of these changes that we, ourselves, are living our individual lives in peace and harmony. When we perceive the confusion and the utter chaos of the pattern of living upon your planet, we can only look with sorrow at the lack of understanding within the soul of Earth man. We can only extend our love, our brotherhood, our Light, at this time and our craft in your atmosphere to be of aid to your peoples as the change comes rapidly now.

Be prepared at all times for the possible necessity of evacuation of personnel, for this may take place abruptly and you will be required to take naught with you save that which is of life, and of life we speak of those beings which are living. That which is inanimate cannot be removed from your planet in terms of goods, possessions, material things, for these will have no value. All that is necessary will be provided for you, as there is an abundance of these things upon our planet and our craft. There is not, however, an abundance of Earth people who carry within their beings the understanding of things Cosmic, and all those whom we can reach and awaken we will: For you are our brothers, our sisters in Light, and we cherish above all things the thought of taking from this planet all Earth peoples who can reach outward and who will be returned in the New Frequency to bring in the Golden Age of Light. We have an infinite regard for you, our brothers, our sisters in Light, an infinite regard for LIFE. Whether it be the spark within the human or animal form, it is a spark of intelligence and life created by the Divine, and as such we respect and extend our love to all these sparks and creations of the All-Knowing One.

Rest assured that you will be one with us in consciousness and being as the changes come rapidly now, that all things will be cared for within the Plan of an infinite all-loving Creator. Hold yourselves in readiness; hold yourselves poised and stabilized that the One Light may permeate your beings and may fill you also with a desire for service to that Light which fills our own people.

In this Light, I, Orlon, leave you in consciousness of great changes and great happenings. May Our Radiant One be one with you, and you one with His Light.

(By Telethought transmission, 22 Aug. 67. Channel: Marianne Francis)

* * * * * * * * * * * * * * *

SIMULTANEOUS UFO SIGHTINGS

Four reports of a brilliant UFO which all occurred at 11:15 pm July 5th over Oregon and Washington states made this an outstanding sighting.

Marianne Francis reported being with Jeanne Hagen at the Center that night when a brilliant white and greenish-blue object like a comet streaked across from East to West, leaving a wide trail of light etched across the sky. The huge head seemed to explode and it was thought this might be one of the energy devices the Brothers spoke of in our Spring issue of STARCRAFT.

Mr. & Mrs. Vern White of Gold Hill reported this sighting at the same time which appeared a brilliant blue with a white tail travelling East to West at terrific speed. It was the size of a basketball seen at 100 feet.

Mr. & Mrs. John Carpenter reported a similar sighting over Puyallup, Wash. at that same time. A huge comet-like object streaked westward across the sky leaving a trail of golden sparks which glowed after the object seemed to explode with a brilliant greenish-blue flash.

In Ashland, Oregon, Harold Brande reported seeing an object at the same time and also measuring its altitude and velocity using two telescopes set up on a known base line. The UFO appeared in the East and travelled Westward over a large arc of sky. Harold and a friend took accurate measurements of time for a given arc and calculated its altitude as 100 miles with a velocity of 52,000 mph. Its length was estimated at 2000 feet and weight a million metric tons (based on construction similar to our Satellites).

SUMMER SIGHTINGS OVER SOUTHERN OREGON

June 17 - Brilliant blinking light, extremely fast, gone in seconds to West.
July 3 - Starcraft over Center seen by Marianne, Kenneth, & Gunnar Merit.
July 5 - Comet type craft described above.
July 7 - Starcraft seen by Dr. Dan Fry and his wife, Tahalita, over Merlin.
July 8 - Starcraft seen over Center at 11 pm.
July 11 - Two Starcraft going at right angles nearly intercepted one another. Half circled each other then proceeded in original directions.

SCIENCE DEPARTMENT   K.M.Kellar, BA, Editor

OCCULT CHEMISTRY AND THE PERIODIC TABLE

One of the first principles the chemistry student learns is that elements are classified according to their positions in the Periodic Table of chemical elements. Science shows that when the elements are listed according to their atomic weight, they fall naturally into groups having similar chemical properties. This cyclic principle is based on the repetition in structure of the outer VALENCE SHELL of electrons which determines chemical properties to a large extent. Atoms of larger mass contain more neutrons and protons in their nuclei. For each positive proton in the nucleus, there is a negative electron bound in one of the shells surrounding the nucleus. Lighter atoms can hold up to eight electrons in the valence shell, then the next heavier atom forms an outer shell with one electron in orbit about the completed eight-electron shell. In heavier atoms, the outer shell can hold up to 16 or 32 atoms before a new shell is started. Thus, there is a cyclic pattern which is repeated as each increases in the number of electrons it contains, depending on the number of protons in the nucleus. This periodic nature of matter has been very well established and accounts for families of similar chemical elements.

Now, how does this modern atomic theory fit in with Occult Chemistry in which data is obtained from direct observation by clairvoyant magnification of atoms and molecules? (See the previous two issues of STARCRAFT.)

Occult Chemistry verifies that the elements are divided into distinct families according to the seven fundamental types. Each type has its distinctive configueration of ANU which are heart-shaped basic building blocks. Various groups of ANU rotate as a whole about their own axis to form subatomic units. Also, as previously described, the ANU itself has three types of motion: rotation, precession, and pulsation. These complex motions generate force field patterns which are classified into seven groups corresponding to the periodic table. Typical atomic shapes are in figure 1.

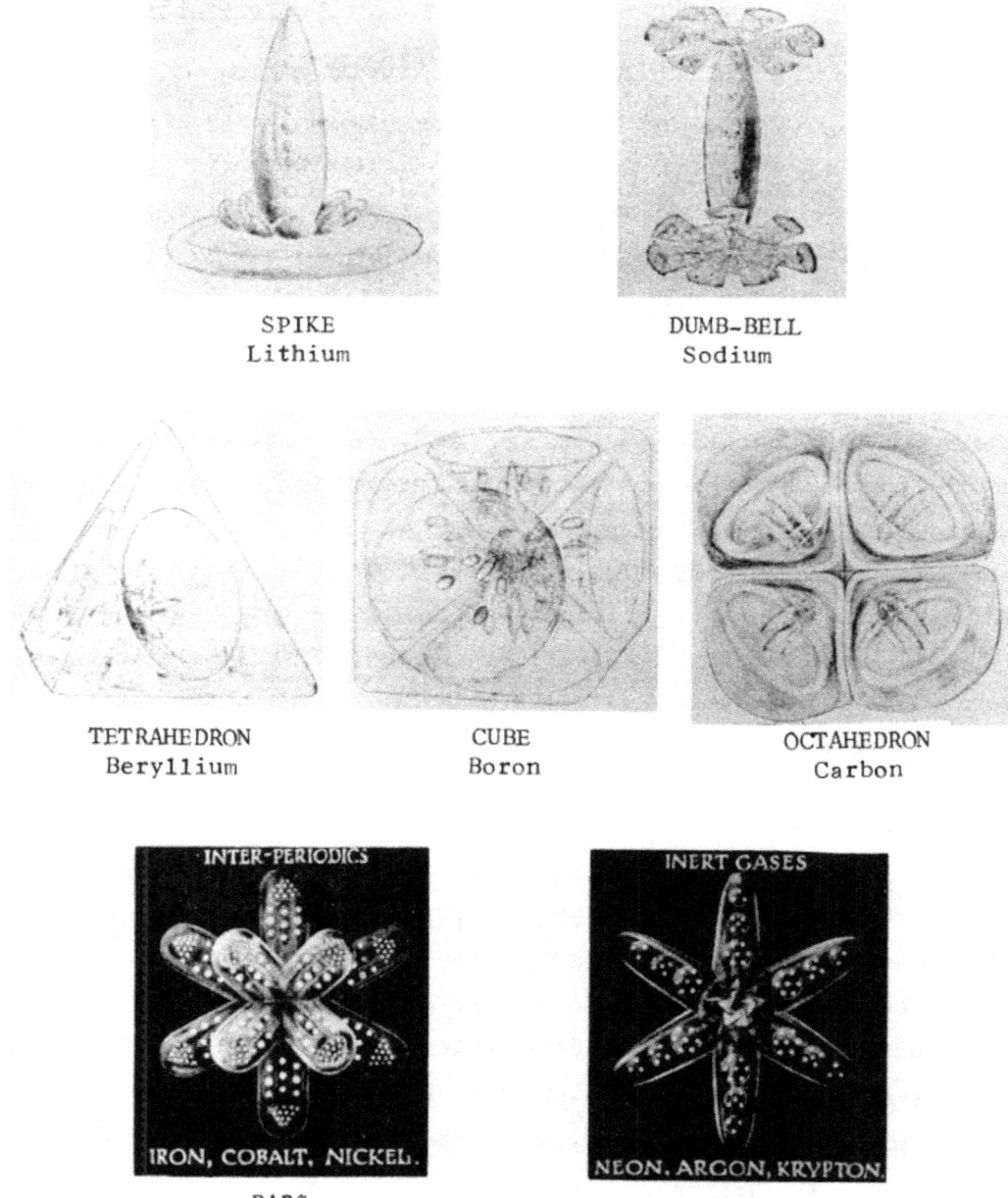

Fig. 1. THE SEVEN FUNDAMENTAL FORMS OF THE ELEMENTS

The seven types of atoms in figure 1 are each represented by a typical atom. The larger atoms are more complex, as is expected, however, the basic characteristics are retained. For example, the potasium atom has nine SPIKES radiating outward from a central globe instead of one spike as in the Lithium atom. Certain of the lighter atoms do not resemble any of the basic types, having their own unique structure. The classification of elements by group and type is given in figure 2.

GROUP	TYPE	ELEMENTS IN GROUP
1A	Spike	Li, K, Rb, Cs, Tm, Fr
1B	Dumb-bell	Na, Cu, Ag, Sm, Au
2A	Tetrahedron	Be, Ca, Sr, Ba, Yb, Ra
2B	Tetrahedron	Mg, Zn, Cd, Eu, Hg
3A	Cube	B, Sc, Y, La, Lu, Ac
3B	Cube	Al, Ga, In, Gd, Tl
4A	Octohedron	C, Ti, Zr, Ce, Hf, Th
4B	Octohedron	Si, Gm, Sn, Tb, Pb
5A	Cube	V, Nb, Pr, Ta, Pa
5B	Cube	P, As, Sb, Dy, Bi
6A	Tetrahedron	Cr, Mo, Nd, W, U
6B	Tetrahedron	S, Se, Te, Ho, Po
7A	Spike	F, Mn, Ma, Il, Re
7B	Dumb-bell	Cl, Br, I, Er, At
8A	Star	Ne, A, Kr, Xe, Rn
8B	Bars	Fe - Co - Ni Ru - Rh - Pd Os - Ir - Pr

Figure 2. Classification of Elements

Note that there are 8 groups in the Periodic Table, but only 7 basic types. The reflected symmetry between groups 1 and 7, 2 and 6, 3 and 5 accounts for this distribution.

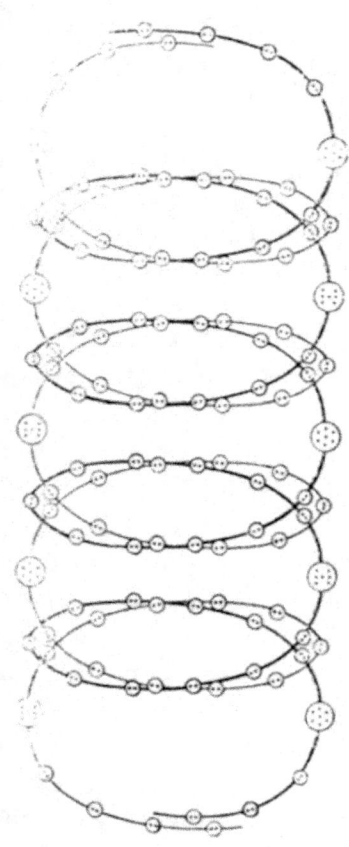

Figure 3. Oxygen Atom

The Rare Gases (8A) are Star shaped and flat. In contrast, the Interperiodic Group (8B) has bars radiating outward from the corners and sides of an imaginary cube, making a total of 14 bars in all. These interlock in molecular combination to give great strength as found in iron (Fe).

OXYGEN (see figure 3) has a very unique structure consisting of two inlaced spirals rotating rapidly in opposite directions. Either spiral consists of a chain of positive and negative ANU pairs linked by five "heptad" units at nodal points along the 5-turn spirals. Forces flowing through each ANU from top to bottom in the spirals bond them together as a chain. In the positive spiral the force flows up to the top then crosses over and flows down through the negative spiral to complete its circuit. A heavier isotope of oxygen has an extra 20 ANU in groups of 4 situated between the nodal pairs along the two spirals.

HYDROGEN (figure 4) is comprised of 18 ANU forming two triangles (one positive and one negative) with sets of three ANU at each corner. Two types of hydrogen atoms have been observed: one with 9+ and 9- ANU, the other with 10+ and 8- ANU forming triangular pairs. This latter type could possibly be the H+ ion. The Deuterium atom appears to made up of one of each type Hydrogen atom set at right angles to each other. The outer shape of the H-atom is ovoid, being formed by a force field generated by the rotating groups of ANU. In compounds, the two triangles often separate as in methane (CH_4) which has one hydrogen triangle over each of its eight funnels.

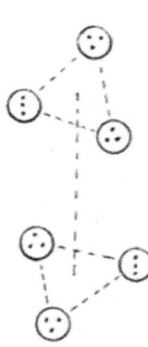

Fig. 4. HYDROGEN ATOM

CARBON is a typical octohedral type (figure 1) with the eight funnels radiating outward, one at each side a an imaginary octohedron, with four ANU making a central focal point. The funnels act in pairs (one being positive, the other negative) to provide the four valence bonds typical of carbon. The octohedral shape and symmetrical valence bonds account for the very close-packed atoms found in diamond crystals of carbon.

Compounds of atoms in molecular structures are considered by modern science as being discrete atoms held together by forces represented as valence bonds. This view is in sharp contrast to that obtained by clairvoyant observations which reveal that atoms are often broken up in compounds. In carbon monoxide, for example, the carbon atom is split in half with the oxygen spirals set between four funnels at either end. Many compounds of both organic and inorganic chemistry have been investigated with interesting results. Those who may wish to study further in this field are referred to "Occult Chemistry" by Besant and Leadbeater. Anyone seeing clairvoyantly anything similar to atomic structures is invited to write in about it. Some of our readers have already reported on this.

A CHALLENGE TO YOUNG PEOPLE
(By the Space Brothers)

Greetings in the Light of Our Radiant One, my brothers, my sisters of the Earth planet. We are very happy and honored to speak with many of you of the younger ones on your planet whose minds are not so formed with the rigidity of many years of false concepts and false teachings. We speak with you in anticipation of much discourse which is yet to come to your peoples and to the minds of the younger ones. We speak in anticipation of meetings between ourselves and yourselves, many, many of you in the times which lie ahead; for soon in the not distant future our craft will be landing on your planet.

Your peoples, many of them...those who can attune their minds with the things of the NEW... will be acquainted with the nature of our coming and the nature of our being. These peoples will meet with us in peace and in understanding and in Cosmic Brotherhood, knowing themselves to be the children of One Creator of all created life throughout the Universes of God.

We speak with you upon this occasion, knowing of many questions within your minds of the newness of that with which you are confronted. We speak with you that we may in some measure bring to you a greater understanding, a greater wisdom of the things which are eternal in nature. Change comes upon your planet. Change comes in the concepts of Earth man. Change is already all about you in the changing patterns of your society, of your moral standards, of the very things of which your traditions and your heritage have been built. Certain of these changes are what might be termed good. Certain of these changes are of degenerative nature. Earth man must choose that which he takes into his own consciousness, that which he makes a part of his own being. Each individual upon your planet is responsible to no one but to God, to no one but the One Creator of his being, for that which he IS, for that which he BECOMES. Therefore, all individuals must choose at this period of time to what they align their consciousness, their mode of life, their very existence, and as they so choose, so will they stand at the time of the Coming Changes, the changes which are already all about you.

Many things of confusion manifest upon your planet. Many concepts beset your consciousness and leave you in states of bewilderment as to which path to choose, which path should be yours in honor, in dignity of being. We state to you that you have, each one, unfailingly within you, a spark of the One Creator and to which, if you will attune, will lead you in the pathway which is leading to the future, the pathway which leads to the stars, to the time of that which has long been forecast by the ancient ones, called in your philosophy, the GOLDEN AGE OF MAN, in ours, the Solar Age, the Age of Cosmic Enlightenment.

The technologies and scientific achievements of your peoples are leading them far beyond the confines of your planet. Yet, these technologies and these scientific achievements are not teaching man of the inherent nature of his own god-being. We speak now in no sense that you might consider blasphemous. We speak of the god-being as that spark within each individual created of the One Creator, that spark which may be expanded and which illumines the being of each so that they become of the nature of the Creator and become co-creators in Light, also.

Your technologies and scientific achievements have been tremendous within the last three or four decades of your time, but the spiritual unfoldment of man has not kept pace with these achievements, and therefore man upon your planet is on the verge of destroying the very ediface upon which he has built his civilizations. Because of the misunderstandings, because of the racial differences, because of differences of creed, dogma, sect, and nationality; because of the nature of many of your races who are backward compared to others, there is great conflict, there is great violence upon your planet and even greater violence is threatening. Yet your peoples may find a path through this labyrinth of confusion which besets them if they will but turn to the infinite nature of their being.

We who come to you from many planets inside of your System and other planets outside, from other planets far distant from our own, have learned to live in peace and brotherhood and understanding with one another upon our own planets and within our System of planets. Such understanding is not difficult, our brothers, our sisters of the Earth planet. When man once masters that nature of his which partakes of the animal and unfolds into a consciousness of the higher self inherent within him, all differences become small factors in the larger scheme of affairs Cosmic in nature. When Earth man realizes he is but not one planet inhabited within a whole Solar System containing no other beings, but is a small planet among a myriad systems teeming with life, teeming with interplanetary travel, then will he understand of the smallness of his concerns and reach outward and partake of that help which we, your brothers and sisters from other planets, offer to you at this time.

We are permitted by the Laws of the Confederation and the Laws of the Saturn Tribunal governing this System to offer to you, planet Earth, aid and assistance to guide you through this period of tremendous upheaval and change. However, we are not permitted to force upon you that which you cannot willingly accept. Earth man must reach out in sufficient number, in consciousness, that our craft may land in peace and may be greeted in understanding, that we may walk openly upon your planet and commune with you even as we do with our brothers and sisters from other planets.

Our purpose at this time is to acquaint your peoples with the nature of changes which come, of the nature of our craft in your skies, and of the necessity for stability of being in each individual; for the vast changes taking place are creating tremendous upheavals within the consciousness of all: upheavals which are difficult to contain within the mind, within the emotions, and many find themselves seeking in strange pathways. Many find themselves left without a foothold upon those traditions and those heritages on which they have built their existence. Now, all is change, and the only foothold of stability exists within the core of each individual, and as each one, so stabilized, so poised in consciousness, links and unifies with others so stabilized, your planet will be held in balance. But if sufficient of your peoples rush in confusions of violence, of destruction, throughout your cities and your nations and wage senseless wars, one upon each other, and know naught of the nature of love and brotherhood, then will your very planet rock upon its axis and we ourselves will, of necessity, remove those whom we term the children of Light from your surface.

You, the younger ones, will inherit the future. You, the younger ones, of necessity, must come to an understanding of yourselves, and it matters naught if your concepts differ from those which have gone before if these concepts are aligned with the principles of Light, of Love, of Brotherhood, of Understanding and Wisdom. For the things of the NEW come in and the things of the OLD crumble and vanish. Each must determine wherein he stands at this time of change upon your planet, and as we find within the heart and the mind of each individual, understanding and the Light of TRUE enlightenment dawning, then shall we in consciousness link with that one and make ourselves known in the days which lie ahead... days of great CHANGE, days of great CHALLENGE... days in which Earthman shall find himself as never before in a changing world, in a sea of utter confusion, in a time of greatest challenge known upon your surface.

We speak with you upon this occasion that we may link with you this first time in consciousness that our concepts may reach you and you may have time to dwell upon these things which we say to you.

Our transmission is by Telethought beam transmission with the mind and the frequencies of this one who is aligned with us in consciousness. The simplicity of this operation is, to us, a matter of little difficulty. Once the scientists have mastered the technology which we offer, such matters will become of commonplace understanding to your peoples. We withdraw our communication and leave with you the Light of Our Radiant One, the Essence of our beings. May you be one with the Light of the Coming Age of Reason.

Adonai vassu, my brothers, my sisters.

* * * * * *

(By Telethought transmission, 26 Aug. 67. Channel: Marianne Francis)

A SPACE MAN'S PRAYER

Oh Radiant One, I your child humbly ask that my vision be not blinded; that my strength be not weakened; that my spirit be not shaken; that my emotions be not stirred beyond control; that I may serve in THY great work to the fullest of my ability. For there is nothing in my heart but the desire that THY will be done. Amen. (Korton of Mars)

CRAFT XY7 CONTACT

Our brothers, our sisters in Light, Craft XY7 identification. Communication channel now open. Recall of certain craft to central area of command is now taking place, these craft to be recalled for specific mission and sent forth again very shortly into your atmosphere. Identification of our craft (XY7) made for a specific reason which will later be revealed.

Your "sightings" (as you term them) of our craft have taken place as we have stated they would over this and other areas. Our craft have been in many vicinities, particularly along the West Coast region, for purposes of stabilization of energies along fault-line localities. However, the stabilization of other more volatile elements in your populace also is requiring the attention of many of our peoples and our command craft. The instability manifesting within the world scene is accelerating and will continue to do so, forming highly explosive situations, as we stated some time ago would be the case in many areas at once, not only in one or two isolated localities.

The disturbance of the fault lines in your planet, particularly around the Meditaranean basin is taking place prior to volcanic upheavals and the greater subsidence of portions of land in those areas and others.

We, at this point, can only repeat the information which has been given to you many, many times. We regret that we may perhaps sound repetitive, none-the-less, it is necessary that you take into your consciousness fully those things which we say and utilise them at this time through which you are now passing.

Stability of being within the individual is of paramount importance, for as the greater eruptions and turbulence take place, all elements will be in a state of chaos and all elements mean elements within the human body vehicle also. Therefore, it behoves the indwelling soul of each to assume mastery and dominion over the elements within their own kingdom or body vehicle of expression: the body vehicle being the physical, emotional, and physical shell. These are the vehicles most apt to cause disturbance and to become out of control unless the indwelling self or oversoul takes command and asserts its mastery or dominion over these elements.

You have been notified (through this and another of our finely attuned channels known to you as Teska) of the coming disruption in the human Kingdom where resistance meets the increased frequencies. We can only repeat that this will undoubtedly take place among many millions of your peoples whose resistence to the coming high frequencies of energy will set up highly disruptive states in their own body vehicles of expression. These will, in turn, cause violent outbursts of emotion ranging from anger, violence, to states of extreme suicidal tendencies. All who do not keep control are subject to these influences and the disruption of their own energy flow of vitality.

We, therefore, do stress the necessity of inner stability, of inner poise despite all appearances to the contrary on the outer scene or within any individuals within the environment of the said individual. We would also repeat at this point that not one of you is responsible for any other being unless that being be a minor or child. All adult beings are responsible only to themselves and none is responsible for another adult being. One may feel love, compassion, a desire to help. These things are admirable, but responsibility is entirely another thing. Therefore, each must recognise that the responsibility for one's self lies only with that self. No matter how close the relationship in the time into which you are now passing, each is responsible to the indwelling soul or overself and to the god-force only. Each will be held accountable by their own thought patterns, actions, behaviour patterns, and only by these.

The time has come, not for that which your Christian religion would call a judgement, but for the final sifting of the "wheat" from the "chaff", as your biblical phrase would have it. The time has come for each individual to make the stand upon the ground which is theirs, in pattern of being, to stand upon, to make the final decision as to _where_ they stand and to _whom_ their allegiance is given. By allegiance we speak in terms of forces of Light and forces of disruption... we do not speak in terms of allegiance to individuals. Individuals may align themselves and stand for forces of Light or disruption, but each must make the choice as to which forces they align themselves with. By this decision the Light within will either show forth from the individual or it will be dimmed. It is by this Light or the lack of this Light that the frequency rates of the individual will show forth at the time of the evacuation from this planet. Therefore, the decision, once more, is an individual decision. Each will decide where they stand and whether they align with the forces of Light who will carry out an evacuation of this planet when the Nature Kingdom and elements reach a point of uttermost chaos, or prior to such point.

If individuals permit chaos and destructive tendencies within their own being, they will simply align themselves with such forces of disruption and bring upon themselves what you might term "Karmic retribution" but which in reality is simple CAUSE and EFFECT.

We would have you give some thought, our brothers, our sisters, to this particular pronouncement for it affects not only all individuals to whom t these words go forth, but it affects all individuals, yourselves included. The Law and the Principles are absolute, the Law being a Cosmic one and mankind upon this planet will learn in a very short period of time the absolute nature of such Law and such Principles and will learn that the individual is a free agent making their own destiny.

The time which has rapidly been approaching is even upon you now and we have spoken of this in many of our communications. That time is here; that time is NOW.

We asked you through Saturn Command communication to be ALERT to this period and to the responsibility which is yours, each one, to yourselves, and as you choose, to the service of the One Light. All who show forth in understanding and wisdom at this time will be given a greater responsibility and will work more closely with us as the time of the evacuation approaches.

The responsibilities which many of our chosen channels and workers are now bearing is indeed a heavy one and this responsibility is one which many upon your planet could not bear at this time. Yet, many, many are being called forth to share in these responsibilities in order that we may reach more individuals... all who can be reached in the time which remains. The program is one of Light dissemination, of dissemination of understanding, of information relating to the changes. This is the program of Space Command of all who work with the Galactic forces and Commands at this time.

Our craft will once more come into orbit of your location within one week of this time and should be observed during your evening and night hours. We transmit on this occasion by direct telethought transmission from craft to channel.

Align yourselves with Light frequencies at all times and permit no negativity of expression within your auric fields. You may then rest assured that we ourselves will draw closer in consciousness to you and to this Center of stabilization and anchor point for Light descent.

May the One Light be yours, our brothers, our sisters in Light. I who speak with you have not previously communicated from this craft in this manner. My name, as far as it is understandable in your language patterns is Byritas. May the One Light be yours and you one with it.

(By Telethought transmission, 8 Aug. 67.   Channel: Marianne Francis)
* * * * * * * *

Underwater Volcano Ready to Erupt?

It was privately reported that Coast and Geodetic survey parties are concerned over a volcano apparently getting ready to erupt off the coast of Mexico west of Baja, California.

PROPHECY OF THE MESSIAH

(Quoted from FATE magazine, October 1967 - "I See By The Papers" column)

"Twenty-four hours before the outbreak of the Arab-Israeli war, the following dispatch arrived in the offices of the Jewish Press, a Brooklyn newspaper, from an Israeli correspondent named Menachem Israel:

'...a story that is sweeping the country and lifting the morale everywhere offers a prophecy.

'Reb Yaakov Ribikov,z.l., was a Tel Aviv shoemaker who enjoyed such an outstanding reputation as a Tzaddil and Kabbalist that even the Chazon Ish referred people to him for help.

'Before his death, less than a year ago, he left instructions that his will be opened after lag b'omer. When it was finally read last week, it told of a war that would take place between the Israelis and the Arabs which would result in an Israeli victory after three days, <u>followed by the arrival of the Mascheach (Messiah)</u>."

The Jewish Press somewhat wryly commented on June 16th, "the first part of his prophecy has come true....". (End Quote) midnight skies, partaking of the thought of a vast Universe to explore with your minds, with your souls, with your beings. Insofar as you can partake of that which is unlimited and consciously UN-limit areas of your consciousness which have been bound by concepts, creeds, dogmas, or traditions, then so will you become FREE-FLOWING in being and flow with the tides of change. Insofar as you can do this, change will meet you and you will meet change without resistance, without pain, and you will become at one with that which has been termed the new consciousness, the new frequency, or NEW AGE.

Those of the peoples upon your planet who are hide-bound in their traditions, in narrowness of thought, in smallness of endeavor, will find the change which is coming of shattering impact and must, of necessity, find themselves elsewhere following this great outpouring of Light. Yet remember, my brothers, my sisters of the Earth planet, each soul or being finds their self where they are equipped to be as this time of change comes upon you. Each soul is an individual being created from the one creator and has Freewill and makes its own decision as to where it finds itself, whether it be consciously aware of this fact or not.

You have a saying of this generation of your nation: to "play it cool" and in the understanding of our peoples, this would be a logical follow-through concerning that which is about to take place. Do not attempt to attach yourself to the things of the old nor to those who cannot meet with change. But KNOW that all things in the One Creator's Universe are ordered, are in harmony, and that these changes which come, tremendous indeed, will bring about a greater harmony in the lives of Earth peoples who can meet them with understanding. Those who cannot will find themselves elsewhere, also in harmony with that state of their existence and that state of their consciousness wherein they find themselves.

All things take place within a law of the Cosmos and it is only Earthman's misunderstanding of these laws, or ignorance of these laws, which allows him in idle regrets for those things which are past or those things which must give way to change. The structural changes which come upon you all are changes of an immensity beyond the understanding of Man on his planet. Until this takes place, there are no words in your language to explain fully to your consciousness of this time. But in the expanded awareness

which will be yours as these changes take place and as these tremendous energies flow in their entirety through the structure of your beings, through the structure of this planet, then understanding will come, JOY will come, LIGHT and ENLIGHTENMENT will come in their FULLNESS.

We therefore suggest in simplicity to you, that as these changes come upon you, that you flow with them, knowing we have communicated with you, knowing we, your elder "brothers" and "sisters", have concern for you. We will do our utmost to assist you at this time and, as you send forth your thoughts to us, many of us and our craft will be with you at this time, standing by ready to assist you into the NEW STATE of AWARENESS which will be yours in the BREAKING of the BARRIER between TIME and MATTER, between ETHERIC SUBSTANCE and that which you know as physical third-dimensional substance.

Our salutations are with you. Many of us are gathered in this craft from which I, at this time, communicate. Many of us send our love and our brotherhood to you, the people of your planet. Many of our craft, a great many, are coming closer within the lower reaches of your atmosphere as the time of your Christmastide approaches. Look for our craft in your skies, as a time will soon come when great masses of these will be seen, particularly in certain areas.

Now we take our leave of you. We are gratified that it is possible for our consciousness to reach outwards to minds which are rapidly becoming receptive to these concepts and to the nature of our coming. Our mission is one, as we have previously stated, of enlightenment under the auspices of the Saturn Council and the Galactic Tribunals governing this section of Space.

I, Orlon, acting as spokesman for many at this time am relaying this transmission from higher levels or echelons under the Saturn Command source.

In the Light of Our Radiant One we leave you. May this Light be one with you. Adonai vassu.

(By Telethought transmission, 7 Oct. '67. Channel: Marianne Francis)

* * * * * * * * * * * *

HELP NEEDED AT THE CENTER

The Solar Light Center is in great need of helpers to assist in the work at the Center. Workers are needed on the grounds, on the mountain itself. Dedicated volunteers able and willing to assist in secretarial and general work are requested to contact us at the earliest opportunity. A man, woman, or couple having talents and service to donate would be ideal. Living expenses are relatively low here, however, a modest private income, pension, or local part-time job would be necessary as well as a car or jeep. The residence listed on the back cover page is available now and we need helpers now.

Please write to us only if you are really dedicated, have ability to offer, and are constant in your desire to assist the Center. We thank you in anticipation of finding the right people soon. The Brothers also thank you, for it is their work we do. In Light,

Marianne Francis and
Kenneth Kellar

CENTER NEWS AND TRAVELS

With the coming of June, events began to move faster and the whole summer resulted in a series of lectures and lecture trips. Unusual weather prevailed here in the Pacific Northwest with high temperatures from mid-June on. Long drives to Conventions were undertaken and the heat proved exhausting and wearying to your editor who likes her scenery green and pleasant!

I drove up to Mt. Rainier, Wash., on June 24th to attend the World Wide Watch. Many UFO were seen during the gathering and many more reported from other states that week.

June 29th was the date set for the Vancouver, B.C. lecture and once more I spoke to a packed hall of over 350 people. Literature vanished in shoals from our book table and many new subscribers signed up. Interviews were arranged by Herbert Clark (Vancouver Flying Saucer Club President) with four radio stations: KARI (Birch Bay, Wash., CKWX (with Bob Bye and Jim McDonald), CKNW (Dave Abbott) and CJOR (Vic Waters) all in the Vancouver area. These interviews and call-in shows ran longer than originally planned, the total time on the air amounting to 6 hours! Though several of the interviewers were somewhat more than skeptical of Flying Saucer contact, at least eighty percent of all call-ins were openly "sold" on Flying Saucers and many had experienced their own sightings.

All that week Starcraft were seen over Vancouver and also in Washington and Oregon. On the night prior to the lecture I had my own sightings at 11:30 and again at 12.30 p.m. in the company of Mr. & Mrs. Vic LeBel, at their home in Richmond, B.C.

Back at the Center, little time presented itself for remodeling or for painting. Local groups arranged lectures and several people (several of the professional class) requested home group talks. The Kiwani's, Rotary, and Hoo-Hoo Clubs were addressed on the subject of "Starcraft Contact". Sightings of a very interesting nature were made in this area and over the Center as reported on another page.

July saw the Seattle Convention (sponsored by the New Age Foundation, Wayne Aho and Lenora Croft) held at beautiful Rainier Room, Seattle Center. Old friends were greeted and new ones made and a pleasant week spent with Peg and John Carpenter in Puyallup. Other small groups in Seattle were also addressed and interest quickened. July also brought a local reporter, Marjorie O'Hara, to the mountain with a request for an interview. The charming Miss O'Hara did a wonderful story on your editor which appeared in Medford-Mail Tribune (July) and also in "The Oregonian" (Aug. 7th).

August proved to be intensely hot and trying at the Center. Heavy stacks of mail and requests for literature were dealt with--these in response to the lecture and TV publicity. Each afternoon, as the heat increased, we wilted and took long siestas until the blessed cool of late evening revived our flagging spirits. One bright episode was my meeting with David Spangler and Myrtle Glines. David is a charming and highly evolved channel for the

Hierarchal forces and Space beings.   Myrtle, his co-worker, is a gifted Personologist.

Project Prometheus (a special Summer School for 200 top students from southwestern Oregon High Schools) honored your editor by requesting a lecture on extra-terrestrial contact. They stated they wished their students "exposed to the impact of extra-terrestrial intelligence and its implications". Several of these students and their friends have since attended Guest Sessions here at the Center. Their enthusiasm and interest is inspiring and stimulating and the Solar Light Center salutes such youth. The Brothers communicated a special transmission for one such Guest night (Aug.26th) which is reprinted in this issue on page 15.

Labor Day weekend was the scene of the City of Light's Convention at the Alameda County Fairgrounds, Pleasanton. Dedicated light workers gathered and a crowd of about 400 people attended. Photographs of Spacecraft were taken with a Polaroid camera after Elaine Chambers and Bob Short had been impressed that craft would be present over the area.

In the last week of September, once again I drove north to lecture in Vancouver, B.C. This time Kenneth Kellar was able to be present. Radio interviews were again arranged, this time with Emmett Cafferty (CFUN) and Dave Abbott (CKNW). Another interview was also arranged by phone from Nanaimo to a Victoria, B.C. radio station. The hall was packed with over 300 in attendance and others turned away due to a "full house". Ann Lee of Seattle sang two of her beautiful inspired songs and it was a joy to have her present. Our thanks to Hannah Decker for helping with the transportation. Thanks also to Lucy Lusby and others there who helped in various ways to make the meeting such a success. No where else have I met with such open-mindedness and enthusiasm for Flying Saucers and New Age material.

Two pleasant days were spent on Vancouver Island at the home of Mr. and Mrs. Larry Cann in Nanaimo. Several small Saucer groups are on the Island and again, a high level of acceptance and understanding was found.

Seattle was visited on the way home and the New Age Fellowship lead by Dorothy Sinclair was addressed on the subject spoken on in Vancouver: "Men from Space and the Prophecies of Earth Changes". (We would like to add: We salute you, Dorothy, for your great courage and faith. Keep up the good work).

A very special invitation was accepted to lecture to 200 teachers and associated personnel who had arranged a meeting at St. Helens, Oregon, on Oct. 2nd. This proved challenging and interesting. The drive home was very pleasant and cool. Rain had fallen and the leaves were turning softly to Fall. Plans are now under way for a visit to the San Francisco Bay area in November. Other lectures in Klamath Falls and locally are also scheduled.

The telephone company has raised our hopes again: the Solar Light Center may have phone service before Christmas. Perhaps by then we will have a direct line via frequency change, to even more important areas....of Space!!!

Our Love and our Light,

— Marianne Francis

ANNOUNCEMENTS

GUEST SESSIONS, normally scheduled on the last Saturday of each month, may be irregular during the Winter months due to road conditions. Please check to confirm before coming. The regular schedule should be resumed by next March, it is expected.

TELEPHONE service is being planned for our area. We hope our telephone will be installed within a relatively short time. This will be a great boon to our activities and facilitate arranging meetings on short notice.

SECRETARIAL help is in short supply, so correspondence and records are not always kept up to date. Please write if it appears an error has been made or if you do not hear from us in a reasonable time.

HOUSE FOR SALE OR RENT

Another house near the Center on an acre of land is available. It consists of a large living room (with picture windows) built on to a 40-foot trailer. Price: $4,000 or $40 per month rent. A car is essential, as it is 20 miles to town. Small down payment accepted. Write for details.

THANKS very much to all who have made contributions to the Center and to those who have subscribed to STARCRAFT. Extra donations make it possible for us to send out hundreds of free copies as exchange or complimentary copies to interested newcomers. With postage rates about to be raised, your donations are needed even more to defray extra expenses.

PUBLICATIONS

Men from Space and Prophecies of Earth Changes - (Revised) - - - $1.00
    This popular lecture has been updated and reprinted.

God-Man or Animal-Man - By Marianne Francis - - - - - - - - 1.00
    This lecture deals with the raw facts of basic hypocrisies on this planet, as seen through the eyes of the Space People. Transmutation of animal-man to god-man is spoken of as a reality for the "god-within IS at the very core of every individual created of God".

Starcraft Contact - By Marianne Francis (To be printed soon).

CHANNELLED MATERIAL from the Space People:
    Set of ten scripts selected from Channelled Material - - - - 2.90

ALEUTI SCRIPTS (superconscious communication) - - - - - - - .50

STARCRAFT Magazine - 1 year Subscription (4 issues or equivalent) - 2.00

SEND ORDERS TO:

SOLAR LIGHT CENTER, Rt.2, Box 572-J, Central Point, Ore. 97501

STARCRAFT

Vol. 3, No. SOLAR LIGHT CENTER SUMMER 1968

STARCRAFT

SUMMER - 1968 - CONTENTS

EDITORIAL: A CLIMATE OF VIOLENCE	3
GUEST CORNER: SOLAR ECLIPSE - by Tarra Misslich	6
DENSITY LEVEL TRAVEL - by Orlon	7
SCIENCE DEPT: Transistorized Light Beam Communicator	10
CANADIAN AFFILIATES of the SOLAR LIGHT CENTER	11
COSMIC INTERVENTION	12
DEVIC ENERGY PATTERNS	15
PROJECT COVER-UP: The Condon Report on UFO's	17
CENTER NEWS AND TRAVELS	18
ANNOUNCEMENTS & PUBLICATIONS	20

* * * * * * * * * * * * * * *

Director and Editor - - - - - - Marianne Francis, Dr. Sp. Sc.

Science Director & Business Manager - Kenneth M. Kellar, B.A.

Published quarterly by SOLAR LIGHT CENTER
a non-profit corporation.

COPYRIGHT reserved - - - - - Write for permission to reprint.

ZIP CODES are required now, so please include yours when writing.

ADDRESS ALL CORRESPONDENCE TO:

SOLAR LIGHT CENTER
Rt. 2, Box 572-J
Central Point, Oregon
97501

EDITORIAL
—Marianne Francis, Dr.Sp.Sc.

A CLIMATE OF VIOLENCE

"I want you to say that I tried to love and serve humanity. If you want to, say I was a drum major; say I was a drum major for justice. Say I was a drum major for peace; that I was a drum major for righteousness, and all of the other shallow things will not matter". — Martin Luther King.

"Some men see things as they are and say 'Why?' I dream things that never were and say 'Why not?'" — Robert Francis Kennedy.

I write this editorial in the week of Robert Kennedy's assasination. Martin Luther King, exponent of non-violence, has also been assasinated since our last issue. A climate of violence exists, a climate in which deeds of murder are becoming increasingly commonplace in high places. Anger, violence, sadism, murder, and perversion are the fruits of this sick civilization which exists, not only in America but over most of the world.

We of the Space movement, or at least some of us, KNOW that all dross on planet is coming to the surface as a gigantic cleansing takes place. Many souls incarnate here, expressing love, compassion, and concern for their fellowman, exponents of non-violence and peace, are being viciously maligned and persecuted and some already have been murdered. How many yet are to die or be maimed in soul or body as a result of the hate rampant on planet Earth in this year of 1968?

When people ask themselves WHY, WHY do these things happen?...and they are asking, the answer is clear: a climate of violence exists here. A climate of violence exists because hate and violence are a way of life here. Wars are violent; portrayal of war as necessary and patriotic is a sick perverted philosophy existing on planet Earth alone in this system. No amount of justification makes one type of killing good and honorable and another vicious and unlawful.

Mankind is split in nature, allowing the animal self full play on the one hand, killing and maiming viciously, yet attempting to express higher values on the other. A terrible schism, as an end result, is what we have today: schizophrenic Man. No words are too strong to express the conviction of Space people and myself that all killing, all violence has to END. This is the end of the cycle of violence on planet Earth. Obviously, because it is the end, a peak point is being reached in all evil and hatred. Undoubtedly, more outbreaks of violence, killing, and hatred will occur until the "Frequency Change" takes place. Yet, in knowing this, we cannot allow ourselves to become hardened, fatalistic, or resigned.

At every moment of our lives now we must be intensely aware, sensitive, and highly vocal in our expression of the Cosmic values of love, compassion, tolerance, and peace. That many of us will suffer and have suffered deeply from the world in which we dwell and the hatred and misunderstanding of a hate-filled people, is inevitable. Then, if this be so, let us suffer a little longer and transcend it with love and that compassion which is of the Christ consciousness. Suffer and love, for "love suffers much yet is kind". Weep for the world and its peoples; weep for Robert Kennedy and Martin Luther King and for all who die as a result of sick hatred. Weep and in that weeping know that Space men and women gather to assist the children of Light who weep in love. Know that the Space Host, the Angelic Host, and the Radiant Being who created all, decree an outpouring of Light which will bring an end to the sufferings of the children of Light.

It is a common error in metaphysical and Space circles to assume when tragedy strikes or hatred is directed against an individual, it has invariably been karmically caused, therefore, no compassion is needed but a cold impersonal detachment suffices. A selfrightous attitude is observable in people who expound this view. Therefore, it is necessary at this time to point out these facts: two types of souls, at least, are in positions of leadership and authority on planet Earth now. One type consists of those who have been in positions of authority in earlier days and periods of history. These people are playing the old Earth game of power politics, personal ambition, and disregard for human life. Such individuals are reaping and will reap karmic debt, often through strange and violent circumstances. The other type consists of those who came in Love and Light and Compassion from other planets and planes of existence to assist Earth through its period of change. Many of these have no Earth karma whatever, though some have. All of these souls, however, are motivated solely by Light principles. All came with Love in their hearts, some knowing prior to incarnation of their destinies. Martyrdom and sudden death have come to several of these. To awaken Earthman to the full horror of his ways, a path of sacrifice was chosen by some of these great souls.

Christ was crucified for teaching Love, Light, and Compassion. To this day

 # Psychic News

VOL. I, NO. 97 — **SPECIAL EDITION** — **JANUARY 1, 1969**

DR. BUSQUETS TOURS U.S.A.

Amazes SRO Crowds

PUERTO RICO (Special)—Standing Room Only audiences in Latin America, Europe—and now in the United States—are witnessing psychic phenomena occurrent in Dr. Carlo Busquets (pronounced Booze-ket). "I knew E.S.P. existed," gasps one woman, "but certainly not to this extent."

And no wonder. Of the many well-known psychics—e.g., Peter Hurkos, Jeanne Dixon, Richard Ireland—none compare admirably to Dr. Busquets, whose basic function, as he sees it, is to "create in others the psychic gift."

Before his own psychic demonstrations, his pre-emption is always several persons from the audience on whom he ties blindfolds—or otherwise "blinds"— and helps *them* to give psychic readings. "I do this," he explains, "in order for the average person to trust me. I am not God or Superman, and I don't want anybody to think that. My gift is not unusual—others have it, too, as I always prove in my audiences. But," he continues with a smile, "mine *is* perhaps a little more developed."

Dr. Busquets, who has a Doctor of Divinity degree from Iglesia de la Vida Universal de Puerto Rico, is interested in the anti-poverty program in America, flying saucers, traveling, people. "But mostly people," he explains. "They are what

Rev. Busquets delivers a message to his congregation in Puerto Rico. The subject this Sunday is "The Bible and ESP."

life is all about. They *are* my life—and my goal is to help, counsel, direct, influence as many as I can, especially in the realm of the psychic. This is where it's *at;* this is where the action is. Also, I might add, in hypnosis. That's why my demonstrations usually include hypnosis. The world needs more psychic hypnotists!" Asked if he knew of any off hand, he replied: "Only my grandmother, Cuca Trapaga, and she—God bless her!— is dead. Dead to others, maybe. But not to me; she still helps me."

April's the One!

Dr. Carlo Busquets Predicts SF Quake

by Dr. Irwin R. Masters

SACRAMENTO (Special)—Jeanne Dixon said no, but Dr. Carlo Busquets says yes.

Yes to April as the month for The Earthquake. Specifically, but not for certain, April 6, which could put a crimp in the Easter Bunny's style.

"I'm not saying that California will just fall into the ocean," emphasized Busquets, an expert in extrasensory perception (ESP).

"But it will be an earthquake like the one in 1906. It will occur between Los Angeles and San Francisco."

He said he preferred keeping the prediction general to cover all of April, although for some unexplainable reason, April 6 seemed to stick in his mind.

Busquets, 27, is a native of Puerto Rico. In an interview this week, he said he has been touring Latin America, Europe and the U.S. giving lectures and demonstrations on ESP. Most recently, he has been touring the Sacramento area.

1969 PREDICTIONS

Busquets had a number of predictions for 1969:

—"I always like to begin my New Year predictions with a look at the Academy Award winners for Best Actor and Best Actress. This may come as a surprise," he winked, "but in the past seven years, since I began these predictions, I have never missed. Nor never shall! This year Katherine Hepburn will deserve to win, but won't. And taking the laurel from her—who else?—Barbara Streisand. And for Best Actor—Burton? No. Congratulations go to Peter O'Toole."

—President Eisenhower will die the last part of March or early April. "I see a great calendar of 1969, with the months of March and April on it, separated by an American flag with black stars on it. 'Night's candles are burnt out' for the man who lies under it. Who it is, precisely," he continued, "I can't tell, but I see a giant 'E' across the flag and the name that comes immediately to mind is Eisenhower. I see his body being carried by a train, as Bobby Kennedy's was."

—President Johnson will suffer a heart attack in September.

—President De Gaulle will die of natural causes before the year is up. "I see him being carried on a bier but nothing more than that. Thousands of mourners. That's all."

—"Cuban hijackers will take another batch of our commercial planes—precisely 12 of them, an average of one per month. Even so, nothing will be done to prevent it in the future."

Dr. Busquets counsels 10 to 16 people a day—doctors, lawyers, businessmen, housewives, students. He is seen here concentrating between consultations.

—A revolution in Puerto Rico will erupt in defense of independence, but to no avail. Puerto Rico will become a state, just the same.

—Jackie Kennedy will become a widow again.

—A cure for leukemia will be discovered.

—Sirhan Sirhan will be shot.

—Red China will be admitted to the UN, possibly in May.

—The US will place a man on the moon before Russia will—Russia probably not later than June; the US maybe as early as May.

—"Chaing Kai-Chek will lay down his career—and who will rise to power? His son—certainly a more foreseeing and peace-loving man than his father."

EARLY PSYCHIC GIFT

Busquets said he became aware of his ESP powers when he was 10 by being able to predict who was calling on the telephone or knocking at the door before either was answered.

Since then, he explained, his powers have further developed.

Busquets claims that among his accurate prophecies last year, he predicted the election victory of Richard Nixon and the initials "S.S." as being those of Robert Kennedy's alleged assassin.

Here are some of his 1968 predictions, published in "Psychic News," January 1968:

1968 PREDICTIONS

—"Sorry, Miss Taylor, you will not (though you may deserve it) get two Academy Awards in a row. I am almost certain Katherine Hepburn will take it away from you. And as for you, Sir Olivier, no chance. Paul Scofield has you beat by a mile and will take top honors this year."

—Luis A. Ferre will become Governor of Puerto Rico.

—US Astronauts—three of them—will circle the moon but not land, probably in December.

—The Viet Nam war will continue, with more and more domestic opposition. "There will be peace talks," he said, "but nothing remarkable will come of them, except perhaps a bombing halt—and that will not be a direct result of the peace talks but more as a political maneuver on the part of the Johnson Administration."

—The next President of the United States will be Richard Nixon. "He will win by a surprisingly slim margin over Hubert Humphrey, if Robert F. Kennedy is assassinated. Otherwise, Kennedy will take the nomination away from Humphrey (on the first ballot) and will win the election almost automatically.

"But I see, as in a dream, John Kennedy take Bobby's hand and walk silently through a black veil, which I interpret to be death. On *this* side of the veil I see a gun and the initials on the handle are "S.S." Perhaps these are the initials of the assassin, but I can't say for sure. So I feel very strongly that Kennedy will be taken from the scene before he is nominated for President—and Nixon will take the Presidency."

—"Governor George Wallace will emerge as a much stronger candidate than is generally supposed now, but will show as poorly in the actual election as Goldwater did against Johnson."

—The Presidency *will not* be decided in the House of Representatives, as some political leaders believe will or could happen.

—"I cannot tell who the Vice Presidential nominations will be, but Nixon will gamble on a political unknown and Humphrey will take who he can get—certainly not Ted Kennedy or Shriver. Maybe Muskie?"

—Martin Luther King, Jr., will be assassinated. "I see another great leader in our country being assassinated—and the assassin will be caught but with great difficulty. Who the leader is for sure or who the assassin is I cannot say at this time. It will be a Negro, and I have a terrible fear that it will be Martin Luther King, Jr. I pray that it is somehow a lesser man.

"I do, however, see Mrs. Martin Luther King and Mrs. Bobby Kennedy together, as if to comfort each other—or rather Mrs. King is comforting Mrs. Kennedy; so I am going to conclude from this that the Negro assassination will come considerably *before* the White one. Otherwise, Mrs. Kennedy would be comforting Mrs. King.

"For some reason, I see a black rose and a white one floating in water, and—which is sort of interesting—I recall the War of the Roses in England whose opposing rose symbols were Red and White. They stood respectively for the House of Lancaster and York and after decades of fighting were united.

"Now, I see a *Black* rose and a *White* rose, which symbolize to me—as they would, I guess, to anyone—the Blacks and the Whites. Why do I see the roses in water? I don't know exactly, except to me water has always symbolized sorrow and suffering. If Kennedy is assassinated, as, alas, I predict he will be, I would consider him a White rose. And, if Martin Luther King, Jr. is assassinated, as, alas, I predict he will be, I would consider him a Black rose. But, if the two leaders are indeed assassinated, how can they feel sorrow or know suffering? They can't. So I am going to conclude—at the risk of making a logician ill—that the 'black rose and a white rose floating in water' is Mrs. King and Mrs. Kennedy in sorrow and suffering after the loss of their husbands.

"Even as the Red and the White rose were united, maybe the Black and the White will unite. But, of course, not before long, long suffering—and many lives are lost. At least two opposing symbols will become united and the symbol of peace they stand for will, in turn, stand for hope."

INTERPRETS DREAMS

Busquets said he interprets predictions through the dreams he has while meditating.

"There are too many skeptics now. Not everybody believes that people like myself have the power to predict the future.

"As far as The Earthquake is concerned," he mused, "half my friends plan to move in the next three months, at least before April. The other half—well, I guess they're more Jeanne Dixon's friends.

"And don't be concerned about the Easter Bunny. He'll be safe with me—in Oregon."

Dr. Busquets plans to tour Oregon and Washington before returning to Puerto Rico.

evil forces and evil men and women on planet Earth seek to crucify all who follow this path. Therefore, let none among us be complacent or stand in judgement on any. Let us analyse all things from the viewpoint of Light principles.

Souls who are of Light reflect Light in their eyes and their actions. They care deeply about injustice, the poor, the oppressed, the innocent and the vulnerable of Earth. They love and have compassion. These are the children of Light and "by their deeds shall ye know them". Their political or religious affiliations mean little but their <u>deeds</u> do count for much.

As to the "brotherhood of darkness", who destroy and hate and maim on our Earth, the Frequency Change and the great outpouring of Light which is coming will take these out of incarnation. For, in their darkness of soul, they will be unable to withstand the brilliant penetrating quality of the Light. For these, too, let us say, "Forgive them for they know not what they do".

Let us love and cast out hate in all its guises. Let us love so greatly that fear ceases to exist and a Christ-like compassion and Light radiate from our souls and our very beings. For all Light comes and darkness and a climate of violence shall exist no more on the face of the Earth; and Earth shall become the risen star of the Solar System.

Let us "dream things as they never were" and say, IT WILL BE. Let us all be "drum majors for peace and for righteousness...and all of the other shallow things will not matter".

* * * * * * * * * * *

OUTLOOK INN - - ORCAS ISLAND - - LOUIS FOUNDATION
A Space station for Earth People. Catering to New Age individuals.
Groups, Conferences. Fabulous food at inexpensive prices.
LOUIS FOUNDATION Courses: "The Expanded Consciousness Courses!"
(By mail or in person: taught in three-day seminars.)

TEMPLE OF SILENCE: Send your problems, large or small, to
LOUIS FOUNDATION: Box 16, Eastsound, Washington.
(No fees... Love offering accepted.)

GUEST CORNER: SOLAR ECLIPSE   -Tarra Misslich

The Solar eclipse of September 22, 1968 at 6:09 a.m. EST is unique in that this event falls during the equinox which makes it more powerful than an ordinary eclipse. The eclipse is exactly conjunct the eccentric, revolutionary planet, Uranus. This sun eclipse takes place in the astrological sign Virgo which is the sign that represents the working people the world over. The planets Jupiter and Pluto, representing religious mind and initiate mind, respectively, are widely conjunct the eclipse complex.

This September eclipse will be a total eclipse which at its height will cover and momentarily totally inhibit the spiritual rays of the Sun from radiating directly earthward. An eclipse, therefore, is a rallying point for the dark, Satanic forces who are seeking to subvert the human life wave away from decency and Christ to a state of degeneracy and depravity, thereby to rob humanity of its divine birthright which is immortal identity with the Father-Mother God of this Universe.

Following the eclipse, Uranus leaves the sign Virgo to take up a seven year's residence in the sign Libra. Since this is still the Piscean Age, Libra may be considered the 8th house sign of the Age. Thus, you may expect to see in the next seven years a great interest in the occult, in survival after death, in oriental religions such as Zen and Vedanta; also in Spacecraft and ESP; but alas, also an increased interest in negative forms of psychic manifestations such as High-powered Salesmenship and Mass Mind Control.

Since Uranus's entrance into Libra is preceded by the above-mentioned total sun eclipse with its conjunctions, the world can look forward to some very insidious, rank times. Satanic forces working thru the materialistic-minded, power-man leaders of the world will try to lead this earth's inhabitants into worse degradation than ever before in the history of mankind. In the next seven years, sadistic forces will diligently and boldly try to take over and rule most of the political, scientific, religious and artistic fields of human expression. If it were not that Neptune in a few years will leave the sign Scorpio and enter into the sign Sagittarius, there would be little hope for humanity.

The sun in Virgo symbolizes both the morality of the working class and the attitudes of those in authority chosen to rule over them. This eclipse forewarns a stepup of Satanic leadership throughout the world, to further demoralize the human race. Highly intellectual, worldly reasoning will be used to cow the unwary and put to shame the would-be followers of purity and Light. These Satanic forces are subtle. A time for martyrdom for the practicing Children of Light is not far distant. If there is not a general awakening among the people soon, true Christianity may have to go underground.

This is prophecy. With this eclipse, we have well entered into those times for which it was written in the scriptures, "For there shall arise false Christs and false prophets, and shall shew great signs and wonders, in-so-much that, <u>if it were possible, they shall deceive the very elect</u>".

DENSITY LEVEL TRAVEL

Greetings, my brothers, my sisters in Light. I, Orlon, transmit to you upon this occasion with an extension of the transmission relevant to Density Level Transition, entitled: Density Level Travel.

We have previously acquainted you with the information relevant to the coming changes in density...the structure of the plane or subplane on which you find yourselves...that is, the existence which you know as physical plane life at this time. Relative to density level transition will be the secondary matter of density level travel. When the transition takes place between what has been termed differing subplanes, levels, or frequencies, and Man of the New Age finds himself in 4th density, 4th dimension, or 4th etheric subplane (whichever terminology you have found clarity to use) then will come about a new phenomena previously unknown to Man of your time: that of TRAVEL within and between the varying densities or subplanes of the physical plane manifestation.

This, my brothers, my sisters, is not in the far distant future as you might suppose. Indeed, now that you are conversant with the whole idea of some imminency to the actual transition between frequencies or densities, you must make yourselves equally conversant with the idea of density level travel. In the travelling between densities, the vehicle which will be used may not only be a vehicle or craft known as Spacecraft or by other terminologies: Vimanas or Ventlas, but the vehicles may be those of man's own etheric body or bodies.

We would now acquaint you with the thought previously unknown to your Earth teachings. You are already familiar with the idea of the physical vehicle or body which you now think of (many of you) as your selves. You are also familiar with the vehicle known as the etheric which is a duplicate of the physical body. We would, however, bring to your attention the thought that the Etheric vehicle may also be divided. This, we realize, is a new thought. The etheric vehicle may be divided into a higher and lower etheric body or bodies, either of which may be divided by a manifestation of the consciousness or will, so directed, allowing man to travel in either vehicle to the higher or lower etheric subplanes.

In the division of these etheric bodies (which is a commonplace occurrence to our peoples) the indwelling soul may so direct its vehicle that it may move freely between all densities of the physical plane of manifestation: Using the lower etheric and densifying it, lowering its vibratory rate that it may become visible to the physical plane manifestation of your known world and using the higher etheric to move into the upper ethers. Thus, density level travel becomes a possibility.

When man, using these vehicles, also uses, as he does (and we speak now of Space Man) a craft, the structure of the craft, also undergoes a molecular change, a change in vibratory rate of the molecules of the metals under the direction of the will of the individual directing said craft. When an aggregate of consciousness of individuals attuned mentally and spiritually travel within one of these vehicles, they may be thus densified or etherialized according to the nature of their mission. Thus, craft manifest within your atmosphere unseen to your physical eyes, yet registered upon the sensitive retina of your cameras, and craft, thus, may come into density visible to you and may disappear within a matter of moments.

We are attempting to further clarify the picture which is one of extreme complexity regarding the nature of our craft, the nature of our bodies, and those things which man on Earth, New Age man, may find himself a part of as the change takes place. In attempting to further clarify, we wish to bring a greater understanding with as much simplicity as possible out of the hither-to-fore conflicting picture.

Much, as we have previously told you, remains to be given to your peoples as they evolve in consciousness to the point whereby such enlightenment may be a part of their consciousness. Thus, we have stressed constantly and continually the necessity for expansion of consciousness. We cannot, I repeat, we CANNOT hand you information of a scientific or spiritual nature until your own levels of consciousness are prepared to receive them. Thus, the stress upon consciousness expansion. It all depends on you, my brothers, my sisters.

As you (and here we find many minds expanding rapidly in the group who come and go around this Light Center) as you expand your consciousness, out beyond the confines of your own materialistic science, a greater science, a greater spiritual knowledge will be given to you, perhaps you might say in minute doses at first, but as rapidly the consciousness is expanding and ever increasing, knowledge and wisdom will become yours in your relationship with us and the link from Space to Earth

As the New Earth and the New Frequency and the New Density Level come into being and New Age man becomes a part of this, he will find himself in a world of what he might previously have termed miracles. Yet these are not miracles but the natural outworking of Cosmic Law. Only as we ourselves have attuned with Cosmic Law have the wonders of the Universe of One Creator become manifest to us. Prepare yourselves, therefore, in consciousness for the changing in density in the structure of your known worlds and for travel between your known world and worlds of other dimensions. Prepare yourselves in consciousness to meet with those who will come to you interdimensionally and will walk with you and give to you of their wisdom from worlds beyond the known which man in his small knowledge has called the physical universe.

In the infinite Creations of the One Light, the All-Knowing One, Our Radiant One, are wonders beyond the understanding of mortal man: Science beyond the dreams of scientific men, of much knowledge, and a relationship between all life which only the mystic in his most exalted moments may perceive.

You stand, my brothers, my sisters, on the brink of change, great change, and as you stand on this brink, we take you gently by the hand and we lead you forth into the horizon of a New Dawn, an Age of Reason, an Age of Light in the affairs of Earth man. We walk with you in consciousness this night. We speak with you from our craft located high in the atmosphere above this Center. We suggest once more that it will be possible to observe certain of our craft in the days ahead in your night skies, as we are again coming closer into your atmospheres over many localities, particularly over your coastal areas.

In the Light of Our Radiant One, may you, our brothers, our sisters, walk always in the Pathway, in the Wisdom, and Love of His Creation and His Laws.

Adonai vassu baragus.

* * * * * * * * * * * *

(By Telethought transmission, 12 May '68. Channel: Marianne Francis)

* * * * * * * * * * * * * *

RADIO and TV Programs on which Marianne Francis has appeared recently:
- Seattle, Wash.: KING-TV: Howard Hall's Telescope show.
  KTW radio: Call-in program.
  KING radio: Clark on King
- Portland, Ore.: Jim Fenwick, radio Call-in program.
- Vancouver, B.C: CHAN-TV: Mark Raines; CKNW radio: Dave Abbott.
  CKNW radio: Jack Webster; CKWX: Jim MacDonald.
- Victoria, B.C.: CJVI radio: Vic Williams Call-in Program.
- Nanaimo, B.C.: CHUB radio: Larry Thomas Call-in Program.

SCIENCE DEPT.

K. M. Kellar, B.A.

TRANSISTORIZED LIGHT BEAM COMMUNICATOR

The original diagram for a Light Beam Communicator was published in our Summer '66 issue of STARCRAFT. Since then, further experiments have been made to improve the design with transistorized circuits. The advantage of using transistors is that the weight is reduced and the high voltage power supply is no longer needed. The new circuit requires only a 9 volt dry cell battery which will last longer and take less space. The audio output from the Light Beam Receiver can be coupled directly to a loud speaker, earphones, or a tape recorder with proper matching impedance. It is desirable to use a small portable recorder which has a monitoring switch. It is possible, then, to listen in during experiments at some length, but turn on the recorder only when an interesting signal is being received. This will save much tape, and with 3-inch reels, this is important.

The Space Brothers indicated in a recent communication that it is desirable now to step up our efforts in Light Beam Communication research. With the liklihood that wide-scale Earth Changes may occur yet this year, it is advisable that new age groups in many parts of the planet be prepared to receive communications for instruction when the need arises. In the absence of a Telepathic Channel, this electronic device can provide the means to receive communications from the Space Brothers in an emergency providing the group has the right motivation.

The basic circuit shown in Figure 1 operates as follows: Modulated light is focused by a reflector or lense (and filter) onto a photocell, which in this case is a resistive type made of Cadmium-sulphide or Cadmium-sulfo-selenide. The resistance of the photocell changes from about 6,700 ohms to over 500,000 ohms when the light changes from 2 foot-candles to dark. This change in resistance causes a change in the current (regulated by Q1) and thus a signal voltage is applied to the amplifier section, Q2 and Q3. The output stage, emitter follower Q4, applies the amplified signal through volume control, R8, to the output transformer and thence to the speaker or phono-input of a tape recorder. Resistor R1 is adjusted to provide a bias voltage of about 4.5 volts at the collectors of Q2 and Q3. Other type photo-resistive cells might be used to advantage with some circuit modifications.

We are interested in hearing of research from other groups and will welcome any constructive comments for improving design features.

CANADIAN AFFILIATE OF THE SOLAR LIGHT CENTER

A newly formed Canadian branch of the Solar Light Center was organized following the lecture Marianne Francis gave July 4th at the Peter Pan Ballroom in Vancouver, B.C. Those interested were invited to attend a Committee meeting the following evening at the home of Bob and Joan Gale who kindly offered to have the meetings held in their home.

The official name was adopted and officers chosen at a subsequent meeting as follows: Chairman: Bob Gale; Vice-Chairman: Harold Pym, Secretary/Treasurer: Bernice Young; Liason: Frank Russcher; Public Relations: Irene Pym; Appointed Program: Selina Heartwell; Financial Committee: Harold Pym, Laureta Carlson, Louise Blanchard; Welcoming Committee: Joan Gale; Information Telephone: Beatrice Rosen.

Those living in the Vancouver area who wish information about meetings and other activities may call Beatrice Rosen - Phone: 325-0276, Vancouver.

* * * * * * * * * * * * * * * *

TRANSISTORIZED LIGHT BEAM COMMUNICATOR

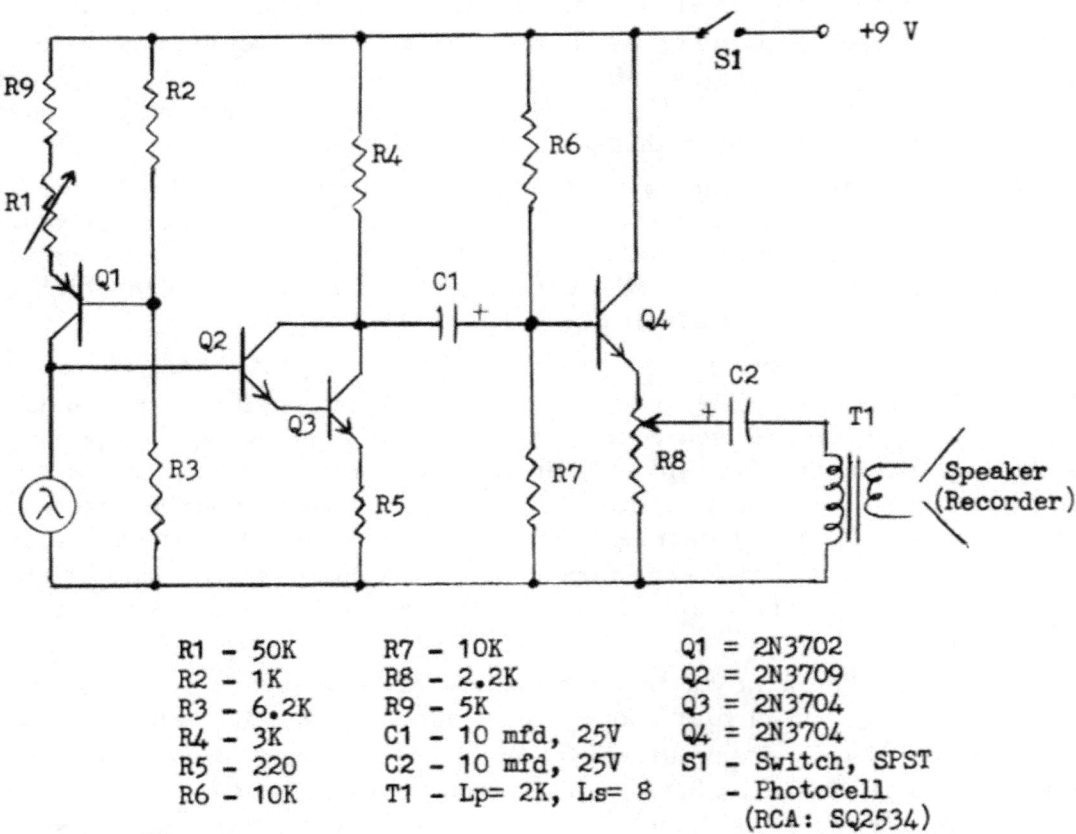

R1 - 50K	R7 - 10K	Q1 = 2N3702
R2 - 1K	R8 - 2.2K	Q2 = 2N3709
R3 - 6.2K	R9 - 5K	Q3 = 2N3704
R4 - 3K	C1 - 10 mfd, 25V	Q4 = 2N3704
R5 - 220	C2 - 10 mfd, 25V	S1 - Switch, SPST
R6 - 10K	T1 - Lp= 2K, Ls= 8	- Photocell (RCA: SQ2534)

Figure 1. LBC Circuit.

COSMIC INTERVENTION

Greetings, my brothers, my sisters of the Earth planet. I, Orlon, speak with you upon this occasion and greet you with much joy in my heart at the coming together of so many minds of common intent.

The subject upon which we converse with you upon this occasion deals with that of Cosmic Intervention, a subject upon which you have most recently been discussing and concerning yourselves. Cosmic Intervention is a matter which we have not discoursed upon at much length in our previous transmissions to you.

Much of the material which has been given to you through the years has been in the nature of 'facets' of information. We have given you a particular facet which your minds could comprehend at that particular time, could ingest, could understand, could dwell upon and enlarge the concept previously held.

Now, we stand at a point of time wherein many of these facets, having been revealed, having been inter-changed among various of our channels and intermediaries upon the Earth, are now making of themselves a whole: A picture, an outline of the events soon to take place upon your planet.

Cosmic Intervention in the affairs of a planet or a Solar System takes place when certain events and certain timing of magnetic cycles coincide. In the overall plan and the overall picture, as viewed by ourselves, we see now such events, such timing of magnetic cycles coinciding at a point in time. We said previously that a day, an hour, a time will come when change of an overall nature must take place, obvious to all men upon this planet called Earth.

We, ourselves, viewing as we do with a perspective unclouded by the misconceptions of your planet's gross density and the concepts held by many of your peoples, see an overall plan: A plan of great beauty and manifestation taking place upon your planet, not only on Earth, but within this Solar System in which you and we ourselves find being and life at this time.

If we were to present to you, people of Earth, our brothers, our sisters, creations of the One God, the overall picture of an immensity so tremendous it dwarfs the imagination of even your most evolved beings, we would, perhaps, overwhelm you with this concept. Therefore, we have sought slowly to bring to you information relevant to the times in which you now find yourselves. We have sought through many of our channels, our peoples walking the surface of your planet, to present through all avenues open to us, whether these be that which you term fiction or fact, data or imagination, something of the change which is about to take place.

We have spoken with you through many years of your time, years which must have seemed long in your concept and your understanding which, however, have passed but briefly from our viewpoint, of the nature of the coming changes which will take place. You have chosen through the use of our terms to employ the expression "Frequency Change", as that which most clearly describes what is about to take place. Others of your peoples, imbued with that of your orthodox religious concepts, have spoken in other terms, have understood in other ways and sometimes, not understood at all.

Now must take place a merging between minds, between understandings: A merging of which some of you have spoken upon this evening in order that all may comprehend at their level of consciousness; all, that is, who are capable of comprehension. It matters not whether your minds have been conditioned through any of your Earth religions if you can but reach beyond rigid doctrines or dogmas to that which is unlimited, beyond the physical composition of Man as he now is and appears to be.

Cosmic Intervention, frequency change, the bringing into being of a new "Race of Man", a new heaven, a new Earth: these are the things of which we speak to you. This is the knowledge which we, who come from Space, came to impart: That you, our brothers, our sisters of the Earth planet, may reach out in consciousness and become as one with us, may become aware of our presence, our mission, as we walk among you and will be with you in the times which lie ahead.

A long hard uphill path has met our efforts in many directions. Vastly entrenched monopolies on the face of your planet have sought to distort the nature of our coming to Earth man and have sought to remain entrenched in their particular ideologies and gods of materialism. Gods truly exist, gods in the sense of the evolvement of the human soul: Gods of Solar Systems, of Galaxies, beings so tremendously evolved in wisdom, love, compassion, understanding, as to be almost beyond the understanding of mortal man of Earth; truly these would be termed as "gods". Yet, beyond all these dwells the One Infinite Being, the source of all life and creation.

We speak, therefore, of gods in terms of gradation, of evolvement. We have spoken before of the godhood inherent within each being and of the necessity for Man of Earth to evolve into this concept of the inherent godhood of his own essence, to reach out to this, to expand, to express, to become.

In Cosmic terminology we speak to you of galaxies, of systems, of worlds, and each of these worlds, these systems, of these galaxies, has a Being, tremendous in stature, who holds authority over that particular dominion. These also are answerable to higher authorities or hierarchies: Finally, devolving into that of the One Being, the Godhead, the Infinite One; and it is as this Infinite One gives forth of His Light and His (shall we say for your understanding) waves of energy, and as these reach out to His creations, His galaxies, His systems, that CHANGE takes place.

Your planet, this System, stands now within such a period of change. Many, many beings on worlds in this system are acutely aware of this coming change and meet it with understanding. It is only your peoples on this planet, in this system, who do not have understanding of the coming change, to whom our attention is directed at this time. We come, thus, in vast numbers from many areas of Space, both within and without this Solar System, to bring the understanding, the knowledge, the Laws, which govern your world and many others, to your peoples in order that at least some segment of them may meet this change with understanding and with joy, may know of that which takes place and may work in conscious accord with these changes.

As the time of the vast and overall change takes place, many millions of your peoples will be filled with great panic; but to those whom we have given of our understanding, of our knowledge, it will fall, for a time, to assume the qualities of leadership, of authority; to assume the burden (if it may so be termed) of responsibility for guiding your peoples aright, in order that they may understand and may be made aware at this time of the things which take place. Therefore, great is the responsibility of those to whom we transmit our understanding, even those among you who count yourselves as the younger ones at this time. It matters little in our understanding whether the soul be housed in a body of 16 or 60 years. It matters only that the understanding of the soul be in evidence.

As a final point of our discourse on the Cosmic Intervention of what might be termed the Space Host: When overall operations take place, there will be little time for conscious direction, or shall we say, choice, or decisions to be made and unmade. We suggest, therefore, that in preparation...and this indeed is a time of preparation for the coming changes... in preparation that you not only consciously prepare your minds for that which will and must take place; but that you attune the frequency of your own individual being, nightly, calling upon that being by whichever name you know that being: The Infinite One, God, the All-Knowing One, Our Radiant One, to send forth His Light to assist you in attuning with those frequencies of Light which are being sent forth now at this time into the very core of your own beings. Become aware of these things; attune yourselves in consciousness that at the time of the change you may move graciously, harmoniously, peacefully, with the CHANGE as it comes and be of help and assistance to those around you who stand in need at such time.

Having said this, we now terminate this transmission, leaving with you the essence of our beings, the Light which flows from the All-Knowing One and His Radiance, we bid you welcome the coming DAWN, for it is, peoples of Earth, our brothers, our sisters, for the greater joy of mankind that this be so.

May the One Light be yours and you one with it.

* * * * * * * * *

(By Telethought transmission, 30 March 1968. Channel: Marianne Francis)

DEVIC ENERGY PATTERNS

We have the authority to transmute energy patterns, energy forces on and outside of planet Earth at this time. What is puny Man in his concept of divinity to assume the authority which is not vested in him, nor his to wield? Who and what is mankind upon this small planet to tamper with the forces which hold together Solar Systems and galaxies: the force within the atom, the world in miniature, the energy from the Godhead!

We, who do have authority to wield these cohesive forces for the evolving of races throughout the galaxies, do so only under the jurisdiction of the Most High and the directives of Light. Wisdom is not the prerogative of this race which dwells upon the planet called Earth. Wisdom resides only in the hearts and minds of a few, yet these few may be exalted in consciousness to a comprehension of their innate godhood of being. At such time and in so evolving, these individuals will assume not only responsibility but authority proceeding directly from ourselves and from the Godhead itself.

When mankind tampers with forces beyond his understanding or control, he does so unknowing of the tremendous majesty and awesome nature of that which he, ineffectively, has confused with his understanding of jurisdiction. Jurisdiction for mankind falls only within the category of mankind's own development within his own being and own social systems. It does not extend to disruption of a planet, the forces of the Devic Kingdoms of nature, nor interference with the patterns of other planets within this system, held in balance by that same cohesive force which manifests throughout the galaxies of God.

When the lesson, which is yet to be learnt by destructive Man in its entirety, is fully absorbed, then will come a certain humility, a certain breaking down of the ego manifestation of Man on this planet. Then, and only then, can the inner core of the spiritual being of Man manifest itself, for this alone is of godhood, of the eternal, immortal nature, and yields from itself the energies and the patterns of supreme beauty and magnitude to which Man may rise.

We who are nameless beings in your concept of names, attune in consciousness upon this occasion and utilise this channel of Light. It is not simply in that to which we give voice, but in the energies which we are grounding and transmitting at the time of this channelling which is of import.

Before too long, many of the areas of weakened fault line activity upon your planet are due to be disrupted by tremendous patterns of...shall we term it...oscillating currents of energy, currents which we might describe as being at cross purposes with the basic forces of harmonics holding together the structural matter of your planet. When these oscillating currents begin to make themselves felt in all their magnitude, then many areas of your planet will feel the tremendous upheavals long prophecied and forecast by our prophets upon the Earth planet and plane. At such time the stability of all Light center areas will need the grounding energies which will be sent down from our realm of divine manifestation in order to act as stabilizing factors, poles of force, shall we say, that the planet itself may not be shaken beyond the stress pattern which it can endure without being completely shaken out of orbit or axial balance.

You have been prepared in consciousness and must continue to prepare in consciousness, yourselves, and those whom you reach, for those things which are about to manifest. Stabilization will be of paramount importance, and stabilized individuals will be rare when this time comes; for the very disruption of the energy patterns is going to cause a tremendous fluctuation of cellular matter and agitation of energies within the body physical, not only the body physical of the planet, but the body physical of the individuals upon it. These thoughts are not new. We are aware of this, yet they must be emphasized as you stand close to major upheavals within the pattern of this your month and year.

The energies which we wield must be grounded in many points by those acting as our channels, must be held at this time. Therefore, now we pour down such stabilizing force into the center of this locality at this time.

In the Light of a thousand suns and the ever-burning radiance of the INNER SUN, we bid you adieu of this time.

Nexus aloria.

* * * * * * * * * * * *

(By Telethought transmission, 17 April '68. Channel: Marianne Francis)

PROJECT COVER-UP

Sub-title; The Condon Report into Unidentified Flying Objects.

In October 1966 an announcement was made by the secretary of Defense that the Air Force has selected Dr. Edward Condon and the University of Colorago for a study into unidentified flying objects. This study was to be "a totally objective scientific investigation".

In May of this year, LOOK Magazine blasted the concept of total scientific objectivity with a sizzling article by John Fuller entitled "Flying Saucer Fiasco". It seems strange, as this may appear to the naive, trusting taxpayer, that this study never was the objective scientific thing it was supposed to be. To date it has cost the taxpayer over half a million dollars and the report is yet to be released!

We in the Flying Saucer field, who are neither naive nor trusting where governments and their scientists are concerned, were not surprised at what was revealed in Fuller's article. It seems that Dr. Condon started in on this project in Feb. '67 with a totally <u>unobjective</u> attitude to UFO. He is quoted as saying, "UFO's are not the business of the Air Force". He further added, just so no one might get the idea he had an open mind, "It is my inclination right now to recommend that the Government get out of this business. My attitude right now is that there's nothing to it... but I'm not supposed to reach a conclusion for another year"!!!!

Many people in the Ufo field felt very sure that this study at Colorado University was merely a clever way to "take the heat" off the Air Force, and Fuller's article bears this out.

In August '66 prior to the signing of the contract, Robert Low, project coordinator, had written a memo labelled "Some Thoughts on the UFO Project". In it he said, "Our study would be conducted almost exclusively by non-believers who, although they couldn't possible prove a negative result, could and probably would add an impressive body of evidence that there is no reality to the observations. The <u>trick</u> would be, I think, to describe the project so that to the public, it would appear a totally objective study, but to the scientific community, would present the image of a group of nonbelievers trying their best to be objective, but having an almost zero expectation of finding a saucer....that one way of doing this would be to stress investigation, not of the physical phenomena, but rather of the people who do the observing...the psychology and sociology of persons and groups who report seeing UFO's." (end quote).

In the Saucer field it has been known for a long time that the official line toward UFO's is to use ridicule. Making the whole affair and the people who sight UFO's look ridiculous has proved quite effective. Scientists with reputations and positions to lose, thus became very chary of doing any serious <u>public</u> research into the mystery of the UFO's.

Dr. James McDonald, Senior Physicist at the Institute of Atmospheric Physics, and professor of Meteorology at the University of Arizone, is one scientist, however, who is bluntly "laying it on the line". When interviewed on Louis Lomax's TV show on July 16th, '67, McDonald had this to say: "After taking a close look at Air Force Project Bluebook, it simply has to be waived aside as not a serious investigation, and this is why scientists such as myself and scientists in other parts of the world have not (previously) taken a look at the problem. We have assumed all along that the Air Force has been checking the cases and doing it with expertise, but that's not the case at all. The CIA asked for and got from the Air Force a debunking policy... the actual wording of the recommendation is 'to debunk the Flying Saucers to decrease the public interest in them'". (End Quote).

This policy has been systematically carried out for twenty years. The Colorado study itself, a $500,000 trick, has undoubtedly "taken the heat" off the Air Force. That's about all it has done. Yet the gullible section of the public will be persuaded that a serious scientific investigation of UFO's was undertaken. This leaves us where we came in, with the individual and not with organized authority. Every single individual on this planet is going home to do their own thinking, draw their own conclusions, and cease to lean on "authorities" of questionable worth.

Vast monopolies on this planet are concerned with hiding, distorting, and perverting the truth about the extra-terrestrial Spaceships. The Space people know this and they are leaving it up to the individual Earth man or woman to find TRUTH It takes courage and strength of mind and soul to do this, yet it's worth it, and this after all, is what the New Age is all about: The evolvement of the individual.

— Marianne Francis

References: LOOK Magazine, May 14, '68.
Louis Lemax TV Show, Los Angeles, July 16, '67.

CENTER NEWS AND TRAVELS

I am writing this on Orcas Island where I am enjoying a few day's rest. So muc has happened since March that only the high-lights can be covered here. I must have packed more than twice the usual amount of lecturing, radio and TV interview and driving into the past three months. April and May saw me touring California where I gave several lectures. In Santa Barbara I visited old friends then on to Los Angeles where I stopped off at Gabrial & Helen Green's where I collected some more bumper stickers saying: "Flying Saucers are Real; the Air Force doesn't exist". These were distributed at strategic points along the way.

One highlight on this trip was a meeting with Anthony Brooke which gave us a chance to exchange all the news of Denmark and England. We also agreed something could be very imminant this year on the world scene.

Following a few days rest at Laguna Beach, I returned to Hollywood to find that the Sunday Forum lecture was cancelled as they had closed down two weeks previously. Mr. & Mrs. L. A. Stevens, where I stayed a few days, arranged for a lecture in their home which proved interesting. The Understandorama in Yucca Valley was my next port of call. There I appeared on the Panel Discussion and made quite a few "waves" and found that I was on the same side of the fence as Col. Burkes on the subject of "Hippies". Visited Teska in her new White Star headquarters and lectured for Bob and Shirley Short at their Solar Space Foundation.

The return trip included stops at Santa Barbara and Auburn again and also at Palo Alto, then back to the Center in time for a hectic Guest Session. Kenneth managed to get down from Seattle for this session (May 12th) at which the Density Level Travel communication was received. (See page 7). Then, with little time to pack, on to Seattle for lectures at the Free University (sponsored by Joy Fullerton) and then the United Brotherhood Convention. The next weekend found us at the Portland Convention sponsored by Universariun after considerable delay due to car trouble about which I won't enlarge on here.

The Canadian tour proved quite important in terms of new contacts. I had five radio interviews and a TV show which stimulated much interest, resulting in overflow audiences, both in Vancouver and Victoria, B.C. I was treated most charmingly by friends who invited me as a house guest along the way, and wish to extend my personal thanks again for all favours received. In Vancouver I stayed with Mel and Irene Harper and with the Schimmeyers at Nanaimo. There were pleasant times as well as hard work. We did manage to spend a day cycling in the park and going to the Zoo. Crossing the ferry to Vancouver Island is also quite enjoyable, and the weather was excellent.

Interest proved so great in Vancouver that it was decided to form a branch of the Solar Light Center there. A committee meeting was quickly called together after the Lecture and met the next day at the home of Bob and Joan Gale who have been most helpful. The result of this meeting is that the Vancouver Affiliates of the Solar Light Center is now well organized to assist in arranging lectures, study groups, and related activities in the Vancouver area. (See page 11).

We were glad to see Lile and Elaine Chambers of the City of Light group at the Portland Convention and also in Seattle and Vancouver where they were of help.

Postscript: After leaving Orcas Island, I drove to Seattle where I was invited to stay in Thelma Wheeler's apartment. This was conveniently located not far from KING radio station where I finally had an interview on Clark on KING program. This drew so much interest that it was extended an hour and a half over the time originally scheduled.

A final lecture booking at Coos Bay, Oregon, then on home where there will be a pile of mail waiting to answer. Luckily, Kenneth has taken care of requests for complimentary copies of STARCRAFT up to now, but more come in, and it seems that the predictions that this will be a very important year are coming true.

-- Marianne Francis

ANNOUNCEMENTS

GUEST SESSIONS: Regular Guest Channelling Sessions will be held at the Center as follows: Saturday: July 27th and August 31st, at 8:00 p.m. (Possibly Sessions will be held on the last Saturdays of Sept. & Oct. also.)

TELEPHONE: At long last the telephone has been installed at the Center. The number is: 855-1956 (Area Code: 503). The best time to phone is in the evening (5 to 7 pm) or 1 to 2 pm. As we do not have secretarial help at present, please remember to keep calls brief and concise.

LECTURES: Several of Marianne Francis' lectures have now been printed as listed below. If you have placed an order that has not yet been filled, be sure to write in about it, giving details.

SUBSCRIPTION: As explained in a leaflet sent with the Spring issue of STARCRAFT, the rate has been increased to $2.25 (USA) and $2.50 (Foreign). This should enable us to cover the extra postage and printing costs and continue to give out complimentary copies as we have done in the past, although extra donations are also needed, as many more are now being given out. If you have friends who are interested, a subscription to STARCRAFT will be a suitable gift any time of the year.

PUBLICATIONS of the SOLAR LIGHT CENTER:

Lectures by Marianne Francis:

FREQUENCY CHANGE AND THE SECOND COMING	$1.25
THE CALL OF THE PHOENIX	1.50
STARCRAFT CONTACT	1.25
MEN FROM SPACE & PROPHECIES OF EARTH CHANGES	1.25
GOD-MAN or ANIMAL-MAN	1.00
THE NEW DIMENSION AND THE NEW AGE	1.00

CHANNELLED MATERIAL from the Space People:

Set of ten scripts selected from Channelled Material 2.90

STARCRAFT Magazine: Subscription $2.25 (USA), $2.50 (Foreign).
(Three or four issues per year plus Newsletters when possible).

SEND ORDERS TO:

SOLAR LIGHT CENTER
Rt. 2, Box 572-J
Central Point, Oregon
97501

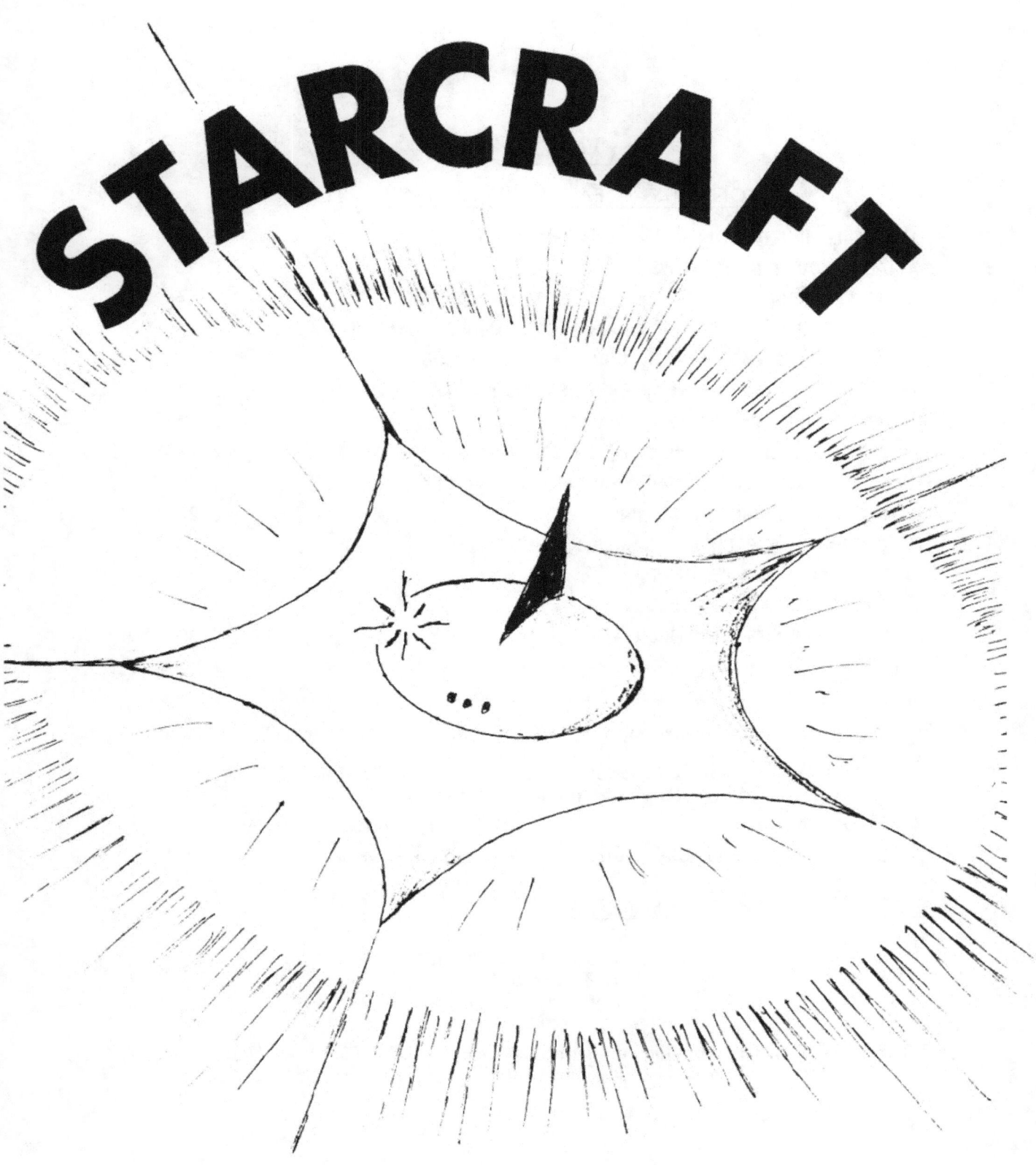

STARCRAFT

VOL. 3, No. 3 & 4   SOLAR LIGHT CENTER   FALL & WINTER 1968

STARCRAFT

CONTENTS - FALL & WINTER 1968

EDITORIAL: INITIATION - by Marianne Francis	3
CANADIAN AFFILIATES NEWS	5
MANIFESTATION - by SUT-KO of the SATURN COUNCIL	6
GUEST CORNER - White Star Release: DESKA speaks on TIME VALUE	8
THE OLD ORDER PASSES - by ORLON, a Space Brother	10
Nevada Underground NUCLEAR EXPLOSIONS and EARTHQUAKES	12
IMMINENT UPHEAVALS???	13
YOURS IS THE CHOICE, PEOPLE OF EARTH - by ORLON	17
SCIENCE DEPARTMENT: THE INVISIBLE UNIVERSE	20
NEW UFO SIGHTING IN SPAIN	22
THE CADENCES OF LIGHT - by JUNE of VENUS	23
LETTERS FROM OUR READERS	25
CENTER NEWS AND TRAVELS	26
ANNOUNCEMENTS and PUBLICATIONS	28

* * * * * * * * * * * * * * * * * *

Director and Editor - - - - - - Marianne Francis, Dr.Sp.Sc.
Science Director & Business Manager - - - Kenneth M. Kellar, B.A.

Published quarterly by SOLAR LIGHT CENTER
a non-profit corporation.

COPYRIGHT reserved   Write for permission to reprint.

ZIP CODES are required now, so please include yours when writing.

ADDRESS ALL CORRESPONDENCE TO:

SOLAR LIGHT CENTER
Rt. 2, Box 572-J
Central Point, Oregon
97501

TELEPHONE us first if you plan on visiting the Center: 855-1956 (Code 503).
(Roads are bad in winter. The Spring is the best time to visit).

EDITORIAL
INITIATION

— Marianne Francis

This issue of STARCRAFT contains data of great importance, received here at the Center during the past three months. If it is carefully studied, it will be found to contain keys to the events which are not only imminent on the world scene, but are already manifesting. In the work which has been done here, we have continually endeavored to present a "whole" picture rather than a single facet. The world scene, the planetary focus, is viewed in its Cosmic perspective, not one clouded by nationalism, politics, or the uncertain values of a materialistic society.

Ever has it been taken into account that few individuals on the face of planet Earth can free themselves from the hypnotic spell under which the masses live and die, to view this life and this period of time as do the Space Brothers. Yet, it has been continually suggested and taught from this Center, that only as a Cosmic viewpoint IS sought, only thus can the individual find real security, stability, and their true place in the eternal scheme of things.

Now it would seem, the time for preparation is running out and the time for facing of realities, at many levels of being, is here. Data from geologists and seismologists is included in this issue to verify the material the Space Brothers have been giving for fifteen or twenty years. Major earth upheavals are taking place and many more are due to shake the civilizations of planet Earth.

Politics will NOT solve these problems, yet several of our subscribers have written in to advocate a candidate whose whole political record has been one of limited vision and on whose face is the stamp of blind hatred and unspirituality. Wealth and materialism will not solve the crisis which is here and grows daily, yet there are those who still believe they can shut their eyes to the world's agony and live in the comfort & security which their wealth has bought. Poverty of spirit will not surmount the crisis nor will false humility. Yet it has been painfully true, for this period of time, that the "children of Light" on this planet have had neither wealth nor position. Their voices have been as voices crying in the wilderness, for they have spoken of things of the spirit.

The appeal to Man's inner self has not been accompanied by outer or materialistic proofs, nor will it be. For the spirit within hears not nor sees as reality the things which are dying. This is why few concrete proofs have been offered, at a mundane mass level, by Spacemen and women from "Light" planets and sources, of their coming

The change which comes is basically a spiritual CHANGE, though it will be accompanied by social revolutions and might upheavals of nature. The change in Man will be a SPIRITUAL change or awakening. It is, in effect, an INITIATION of Earth and its peoples. Therefore, it is not permitted that mass materialistic proofs be offered, for this would not fulfill the purpose of the initiation.

The appeal itself is basically directed to Man's soul and only Man's soul CAN or WILL respond. Those who do so respond will then use their intelligence and their emotions to express the inner conviction, the KNOWING which "knows because it knows. So will come about the separation of the "wheat from the chaff" spoken of in the Christian Bible.

WARNING

A question was asked at the Victoria, B.C. lecture regarding the advisability of anyone attempting contact with the Space Brothers telepathically or physically. Here is my answer, somewhat enlarged upon for the benefit of all our readers.

I will no longer suggest or recommend interested people attempting such contacts unless they are willing to put themselves through a specific kind of program of self-discipline and self-knowledge. Over the last few years I have observed such juvenile antics and ego-inflation taking place on untrained and unprepared mentalities as to be downright dangerous, both to the cause, and to the individuals themselves.

If the Space intelligences want to contact you, they will do so; they do the choosing. If you wish to make yourself a fit candidate to be chosen, then I would ask the following questions:

1) Have you dedication of a spiritual nature?
2) Have you courage to stay with your convictions without bravado, quietly, reasonably, peacefully?
3) Do you really know yourself inside and out, through hell and high water? If not, start a self-knowledge program.
4) Have you an inferiority complex or a secret desire for power? If so,

forget about Space people and go to work to balance your ego and attain inner poise. When you truly know self, you will find knowledge of others follows.

The Space Brothers need highly stable individuals. Are you one?

Astral interlopers, masquerading as Space intelligences, clutter up the Space field. They flourish in the purely psychic realm. They feed on vanity and ego. Organizations have even been formed around power mad individuals claiming Space contacts from such sources. BE ALERT! BE AWARE!

Space men and women from the Solar and Galactic Confederations are concerned with the good of all peoples, of any nationality on Earth, whom they can reach. They preach no dogmas nor creeds, nor do they feed "ego food" to their channels. All True channels are part of a Plan to assist the Earth and its peoples through the great change or initiation. Some play a greater part, some a lesser, but all are part of the Plan, Cosmic and spiritual in nature. The desire to serve, to love, and to understand, is the real mark of a true Light server. "By their deeds shall ye know them".

* * * * * * * *

CANADIAN AFFILIATES NEWS

"Mr. H. A. Pym has been elected the new president of the Vancouver Associates. Temporarily, meetings will continue to be held at the home of Mr. Bob Gale, former president, but this can be altered at short notice, due to Mr. Gale's uncertain health.

When Miss Francis came to Vancouver, a special meeting was held at the home of Mr. Gale which was very well attended. Following the playing of a Space tape recording, Miss Francis gave a short channelling session on the subject of unity, followed by an interesting question session.

After the channelling, two members reported seeing something unusual just before Marianne began. One man said he saw a beam of light surrounding Marianne from above and it reached out into the room as if scanning the audience. He felt it was from a Spacecraft immediately above the area. A lady reported seeing what appeared to be a type of television camera, switched on and all ready to go.

The Vancouver Associates extend their thanks to Miss Francis for both this session and the lecture at Oakridge Auditorium, and wish her speedy return once more."

Information about future meetings in Vancouver can be obtained from either:

    Sec.-Treas. - Mrs. Bernice Young, 156 West 12th Ave., Vancouver 10. B. C.
    President - Mr. Harold A. Pym, 2907 West 6th Ave, Kitsilano, Vancouver.

MANIFESTATION

Greetings, our brothers, our sisters in Light. The title of our talk with you is Manifestation. At this particular time in the affairs and events of mankind upon planet Earth, a period has been reached which is difficult to define in our terminology; perhaps even more difficult to define in yours. For many years we have communicated to you, our brothers, our sisters, of the imminence as seen through our eyes and our recording equipment, of <u>change</u>: Change in all its aspects, overall change on the face of your planet. Now, <u>change is all about you in the consciousness of Man,</u> in the changing standards, ethics, moral patterns. Change is, indeed, all about you and is fast taking place <u>geologically</u> even as it is in consciousness.

We find ourselves now in the position of looking on at affairs as they move on their appointed pattern and of communicating to you our thoughts of the next phase of operation: that phase we have entitled MANIFESTATION. We have entitled it this for a very good reason.

The time for consciousness adjustment, balancing, unlimiting, is <u>almost over</u>. Those who have not adjusted, unlimited, and balanced in consciousness have very little time left to do this before the mighty changes of a very physical nature make themselves felt. In the meantime, manifestation of not only our intent, but <u>manifestation</u> of <u>our</u> <u>presence</u> and of energy, of power, of Universal Light, is <u>about</u> to <u>begin.</u> By Universal Light, by energy, we speak of that power which permeates the Universes of God, which flows directly through all systems: Power from the Creator, from that being itself:

Manifestation of the substance of Light, manifestation of its workings in the hearts, minds, consciousness, souls, of those who are our own upon this planet and those who aspire to be as the children of Light and walk into the new radiance of a New Dawn.

Manifestation is beginning in its <u>first phase</u> with the outpourings of energies through the vehicles or bodies which are being used at this time by our peoples on this planet. Manifestation of ENERGY .... what does this mean? It means, my brothers, my sisters in Light, that <u>as this energy is tapped</u> in all its majesty, magnificance, unlimited quality, as it pours through the vehicle or vehicles of our peoples and of the children of Light upon this planet, that those things <u>which were previously impossible</u> will become as simple child's play; that herculean tasks will be performed with ease, that <u>mountains</u> <u>will</u> <u>be</u> <u>moved</u> as molehills; that the consciousness of those who might be termed hard in heart, closed in mind, will be reached and will be shaken as by a great force, by a power which, as the tape you have just heard has said, may not be gainsaid.

The energies of Light pouring through in their purity are energies of <u>untold</u> <u>potency</u>, <u>vibration</u>, and <u>power</u>. The mountains of Man's consciousness may be scaled, may be looked upon <u>in a light previously unknown</u>.

When the Light of the Universal vibration pours forth, changing the molecular structures, the cellular structures of all physical matter, the vibrating atoms spinning then at higher frequency vibrations, will incorporate within themselves the god pattern of being; and manifesting this in all its intent upon that level, will produce what mankind of this time will call miracles. Miracles, being but the outworking of Cosmic Law, will become the new order of the New Age. Manifestation of Universal Light is the phase and the pattern now commencing on planet Earth.

It is of no moment, my brothers, my sisters, as to the name of beings manifesting from high realms of spiritual identity. It is of moment and import as to the validity of that which cannot be gainsaid. Names are of small importance viewed from the higher realms of Man's consciousness, both discarnate and incarnate, both Devic and Space. Those who would proclaim that within a name lies import, significance, are deluding themselves with the importance of their own small concerns.

We who speak from Space, from the craft stationed above this mountain locality, the Saturn Council directives, speak of energies, of Universal Light, of beings of Light and sons and daughters of Light. We speak in terms of Service, of manifestation of Service, of manifestation of Love, of manifestation of Compassion. We speak not of identities. Those highest beings, by whatsoever name they choose to manifest to various groups, carry significance only within the vibration of that which they bring and that which they, in essence, ARE.

These things are undeniable, these things are the stamp of an evolved being or soul. Be not, therefore, deluded by the noisy concerns of those who would bring upon this field of endeavor, confusion and concern for small things. The concern now is placed upon the VIBRATION ITSELF, MANIFESTATION OF UNDENIABLE SPIRITUAL POWER and IDENTITY. All who carry this stamp, carry it in their actions, in their eyes, and in their words, but not in one only, but in all that they are and they do.

Manifestation of Divine Light, of Universal Energy, takes place in this your year of 1968 in its first and primary phase. From this point onwards it moves forward into other phases, carrying those of you who are prepared in consciousness into the etheric levels of existence and that which you have been taught to understand as the Frequency Change.

My brothers, my sisters of the Earth planet, I speak with you in love, in Light, in understanding, in brotherhood. I speak beyond you also, to those to whom my words will reach. I speak now to many thousands for the words which we utter go forth through this and many channels of Light to the children of the Earth planet, to prepare them, to assist them, to comfort them in the time ahead.

Great changes are upon you and manifestation of the Light energy will uphold all who turn within to the source of the god self of the Divine and the Christ consciousness of being. For the rest, as they turn into the pathways of greater destruction, that which has been termed the separation of the wheat from the chaff on planet Earth takes place, in all its divisiveness, in all its final rending, even as the substance of the Earth itself divides between Light and dark.

This which we say to you upon this occasion is of import; carries with it the authority of the Saturn Council and the imprint of truth in its vibratory quality. We urge that you study our words, for soon it is our intention to reach out also by means of tape recordings through this our channel, as the new phase enters in and takes its manifestation also. The time for talk of change is ended. The time for manifestation of change is with you.

Talk no more, our brothers, our sisters of the Earth planet, but ACT. Cease to bewilder yourselves with the confusions of a confused planet and walk your pathways directly in confidence, in love, in compassion, and in surety of the energies which you draw about you and within, and emanate to all in your environs.

Our brothers, our sisters, I have spoken on this occasion at some length. I identify solely at the wish of those present as Sut-Ko of the Saturn Council. Truth, however, bears its own stamp within the soul of those who hear. Truth most certainly rings its own answering chords within the soul of the evolving ones and needs no names for guarantee.

In the Light of Our Radiant One, I bid you, Adonai vassu baragus.

(Telethought transmission, Solar Light Center, 27 July 68. Channel: Marianne Francis)

* * * * * * * * * * * * * * * * * * *

GUEST CORNER — From: TESKA

WHITE STAR RELEASE

DESKA SPEAKS ON ——— TIME VALUE

Changes have been rapid since the turn of your Planetary Year which took place at the time of your Winter Solstice. All factors which involve the evolutionary progression of your planetary cellular life have been accelerated, creating reactions in all human and sub-human intelligences.

The affect of such acceleration is felt and responded to by all energy fields involved upon Earth; in ALL her life-energy levels-- from the lowest vibratory densities of life-streams unto the highest. LIFE on all Planes of Expression..likewise... in ALL its Degrees of Awareness...has responded. Some toward constructive progression -- others toward destructive chaotic purpose.

To find balance, in the shifting elemental, psychic, and mental fields of influence, presents a great challenge to those mentalities which, having Power of Choice, can rectify adverse conditions by their attitudes of firm, positive stand toward Stability. But those, who have little awareness of what is transpiring, give vent to accumulated emotions through acts of violence and expressions of abandonment.

The speeding up of vibratory conditions -- likewise, brings forth a New Concept, wherein the command of a stable mind, produces quickly, desired results. While the unstable can likewise create chaos as rapidly.

The Time Factor, which has been a blessing to humanity, allowing for rectifying of energies of thought before the manifestation of their results, now lessens in its length, bringing forth with rapid manifestation, those conditions which are dwelt upon, both of a positive as well as a negative value.

It has been taught that...Energy Follows Thought...and the Result of Thought is its IMAGE. The Creation of circumstances follows after the Pattern of Energy Concepts. However, the Time involved for culminating an Energy into a Result of its Content, has been of a Frequency-Duration, and end results have been a conglomeration born of consistent variations of Thought Patterns which rapidly change in man's awareness, and constantly play upon each other, modifying original concepts with conditioning compensating energy wavelengths. A thought Image, before fully manifesting a reality of itself, has been changed and modified by Changing Concepts.

New Energy Potentials now bring forth the closing in of TIME, allowing less opportunity for change of mind before Results of thoughts set in motion. The awareness of this advent of Conditions have been given, plus the Methods which man must learn to use to keep Attuned and properly prepared to handle his Mental Energies in order to maintain himself in the New Age Consciousness.

Special Issues which have given Keys for Mental Attitudes, have been given forth, not in a sense to spiritualize man's soul, for that comes with Growth and Unfoldment, but Methods of Thought Attitude to assure him a retention of sanity and living balance.

The NOW of thinking has become the Now of experience...and the ensuing days will bring Time into a contraction which will bring about INSTANTANEOUS RESULT. An energy of thought creates a chain-reaction after its Kind...which, if Negative, swallows up a man's Victory, once it gains its action.

Thinking NOW, with POSITIVE CONSTRUCTIVE POWER, will bring PEACE into the Eternal NOW of experience...but to think NOW of a negative past, or a fearful tomorrow, brings the Reaction into the immediate field of experience..emotionally immediate, if not materially immediate...but, the Material becomes ever more rapidly a NOW EXPERIENCE.

GUARD YOUR THOUGHTS, and KEEP EVER IN THE LIGHT OF WISDOM!

From: WHITE STAR, P.O. Box 307, Joshua Tree, CA, 92252. Aug.-Sept. 1968.

THE OLD ORDER PASSES

Greetings, our brothers, our sisters in Light. We have spoken to you on the last occasion of our discourse on the subject of Manifestation. During that discourse we acquainted you with the fact that Time as you know it for the expanding, the unlimiting of consciousness was, shall we say, "running out" on your world scene. We did not wish to convey the thought that at the time.. at the future of manifestation there would no longer be expansion, unlimiting, evolution of consciousness. Obviously, this could not be so, however, that which we did wish to convey was the imminence of CHANGE in its overall aspect and manifestation of Light energy, frequency change upon your planet, your world scene.

When we spoke of the running out of time, we spoke in terms which, perhaps, might be better understood if we elaborate to a certain extent on this concept. We have stated that the period through which your peoples have passed was one wherein a speeding up of the processes of consciousness was taking place. Through many means your peoples have attempted to unlimit, to evolve, to experience. The innate being of mankind upon planet Earth has, for many thousands and thousands of years, experienced through the rawest of conditions many things which have brought about a slow and gradual understanding within him of the forces by which he has felt himself controlled. Yet, in the last twenty-five of your years, an awakening has come to some of your peoples that these forces do not control but may be controlled, even as Man himself reaches out and expands in awareness to become the master of that which he surveys.

Certain of your peoples, in misunderstanding this concept, have attempted to force upon their surroundings and their fellowman in dictatorial manner their own aspects or concept of ego. This concept is false in that it does not take into account or understanding the divine nature of Man in his eternal, immortal being. Only as man, in that immortal being expresses, may he become lord of that which he surveys. You have listened to a tape which spoke to you of love, of beauty, of service and of compassion and of consideration. Only as Man understands of these attributes of the God-self, does he become consciously at one with his own divine essence, And in becoming one with that essence, he then is able to manipulate the forces of Nature and to live in harmony with himself and his fellow beings of all gradations of consciousness upon this planet.

In the period of time through which you have recently passed, of two of your so-called world wars, a tremendous acceleration of consciousness has taken place, due to great negativity and destructiveness which Mankind has been combatting within his own nature and with the conditions within which he finds himself at this time.

Now, in the last five of your years, attempts have been made by many of your peoples to expand the consciousness through means other than that of mysticism, philosophical discourse, or so-called religion, and through the use of drugs, an attempt has been made by Man who is seeking, to force upon the doors of consciousness or perception to other realms or levels of being. We have touched on this subject previously. We understand of the reasons WHY man has reached outward and, in impatience of thought and of being, has thought to throw open the doors of perception. No longer content with the three-dimensional world in which he physically finds himself, he has sought the other worlds from which his immortal being once came.

At this time we do not speak in terms of that which is advisable or inadvisable, but what he has sought to experience. Experience being the great teacher upon your planet for the many, it has been necessary for those who sought to know from the very essence of their beings of the reality of other worlds, for soon will come the time of the frequency change, and the catapulting of the New Race of man into a state of etheric, or partly etheric, vibratory existence. This New race of Man will be comprised only of those souls who have, as you would say in your terminology, made the grade in consciousness. It is of this subject, this evolvement, unlimiting of consciousness, of which we have spoken so constantly in our discourses with you.

Even as Man is reaching outward, rapidly now comes the molecular change which will affect all molecular structure upon the surface of your planet. Only those who are so prepared and adapt to this change, to this higher vibration and become the New Race of Man, will move into the new density of the frequency change which is taking place, not only on this, but on all planets in the system. Because Time, even as you know it in your computation of years, is rapidly running out, we have stressed the consciousness evolvement, the unlimiting of the areas of mind previously closed with dogma, with rigidity and with lack of plasticity.

Now we have spoken with you of manifestation of Light energy, beginning in its first and primary phase in this year of 1968. We have rarely (though we sometimes indulge in this) put a date upon the beginning of a cyclic time in your calendar time. We have done this for a very specific reason. As the universal energies of Light pour forth from the Central Sun throughout this system, and throughout all planets in this system, the very molecules vibrating at an increased frequency will force Life, and the Life waves on this planet and others, into a new reassessment of all values previously held.

Other planets in this system, as we have previously told you, are prepared, and are aware of this coming change. Yet the great masses of your peoples, except in a sub-conscious manner, are not. Now, as this change begins in its first phase, those on your planet who have understanding, who are aware of the nature of what is taking place, will be called upon to act as leaders, directors, comforters, wayshowers, to those who are stumbling, yet who seek the new awareness.

We do not speak now of those, and there are many, undoubtedly many millions, who will not, again to use your phrase, make the grade at this time. We speak only of the on-going ones who move forward at this time of cyclic change. We speak at this time to those who have understanding, to those who have ears to hear and eyes to see, to those who are aware of what is taking place in its many manifestations and guises.

As the great outpouring of Light flows in with the waves of energy, the changes will be rapid indeed, and many of your peoples who are only half prepared, will find themselves caught up in conditions of which they have little understanding. Then will come the time of the wayshowers, of the Lightbearers, to hold forth what must become the torch of understanding, of love, and of compassion to the children of the Earth planet in order to assist them through the change.

Once again we make mention of that which has been termed in your Biblical phraseology the separation of wheat from chaff. Knowing that this will take place, we do not need any longer to dwell upon the destination of those who are not as the wheat. For these things follow the outworkings of Cosmic law on this and any other planet. As the times change, and as the consciousness of Man adapts, so do the bodies or vehicles which are no longer required, or cannot withstand the increased energies, lay themselves down to be reactivated in another form, in another season of time.

Time is cyclic, my brothers, my sisters; time marches onwards throughout the galaxies of God, in cycles beyond cycles and in vibratory waves of energy, bringing forward at each new casting upon the shore those treasures which exist and have been garnered from the great sea or ocean of consciousness. At this time, the waves casting forth upon the shore, break and reveal, perhaps, but a few treasures, brightly gleaming in the sand of Earth, yet these few, this humanity, is the beginning of the New Race of Man, of the new consciousness of the dawn of the Age of Enlightment, of the age of interplanetary brotherhood and travel. If you would be one with this and with these, know that your consciousness of being alone, and the love which resides within you to give unto others, is the key, and THERE IS NONE OTHER.

The time has gone for the buying and selling of souls. The time is past for the buying and selling of Man's birthright. The time is past for all things of the old order. In consciousness of being, in the Light of Our Radiant One, we see Mankind of planet Earth, moving forward into a New Dawn of an Era of Light. We who walk in consciousness with you from many planets from within your system, coming at this time to impart that essence of our beings, that love from our very souls, walk with you and will be as one with you at the time of the manifestation of universal Light energy.

With those thoughts, and with that essence and outpourings of our beings (for I speak for many on this occasion) I leave you, my brothers, my sisters. Yet are we with you many times in consciousness as we gaze upon the surface of your planet.

I, Orlon, transmit upon this occasion from Saturn Command sources. Adonai vassu.

(By Telethought transmission, 31 August '68. Channel: Marianne Francis)

* * * * * * * * * * * * * * * *

NEVADA UNDERGROUND NUCLEAR EXPLOSIONS BELIEVED CAPABLE OF TRIGGERING BIG QUAKE

The Atomic Energy Commission has set off two undergound nuclear explosions from its Nevada test site this year and while they hardly have disturbed the gambling habits of Las Vegas residents, the blasts are becoming a controversial issue, particularly among people who feel they may provoke a major earthquake....

The trouble is that scientists have just learned, somewhat to their surprise, that large underground explosions are followed by a swarm of small earthquakes, unfelt but measurable on delicate instruments called seismometers. Since tremors have been known to trigger other tremors with cumulative effect, some experts are beginning to wonder if some day a thumper might trigger disaster.

On one side of the controversy are civic leaders who want undergound testing of superweapons halted pending positive proof that it is safe. Ranged against them are makers of government policy who insist the risk is far outweighed by the need to perfect nuclear weapons....

The thumper that started all the furor came last Jan. 19. Although not the most powerful of the more than 250 undergound blasts set off in Nevada up to that time-- one in December 1966 had a bit more yield-- it unexpectedly jolted buildings as far away as Salt Lake City and Los Angeles. It registered 6.2 on the Richter magnitude scale, which pegs major earthquakes at 7.0. For some unexplained reason, it was called Faultless. ---

Flying over the scene later, geologist David Slemmons of the University of Nevada photographed giant cracks in the earth three miles long and with an upward thrust of more than 15 feet.

TREMORS INCREASED

In addition to these tangible effects, Faultless triggered other events. Seismologists intensified their studies of earthquake activity after blasts, and big landowners demanded that future megaton testing be postponed until results were known. Nonetheless, an even bigger blast 100 miles closer to Las Vegas was set off April 26 at a slightly greater depth, 3,800 feet. It was called Boxcar and had a magnitude of 6.5.

After checking Faultless and Boxcar, Dr. Alan Ryall of the University of Nevada privately circulated a report showing that all explosions of magnitude 5 or greater were followed by an increase in seismicity — earthquake activity — for at least one day and in some cases up to five days.

Seismologist Ryall also found that after five recent explosions, the number of earthquakes recorded was at least twice as great as normal. Ryall's report concluded that effects of continued firing could be cumulative, "possibly resulting eventually in a sizable earthquake." - - -

Last Sept. 30 the AEC issued a statement that it "recognizes that some seismic energy releases occur shortly after, and in the vicinity of, underground nuclear detonations."

(Quoted from The Sunday Oregonian, November 3, 1968)

IMMINENT UPHEAVALS ???

The data here presented is a complete verification of material received through the Tele-thought channelship of Marianne Francis over the last ten years concerning major geological upheavals. Data of an identical character has been received by many valid contactees (both physical and telepathic contactees) since 1947.

Quotation from an article entitled "UFOs, Earthquakes and Volcanoes" by Gordon Creighton, published in FLYING SAUCER REVIEW, Vol. 14, No. 4:-

"Many people have criticised our governments because, as is alleged, they are so 'cagey' about this business of the UFO's, but we should bear in mind, too, that there are plenty of other topics on which our political and technological rulers prefer the policy of the immortal Br'er Rabbit."..."I have a feeling that one of these "delicate' matters upon which we aren't being told too much relates to the question of whether there is good scientific evidence that planet Earth is headed for another spell of immense geophysical upheaval, and that in no remote geological future either, but perhaps in the lifetime of some of us now here."

"I know that geologists, from Lyell onwards, like to be preachers of the gospel of 'gradualism' in these matters. But I notice that, during the International Geophysical Congress held in Helsinki, in 1960, a sensation was created by the top Soviet delegate, Belouzov, who declared, in a paper read before the gathering on July 26th, that vast quantities of magma are now on the move within our planet and that titanic upheavals, involving vast areas of the planet, are at hand.

Belouzov, chairman of the USSR's Committee for the Geophysical Year and one of his country's most distinguished geophysicists, does not exactly fall within the category of 'small fry". I have press clippings from European newspapers about his bombshell lecture, but so far as I know, nothing about it got into the British press. (In subsequent correspondence with the Soviet Committee for the I.G.Y., I received from him what may possibly be the 'official' version of his talk, but there are discrepancies and I think he perhaps went much further at Helsinki than the authorities would like)."

Quotation from PLAIN TRUTH magazine (Sept. 68):-

"Scientists had believed that volcanoes in Antartica were dead...not merely dormant. Until early last year all reference works could only point out one active volcano in all of this southernmost continent. But, in January of 1967, New Zealand geologists revealed the amazing discovery of a second active volcano on the rim of Antarctica. Then in the following December, the volcano on the appropriately named "Deception Island" exploded. So suddenly, in fact, that trained scientists, lacking the discernment of penguins, were completely caught off guard. This third volcano, the second within a single year...had suddenly mushroomed and sent a jolt through the world's scientific community!

Something BIG, it is now admitted, is beginning to happen under the Earth! Scientists are concerned. They know that volcanic activity in the otherwise seismically quiet continent of Antarctica heralds TREMENDOUS significance for the rest of the world! It means we have entered the age of unusual earthquake activity. Antarctica is the barometer of world-wide seismic activity. Once volcanoes on Antarctica begin to erupt.... LOOK OUT!"

"Worldwide Underground Revolution"

"Scientists from many nations are now busily trying to discover the import of these subterranean happenings. The 'International Study of the Upper Mantle' is now in progress...... Paradoxically, 1967 was, overall, the earth's quietest period in more than 70 years! Only six major quakes occurrred. The average is 16 per year since 1897. Good news? No... rather an ominous development! 1967 was merely a quiet period in which subterranean stresses were building up for future tremendous volcanic and earthquake activity! <u>A worldwide earth revolution is now beginning to take shape.</u>"

"Dr. Perry Byerly, a former professor of seismology at the University of California, admits: 'Something world-wide is going on, but it is hard to say just what it is... we don't know what. But Great Forces are at work in relative patterns, trying to pull out continents in one direction or another. This is due to something below, a GREAT STRAIN THAT IS ACCUMULATING...' (emphasis ours)." - End quote.

Quotation from SAGA magazine, July 1968:

"KILLER QUAKES"

"A catastrophe, say the geologists and seismologists, is inevitable in this country. In fact, they say it is long overdue".... "According to experts in seismology, like Dr. Clarence R. Allen, a geologist with the California Institute of Technology, it WILL happen." ... "California is literally a state living on top of a time bomb. In a remarkable survey, the nation's most prominent geophysicists were asked, a few years ago, 'Do you believe a major quake is due in California?' Nearly two-thirds answered with a resounding YES!"

"The next one is expected to strike within the continental limits of the U.S. where, in most areas vulnerable to earthquakes, population masses have built up to huge proportions. Obviously, the more population density, the more potential loss of life."...."Aren't there any spots in the U.S. that are, by reason of their geology, completely earthquake-proof? The answer is, sad to say, NO. True, the area that binds Alaska and the Aleutian Islands is the most active and dangerous earthquake area of any affecting us directly, with close to 50 major convulsions creating upheavals since the turn of the century. Equally true, the West Coast region with its massive San Andreas fault--running an awesome 2,400 miles from off the Oregon coast, down the Golden State to the Gulf of California--is a potential quake disaster area of massive proportions. SCIENCE NEWS reports that in California alone, over 10,000 earthquakes have occurred in the past 30 years."

"Want more? The entire southern coastline is an earthquake zone. So are the mid-Mississippi and St. Lawrence River valleys. There is a seismic region in New England and--few people are aware of this--New York State had a severe earthquake all its own less than 100 years ago."....

"Furthermore, the science of seismology has become much more sophisticated in recent years; as a result, old theories are being questioned and startling new discoveries are being made. There is more going on underneath the ground than even the most astute scientists of yesteryear dreamed of. The upshot: poor old Mother

Earth--already wracked by wars and revolutions, ravaged by hunger and disease-- is now felt to be much more vulnerable to natural catastrophe than it was previously thought to be."

"Consider these astonishing, alarming observations made by geologists and seismologists within the past eight years: (1) At the present time in England, some land is inexorably sinking into the sea. (2) Simultaneously, land in Scandinavia and Canada is steadily rising to higher levels. (3) The land masses encompassed by the continents of Africa, Australia and South America are moving, imperceptibly, in a northerly direction. (4) A section of California is sliding into the Pacific Ocean at the rate of two inches a year."

"But the traditional earthquake belts are by no means the whole story. It was during the International Geophysical Year, 1957-58, that scientists concerned with the workings of Mother Earth received as much of a shaking up as Mother Earth herself has gotten on some memorable occasions. That was when the Lamont Observatory research ship VEMA, as well as other vessels fitted out for research work, made the rounds of a system of seismic recording units newly-installed on a global basis. What the researchers found out had only been suspected before. Stretching some 40,000 miles under the world's oceans is a fantastic chain of mountains and valleys, peaks and canyons. Some higher than the Himalayas, some deeper than the Grand Canyon, they practically encircle the Earth twice over."

"Their significance? These submarine trenches, these rifts some 6,000 feet below the ocean's surface, stretch and strain and gorge up matter from the mantle below. In effect, submarine trenches are 'tension cracks' in the Earth's crust and, according to Leet, 'places of greatest instability in the rocks of the Earth.' They trigger off earthquakes and volcanoes; furthermore, over a considerable period of time, they put pressure on the continental crust, contributing to earthquakes there."

"And what does this new discovery mean? Obviously, that the Earth's underpinnings are even more shaky than was thought.".... End Quote.

Further to this data, we have the channelled material from one of our subscribers who visited the Center last September. This is presented here as additional data:

"June 22, 1967. - Father within:-
Seismologists are beginning to be apprehensive over the 'ominous silence' of the San Andreas fault, fearing it is building up to a tremendous upheaval in the earth soon. Are their fears groundless or are we to experience a real earthquake soon? Please. There are no fears in me, as you know." Answer:

"Your earth is in a state of agitation everywhere, in men's mind as well as in the earth, and this can be seen by your many wars as well as the many floods, tornadoes, cyclones, fires and eruptions in the mountains, but this is to be expected at a time when the earth is reaching its climax for entry into a newer and higher vibratory rate. It is a time of revolt in nature and all old things must pass away that the new can take its place. So must it also be in the world of man. All who are unprepared to live in accordance with the laws of God must be removed from the earth that they do not bring their discord into the new world so soon to come."

"The San Andreas fault has been inactive for a long time. Not since the 1906 disaster has it been actively engaged in changing the surface of the earth but soon, soon it will again revolt over man's method of extracting from the earth the wealth it has to give and once more it will 'revenge' itself by sundering itself from its moorings and this time will the destruction be so devastating that few will remain to tell of its power. For much of the coastal earth will slide into the sea, leaving so wide a gap between earth and water as cannot now be imagined. When this time comes, then will all things of earth be changed, for everywhere on earth there will be chaos, chaos of the most horrible kind, chaos which God in His mercy must bring to an end quickly lest all innocents are lost with those who brought about their own destruction."

"Hold fast to your faith in God's love to bring you through the period so soon to come. It is fast reaching its climax."

"Thank you!" * * * * *

Quotation from SCIENCE NEWS, October 7, 1967:

STRAINS SHOWING IN SAN ANDREAS FAULT

"Definite signs of strain that may indicate the imminence of large scale displacements are showing up in two places along the San Andreas Fault. The two areas are near Cholame, Hollister and Paicines in California's coastal range, and the Santa Cruz mountain area near the towns of Felton and Ben Lomond."

"They were identified in papers presented at a conference last month on Geologic problems of the San Andreas Fault system, sponsored at Stanford University and the Geological Survey, and held at Stanford."

"Near Hollister, according to a paper read by Robert A. Wallace of the Survey's Menlo Park office, the fault has been moving 0.45 inches a year for the past seven and a half years. In that area, he says, 'chances are great...that the most recently active strand will again be the sight of...surface breaks.'"

"In the Santa Cruz mountains, according to Professor Joseph Clark of the University of California at Santa Barbara, 'geologic evidence does not preclude large scale later displacement...'" End Quote.

EARTHQUAKE FELT IN MIDWESTERN STATES

Associated Press (Sun. Nov. 10, 1968). A strong earthquake centered in Southern Illinois shook more than a third of the United States yesterday, rolling across at least 22 states. The shock was felt by millions of persons. It swayed numberless buildings. But there were no immediate reports of serious damage or of any casualties..... Carl von Hake, acting chief of the National Earthquake Information Center, said the quake had a magnitude of 5.5 on the 10-point Richter scale, which is just under the usual damage level of 6. -- The quake was the most severe in the eastern half of the nation since 1944. The quake was centered near the fault in Missouri that caused, perhaps, the nation's worst quake back in 1811 which reversed the Mississippi river by shifting earth and causing it to run upstream!

YOURS IS THE CHOICE, PEOPLE OF EARTH!

Greetings, our brothers, our sisters in Light. I, Orlon, speak with you on this occasion as you stand on the very brink of MANIFESTATION itself.

Much data has been given to you, in the last three of your months, of quality, if not quantity, concerning the changes which are all about you. Now we speak at the very brink or edge of CHANGE in these last three months of this your year of 1968.

The tremendous energies now being released through and from the Central Sun source are reaching into this Solar System and are vitally affecting planet Earth. You will be aware of these energies, as we have told you for the last year of your time, in what might be termed a higher and a lower octave of frequency. We will speak first of the higher octave.

This will be what has already been termed MANIFESTATION, manifestation of the LIGHT ENERGY in all its most creative phases, releasing powers of Light and of Love within the individuals so attuned and recognized as our instruments upon the surface of the planet. Miraculous events will take place: That which has seemed outside of natural law and has been called miraculous, however, which we know of as the outworkings of a higher or more universal Law, and therefore, in our understanding, within the scheme of things COSMIC.

As you attune with the higher vibrations, you will feel yourselves at peace, at peace within the heart, the mind, and the soul. You will find yourselves attuning with what has been called the music of the spheres, and you will hear sounds in this stillness that you have not previously heard, sounds of great beauty, the Symphony of the Spheres!

Take time, our brothers, our sisters of the Earth planet, to attune in the stillness, in the quietness of your own souls and in the still places of Earth with these higher octaves of frequency as they flow in now in their fullness, for in so doing, you will assist in stabilizing and clarifying your own beings.

Now, I speak of the second phase or the lower octave, rather than phase, of this frequency inflowing. This will bring about, and already is bringing about, a tremendous increase in what could be termed destructive type geological and related changes. These changes are intensifying both as to quality and quantity, and many areas of your planet are experiencing and will experience tremendous and overpowering effects of weather, unrelated apparently, to normal cycles or patterns. Earthquake activity is now manifesting around what you have termed the "Circle of Fire" and will follow a pattern around this circle as of an impulse being directed around and around this area.

First one location will be affected and then, as if the impulse moves on, another, and another at varying poonts around the circle of fire. Your own West Coast line is due to be affected in the not-distant future to a considerable and, what might be termed by your peoples, disastrous degree.

For many, many of your years, we have warned your peoples and we would have prevented what will, undoubtedly, be a tremendous disaster to many of your large coastal cities. However, it is impossible for us to intervene further in the free wills of your peoples. We will do all that we can do to assist at the time of the upheavals, that is, that which we are allowed to do within the framework of Cosmic Law, in the internal affairs and karmic outworkings of another planet.

Other events, even more catastrophic, could be and may be triggered off by the breaking up of land masses and the resultant inrushing of tidal waters into areas previously untouched by these. Do not expect your policital machinations to proceed along their predestined paths. The economic disturbance which will ensue following the greater catastrophic events will be such as to precipitate chaos, not only within the scene of this United States, but within the world scene or pattern of events.

Three months remain in the time of this your year, and within these three months much will be precipitated and will continue on in manifestation into the year of 1969, of those events of which I have just spoken.

Those who are our channels, our emmisaries, our peoples upon this planet, working in their varied catagories and performing their appointed missions, will be sent and directed into specific areas to act, in a sense, as catalysts in those areas. For those of you who remain here in this area of anchor point or Light descent, it is well that you unify at all costs and pool your Light energies, for the stabilization of areas such as these depends to the highest degree upon the stabilization and unification of the individuals so involved.

Where there is an area of Light descent by energy anchor point, it can only function to its optimum efficiency according to the efficiency and functioning of the human vehicles who reside in said area. The stabilization of individuals and the indrawing and outpouring of Light and Love from the soul center of every individual concerned, regardless of personality, is a minimum requirement...a minimum requirement, my brothers, my sisters, for the performance of the mission of Light bearers.

Such will be the disturbance which is coming on your world scene... such will be the chaos within individuals, that only those who function from their own point of stabilization, their own point of Light within, and who function through Love, will remain uplifted and in the higher vibratory frequencies, protected against all onslaughts of all forms of destructiveness.... and there will be many!

I speak upon this occasion with much solemnity to you gathered here this evening, as this is the last occasion for some weeks that I may converse with you in this manner. My channel had no knowledge of my communication, as is usual, upon this occasion, however, we have been attuning with her for many hours of this day in preparation for this particular contact.

The many demands of the world scene which will be put upon all Light bearers, all chanels of Light, in the coming weeks and months, will draw greatly upon you all. Even as you give forth of Light, stabilization, and energy of Love to assist others, draw in to your very beings from the highest realms and from the Universal Light which is flooding your planet, to replenish yourselves and to remain vitalized and, shall we say, re-fueled.

I am transmitting upon this occasion from Saturn Command Source, from the

Communication Craft stationed above this mountain locality. I transmit data of import and suggest that it be issued to each before my channel leaves in order that it may be studied and utilized in the time ahead.

The Solar eclipse which occurrred recently has been as a trigger point for certain energies which are now, and I do not have the word within this one's vocabulary, shall we say: are acting as contact and release points for the many disturbances within the Earth itself. Do not be surprised at the erratic behavior of those within many of the larger cities due for upheaval, for these individuals as a mass are already within the vibratory pattern of molecular disintegration and are experiencing this reality within their beings, whether they are consciously aware of this or not.

Individuals who are now within such areas and are not destined to be part of the destruction, will either be removed by direct impression to so remove, or will be placed in areas where they may assist in holding some point of stabilization in such case. They are part of our pattern for stabilization and will be protected. For the rest, their own particular destiny or karmic patterns will manifest at the time of the upheavals.

Having spent some time discoursing upon the lower frequency outworking, I would again draw your attention to the tremendous upliftment of attunement with the highest frequencies of Universal Light as they now flow in. Attunement at these levels may bring about spiritual experiences, spiritual rebirth, and what could be called, a type of spiritual ecstasy. You have, therfore, the two extremes: Yours, oh people of Earth, is the choice! Yours alone is the choice. We know which choice we would make but we cannot choose for you.

I speak with much love, much feeling for my brothers, my sisters of the Earth planet, on this occasion. The outpouring of Light and Love which we feel in its entirety is of such magnificence, such beauty, such warmth, that we would share it with you if you will but permit us.

In the Light of Our Radiant One, I leave you. May you be encompassed with that Light, at one with it, and enfilled with its radiance.

          Adonai vassu, my brothers, my sisters.

* * * * * * * * * * * * * * *

(By Telethought Transmission, 28 Sept. '68. Channel: Marianne Francis)

* * * * * * * * * * * * * * *

"The spiritual spindles are actually weaving the web of a universal history; the spiritual shuttles are threading the warp and woof of a new garment to be worn by the children of a New Creation, whose aim will be the union of all the souls of the inhabitants of the Stars in the religion of Love."

  --Song of the Caravan, by Mirza Ahmad Sohrab

SCIENCE DEPARTMENT   K. M. Kellar, BA, Editor

THE INVISIBLE UNIVERSE

Recent scientific research has revealed that much of creation is not visible to the human eye but is radiating at frequencies outside the normal range of visibility. Most people can observe light waves in the narrow range from 5,000 to 7,800 Angstrom Units. This is only a very <u>small</u> <u>part</u> of the known electro-magnetic spectrum as can be seen in Figure 1.

Science has made much progress in extending the range of frequencies which can be observed and measured. Infra-red photography and radio telescopes have widely extended our observations of the Cosmos, while electron-microscopes and particle accelerators have extended the range into the sub-microscopic and sub-atomic range. Special techniques using various types of detectors enable us to measure radiations from the lowest sub-sonic range to the highest Cosmic Ray frequency.

Studies made at the Mount Wilson Observatory by California Institute of Technology have revealed that the night sky <u>would appear remarkably different</u> to us if our eyes could detect <u>infra-red</u> radiations as well as visible frequencies. The well-known constellations would no longer stand out due to the addition of <u>thousands</u> of <u>unfamiliar</u> <u>stars</u> whose radiation in the infra-red range is <u>much</u> <u>greater</u> than in the <u>visible</u> range. If man's vision were extended only a little further, into the infra-red range, think how different Greek mythology might have been!

An interesting article on Infra-red Stars appears in the August 68 issue of Scientific American magazine. Experiments are described in which infra-red radiations in the two-micron range were measured using a 62-inch plastic mirror to scan the heavens. This wave-length is about four times that of yellow light. Several basic problems make it more difficult to study infra-red rays than visible light. Earth's atmosphere absorbs much of the radiation from outer Space. Fortunately, however, there are certain "<u>windows</u>" which allow some frequencies to pass through. Such windows exist at wavelengths of 1.65 and 2.2 microns as well as at 3.6 and 4.8 microns. Broadband windows also exist between 8 and 14 microns and between 17 and 22 microns. The 2.2 micron range happens to be the most convenient to use.

ELECTROMAGNETIC SPECTRUM	
'REQ.	RADIATION
	Cosmic Ray
$\cdot 10^{20}$	Gamma Ray
$\cdot 10^{18}$	X-Ray
$\cdot 10^{16}$	
	Ultraviolet
$\cdot 10^{14}$	Visible
	Infrared
$\cdot 10^{12}$	
	Microwaves
$\cdot 10^{10}$	
$\cdot 10^{8}$	UHF
	Television
$\cdot 10^{6}$	Radio
$\cdot 10^{4}$	Supersonic
	Audio
$\cdot 10^{2}$	
$\cdot 10^{0}$	Subsonic

FIGURE 1.

Another problem with infra-red research is that detectors for this frequency range are only about one-thousandth as sensitive as those used to measure visible light. To compensate for this, it is necessary to use a large reflector. Also, there is more "noise" from background radiation due to thermal energy in the environment. Even the body temperature radiates and must be shielded during experiments.

Results of the studies made at Mount Wilson show some very interesting features. Visual observations of the night sky reveal about 6,000 stars normally seen by the unaided eye. Of the 5,500 infra-red stars which have been plotted, only about 30% can be seen from their visible light. Thus, if our eyes were sensitive to infra-red, we would see an additional 3,850 stars or 65% more than we now see in our night sky! Imagine what new constellations would appear!

Radio astronomy has revealed even more unusual sources of radiation called Quasars. The nature of such invisible stars or energy sources is not well understood as yet. The Galactic Center of our system has been the object of special studies. The position has been determined by measurements of the "Milky Way" rotation, however, the center itself is not visible. An infra-red map of the center shows a strong point source near the center with a wavelength of 2.2 microns. Radio measurements at 1.9 centimeters also show a radiation source in that area. It would appear that a very large star might be expected at the very heart of our Galaxy. However, from the scientific research so far, it appears that the Central Sun of our Galaxy may not exist on the strictly physical level at all.

Thus, could it be that our Central Sun exists only at the ETHERIC or higher levels of manifestation???

NEW UFO SIGHTING IN SPAIN

MADRID (UPI)— A Spanish meterological station Saturday reported a fresh sighting of an unidentified flying object. The report came shortly after a flying object had been witnessed by thousands of Madrilenians Thursday night.

The Meterological station at Cuenca, northeast of Madrid, said it kept a UFO under observation for several hours. It said the object remained stationary at a great heig for more than three hours, then moved off in a westerly direction. The station said the object appeared bo be triangular, the same shape as that seen in Madrid.

The report was the latest of several from different parts of Spain in recent weeks. The Spanish Air Force has sent up aircraft in unsuccessful attempts to get close to ob jects picked up on radar screens. But the things were reported high above the range of conventional jet fighters.

The air force suggested in a communique that the latest sightings may be of a meterological balloon making tests for future flights of supersonic aircraft. One such balloon came down in Logrono, northern Spain, Friday. It was quickly reclaimed by technicians from the French National Center for Space Studies. The technicians said they had followed the balloon from Pau in France by car and plane and that there was no possibility that it could have accounted for the UFO sightings in Madrid and Cuenca.

The Spanish Air Force said Friday that the unidentified flying object easily eluded a supersonic F104 jet fighter scrambled to intercept it Thursday night. An official announcement said the pilot climbed to an altitude of more than 50,000 feet and reported the object was still above him when he had to return to base for fuel. Another pilot flying at 36,000 feet reported seeing the same UFO.

"BLINDING LIGHT"

Air Force radar screens tracked the mysterious triangular object which some observers said gave off a "blinding light". Radar men said the object was flying at 90,000 feet and moving slowly when picked up.

The Air Force announcement said it had no scientific explanation but suggested the object might have been a metereological ballon. The Madrid Weather Bureau said it had no lost balloons and offered the theory that the object was part of a Space Satellite returning to Earth.

Radar operators and the nearby U.S. air base at Torrejon, and at Madrid International Airport reported nothing unusual on their screens.

(Quoted from the Medford Mail-Tribune, Sunday, September 8, 1968)

* * * * * * * * * * * *

VICTORIA SOLAR LIGHT ASSOCIATES

Those in the Victoria area who are interested in receiving notices of meetings and activities, or help in organizing meetings, please contact the following:

Mr. & Mrs. J. L. Squance
445 Brookhaven Dr., RR 7, Victoria, B.C. Canada

THE CADENCES OF LIGHT
By June of Venus

Greetings, our brothers, our sisters in Light. I who speak with you upon this occasion, have not spoken for some space of your time. I am June of Venus, as my name is known to you at this time. I speak to you on the cadences or tones of Light, relating to you a concept of the varying gradations or tonal qualities of Light energy or Light outpouring.

As I speak with you by tele-thought transmission, as I transmit my thought impulses and receive those flowing out from you in my direction, I see many colors; colors which interpenetrate, which move, which flow outwards, constantly changing. As these colors flow out into the ethers, they bring with them the energy of the Light Force inherent within the individual from which they came.

Light cadences, or tonal qualities, reflect the soul, the entity, the being, around which they are built, created, brought into being; for from Man flows many levels of expression: conscious, unconscious, superconscious. And on these many levels, or cadences, or tones of being, Man expresses himself through the Universe unto other forms and levels of Light. When the highest radiations pour forth in softly subtly interwoven hues of brilliance, density, manifestation, then flows through that being the pure white Light or energy from that Source we speak of as Our Radiant One or Being of Light, the All-Knowing One, Creator of All.

When these cadences, or tonal qualities of Light, become distorted from their purity of source by the coarsening of the lower earth mind or consciousness or mentality, then flow forth cruder, less subtle, less softened hues of expression, bringing into being or manifestation actions and reactions of violence, of enmity, of confusion. Thus it is that the Light energy, the cadences of Light flowing from their highest source, must be received down through what is known as the Crown Chakra and, thus permeating the being, they issue forth unsullied by the coarser vibrations of what has been known as animal man.

In this period of time, energies flowing, crossing, interweaving, are those coming from the highest sources of being and those rising from the lower consciousness, from the earth animal-man mentality into the ethers of planet earth. Though it may appear that the more dominant coarse qualities of Light predominate, and that the subtle, softened hues are delicate and fragile, it is but that one is of a higher vibratory composition than the other.

The more spiritualized nature of Man in responding to the higher vibratory call, is calling down the white Light energies from the Godhead, and in calling this down, it issues forth from the Children of Light on the planet, and though appearing subtle, fragile in hue, gentle in composition, it has a tenacity and a spiritual strength of energy composition which allows it to permeate into areas where force could not; softly flowing, issuing forth interweaving itself, and leaving its essence in the workings upon consciousness. Consciousness itself, in its ever-changing expression, guided many times by the emotional nature of Man, sends forth at another level of expression, these same energies into the world of concrete thought and concrete action, and in the emotional nature of Man once again is found the same divergent energies, from those of the coarsest passions to those of the highest, purest, most elevated expressions of love, compassion, tenderness, harmony and beauty. In that this time, into which Earthman moves, is the time of sudden and abrupt changes, it behooves him to manifest within his auric patterns at all levels of being or expression, the pure cadences of Light, that these may flow forth into the world of <u>manifested endeavor</u>, and produce an edifice of etheric composition, building upon this an actual bridge or energy field between third-density Man and fourth-density Man, so that across this bridge, Man of the New Age, the New Race of Man, can step into the world of the manifested Light.

The concepts which I am attempting to convey are conveyed with some difficulty, as the planetary conditions and areas through which I transmit are not most conducive to the transmission of free-flowing thought energies. I ask your indulgence, that my discourse has been somewhat halting. I have endeavored to present a clearer concept, albeit somewhat subtle, of the confirmation and conjoining, in a sense, of Light, color, sound, and action: These are but manifestations of the one, original Energy: all energy flowing directly from the God-source or Creator, Our Radiant One, aptly named by us Our Radiant One, unto all manifested life and creation.

I, June of Venus, attune with you upon this occasion, bringing in the Venusian ray through this my channel of Light expression, grounding the energies from our own planet through the vehicles of those who can so recieve these energies, these energies of love, of beauty, harmony, compassion, and creation. Endeavor in consciousness to carry these attributes into your conscious expression in the days through which you walk. For LIGHT IS, and all else is illusion.

With the love and the Light of my planet, of myself and my daughter Gloria, I leave you. May Our Radiant One be at one with you.

(By Telethought Transmission, 21 Sept. '68. Channel: Marianne Francis)

* * * * * * * * * * * * *

WANTED: MEN and WOMEN

Single or married, young or retired. Willing to work and willing to live an almost monastic life on Orcas Island, located in beautiful Puget Sound in the State of Washington. All kinds of work to be done: building, gardening, printing, office work, maintenance, cooking, etc.

NO PAY.... but all personal needs taken care of. Do not apply if you have strong family ties now, or cannot transfer your love and loyalty to a new family-- and work...and share in God's Plan for the LEWIS FOUNDATION. You're needed; you're wanted...and you can help. Write us about yourself.

OUTLOOK INN, EASTSOUND, WASHINGTON

LETTERS FROM OUR READERS

16 Sept. 68

Dear Marianne Francis and Others of the Solar Light Centre:-

You may enjoy knowing that I was healed of a thought-to-be incurable mental and emotional illness of many year's standing at your (Marianne's) beautiful, wonderful lecture at Victoria.

I am most grateful for this healing, and for the wonderful messages of Hope and Life received from your Centre since. Your little STARCRAFT magazine is the most vital and timely publication in this field that I know of anywhere.

Will you be so kind as to send introductory copies to the persons on the accompanying list? I am sending you ten dollars and many, many thanksgivings and good wishes to help you with this so important work.

        With love and best wishes,

                (signed) Owen D. LeBaron

                Victoria, B.C.

* * * * * * * * * * *

(The Healing Mr. LeBaron received has been confirmed by friends, and by his daughter)

— — — — — — — — — — —

THANKS FOR YOUR LETTERS AND SUPPORT

Thanks go to all who have subscribed to STARCRAFT and/or made contributions to further the work in any way. Since we are still very short on secretarial help, we have not been able to answer all letters personally, but try to keep up with orders for lectures and material. Special thanks also to those who have helped organize public meetings and lecture tours.

We appreciate receiving informative letters and clippings of general interest, however, due to lack of space, only a few can be published. Some are printed in Starcraft from time to time if they are not copyrighted. Our apologies for delays in filling orders and for any mistakes made. Please let us know if you do not receive your order in a reasonable time.

CENTER NEWS AND TRAVELS

After returning from the June/July lecture trip, I promised myself to relax and swim and generally catch up on nervous energy. Some of this was achieved despite the heat of August and the long dry days. Fired with enthusiasm by the sight of the new carpet, I determined to finish the redecorating of the large room here in which all our Guest channelling sessions take place. As of this writing, it is largely completed and much admired by visitors. The color scheme of green and white is cool and restfull and the amethyst accents complement my large collection of African violets. Still needed is $500 to $1000 and a volunteer carpenter to build on the extra bedroom so badly needed, and the remodeling of the kitchen area. But progress has been made. The planting of next Spring's bulbs is next on the schedule.

All Guest Sessions of July, August and September were very well attended and many new faces, plus our faithful supporters, were greeted. Material of much importance was received is included in this issue of STARCRAFT. September passed in a blur of activity preparing for the Fall lecture trip. One highlight just a couple of days before leaving was the lecture I gave to 1500 students at the Medford Senior High School on "Telepathic Contact with Space Intelligences".

October 6th saw me leaving the Center for Portland where I stayed the weekend and then on to Seattle and Vancouver. A miserable virus of the sneezy type made the first six day rough going in spite of quantities of vitamin C. It seemed to be an epidemic.

A ten-minute interview on Television in Vancouver opened the publicity, followed by radio interviews on the Jack Webster (CKWX) and Mark Raines (CJOR) shows. The interview with Mark Raines was particularly well conducted and allowed me to bring out much data of value. Finally, the lecture on the 14th at the Oakridge Auditorium arrived after a busy week. Due to a slight oversight, the hall was booked for the Canadian Thanksgiving evening and this cut the attendance somewhat. However, much literature was sold and an enthusiastic question session followed the lecture. Thanks go to my hosts and dear friends, Irene and Harold Pym, and to all members of the Committee who worked so hard and efficiently to make the meeting a success. Special thanks also go to Bob and Joan Gale for their help and use of their home for meetings.

The ferry trip to Nanaimo on the 15th was stimulating: cold fresh air, a blue sky with great white clouds, and grey gulls following the boat. A pleasant stay with my hostess, Elyse Dial, who arranged the lecture in Nanaimo and the radio interview on CHUB with Larry Thomas, another interviewer who really gets down to the "meat" of the subject. Chemainus on the 16th and the opportunity to share material with the delightful and enthusiastic group who meet at Joan Carnac's home.

Dr. Leslie Lambert, very beautifully and expertly chaired my lecture in Nanaimo, leaving little room in his opening remarks for critics. On to Victoria the 18th and a three-hour stint on Ralph Pashley's radio show. I shared the first twenty minutes with a couple who travel, make movies, and have twin lion cubs aged 5 months. Later I saw the cubs and fell in love with the boy lion! I suggested they mail me a lion for Christmas, for I have always longed to own one again...shades of Egypt! Now, I am afraid I might get my wish! The inhabitants of this mountain have had many problems with skunks (both the two legged and four legged kind) and I am afraid a baby lion might just prove too much for them! In any case, Precious Jade, my "littlest lion" (he thinks he is) takes a rather dim view of his larger cousins of the cat tribe!

My thanks to Capt. Christofferson who arranged the lecture in the theatre of the New Provincial Museum in Victoria, and to Owen LeBaron who assisted. A long question session and then on to talk further with interested people from the audience wanting to form a group of Solar Light Associates in Victoria. Lovely memories of love expressed and shared, especially with the younger set and the hippies who attended the lecture. Kenneth Kellar was able to come up to Vancouver for the lecture weekend. Also, Harold and Irene Pym crossed to Victoria for the lecture there and Kenneth joined us too. All that extra help and support was of tremendous assistance.

Orcas island again...and a few days rest at Outlook Inn. Louis was on tour, so Stephan, Laura and Jeannie held down the fort. Rain and sunshine, misty sunsets, and a freen island nestling in the grey waters of the Straits...moss and waterfalls, writing letters and generally lazing around....a peaceful time.

Seattle, and the last lecture at the Aquarian Foundation with capable Dick Kiltz chairing. The "Call of the Phoenix" lecture was requested and very well received. An "alive" group and most appreciative. Many thanks to Thelma and Zady for hospitality.

Friends to visit in Puyallup on the way back: Rachel and Loren - keep up the New Age research...we need you in today's world. On to Portland and some time with old friends and new. A long-held wish to meet Erica Strath-Gordon at last realized; also her friends: Lu and Monty Woolly. Thank you, Erica for a wonderful evening and a new and dear friendship.

Home at last, via Roseburg, and the mountain and its peace and quiet, so welcoming after the noise of the cities. Did I say peace?? Well, there were problems on the mountain when I arrived. Yet I can't help feeling the largest problem is removed at last from this locality, even as the Brothers said it would be.

The Winter is nearing and monthly Guest channelling sessions are discontinued. Please phone us to check on snow conditions if you wish to visit. Also, I may not be here all Winter as I am planning to do some research, writing, and catching up now that the lecture season is over for 1968. It has been a year of discovery, challenges, long trips,.. the ending of one phase and the beginning of another, in all, a wonderful year.

                In Light,   Marianne Francis

ANNOUNCEMENTS

GUEST SESSIONS: Regular Guest Channelling Sessions will not be held at the Center during the Winter months due to weather conditions and bad roads. Also, Miss Francis is expecting to be away part of this period.

LIGHT WORKERS NEEDED

Older couple wanted to live on mountain and assist with Solar Light Center. Must have own car and pension or small income, as all work is on a volunteer basis. Help is needed with clerical and domestic work and some gardening. Hours would be short and help needed only three or four times a week. Excellent opportunity for service-minded couple to give much-needed assistance NOW when it is so urgent. A single, strong woman might be considered if used to living alone and in the country. Trailer space possible, but septic tank and well need developing.

HOUSE FOR SALE

A house is now for sale on the mountain for a total of $6,000 with only $600 down payment and $60 per month. Also, a wooded lot is for sale in a good location near the Center. Electric power is available for all lots in the area as well as telephone service. Water can be developed by shallow wells. Most homes in the area use fuel oil for heating. If interested, write us for details.

PUBLICATIONS of the SOLAR LIGHT CENTER:

Lectures by Marianne Francis:

FREQUENCY CHANGE AND THE SECOND COMING	$1.25
THE CALL OF THE PHOENIX	1.50
STARCRAFT CONTACT	1.25
MEN FROM SPACE & PROPHECIES OF EARTH CHANGE	1.25
THE NEW DIMENSION AND THE NEW AGE	1.00

CHANNELLED MATERIAL from the Space People:
Set of ten scripts selected from Channelled material 2.90

STARCRAFT Magazine: Subscription $2.25 (USA), $2.50 (Foreign).
(Three or four issues per year plus Newsletters when possible).

SEND ORDERS TO: SOLAR LIGHT CENTER, Rt. 2, Box 572-J
Central Point, Oregon, 97501

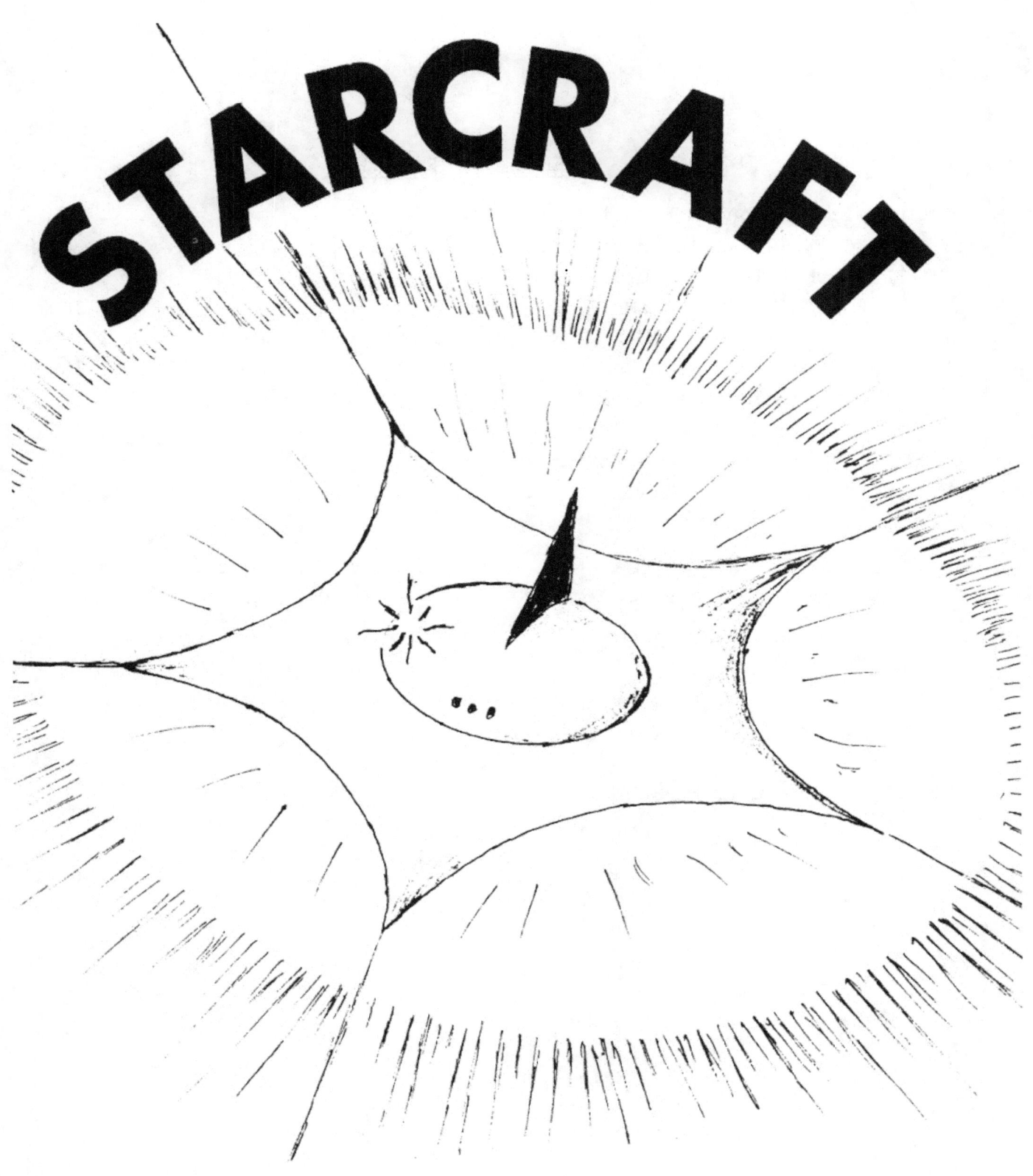

VOL.4 No.1   SOLAR LIGHT CENTER   SPRING 1969

STARCRAFT CONTENTS — SPRING 1969

EDITORIAL: The Condon Report & Managed News 3
A NEW BEGINNING - Solstar of Saturn 6
INTERFERENCE PATTERNS - Orlon 7
SOME MARCH THOUGHTS ON LIMITATION - Marianne Francis 10
REACTIONS TO LIGHT ENERGIES - Xyclon, a Space Psychologist . . . 13
SCIENCE DEPT: Light Beam Communicator Report, - K. M. Kellar . . 16
GUEST CORNER: Ann Lee: New Age Songs - ETERNITY'S SONG 17
EARTHQUAKES in the News 17
CENTER NEWS and TRAVELS - Marianne Francis 18
ANNOUNCEMENTS and PUBLICATIONS 20

* *

Director and Editor - - - - - - - - Marianne Francis, Dr.Sp.Sc.
Science Director & Business Mgr.- - - - - Kenneth M. Kellar, B.A.

Published by SOLAR LIGHT CENTER, a non-profit corporation.
COPYRIGHT reserved.   Write for permission to reprint.
ZIP CODE is required, so please include yours when you write.
TELEPHONE us first if you plan to visit. Phone: 855-1956 (Code 503)

ADDRESS ALL CORRESPONDENCE TO:

        SOLAR LIGHT CENTER
        Rt. 2, Box 572-J
        Central Point, Ore.
        97501

* * * * * * * * * * * * * * * *

The New Age program is to

LOVE

UNDERSTAND   EDUCATE

RELIEVE SUFFERING   CREATE BEAUTY

3

EDITORIAL —Marianne Francis

The CONDON REPORT and "MANAGED" NEWS

In January the long awaited Condon Report was made public. Its conclusion: "No direct evidence whatever of a convincing nature now exists for the claim that any UFO's represent Spacecraft visiting Earth from another civilization".

Further observations from the report were as follows: "It is regarded by scientists today as essentially certain that ILE (intelligent life elsewhere) exists, but with essentially no possibility of contact between the communities on planets associated with different stars". "We therefore conclude that there is no relation between ILE at other solar systems and UFO phenomena as observed on Earth".

"Our general conclusion is that nothing has come from the study of UFO's in the past 21 years that has added to scientific knowledge. Careful consideration of the record as it is available to us leads us to conclude that further extensive study of UFO's probably cannot be justified in the expectation that science will be advanced thereby". (End quote)

A panel of the National Academy of Sciences reviewed the methods used in the Colorado study and upheld its formal findings. To quote the Acadamy panel: "On the basis of present knowledge, the least likely explanation of UFO's is the hypothesis of extra-terrestrial visitations by intelligent beings" !!! (End quote)

So, to add to the general confusion and lies which beset the average citizen, we now have wide-spread publicity given to Dr. Condon's half million dollar "trick" and the National Academy of Sciences endorsing it.

All the sightings of UFO's, performing fantastic maneuvers at incredible speeds, in silent flight, observed by the military, the Air Force and civil airline pilots and millions of citizens, are then just a gigantic hallucination! If this were true, then hallucinations must be on a gigantic increase and in this age of "science"! Obviously, an awful lot of people and nations are sick, but not that sick!

When the Air Force arranged for a group of scientists, led by the eminent Dr. Condon, to take over the highly controversial investigation of Flying Saucers, they also arranged to "take the heat off" of themselves. The half million dollar "trick" did that very nicely. Many scientists, it seems, can still be counted on to stick their heads in the sand, disregard volumes of evidence, and observe the status quo.

The Condon report, however, went even further than simply denying the existence of UFO's. After deciding that no UFO's from another civilization were visiting this planet, this august and "scientific" body of men announced they "do not see any such comings and goings for another 10,000 years! Surely Earthman's supreme egotism is reaching its height of folly!

Hypnotised, brain-washed, and generally in a state of coma-conscious as they are, undoubtedly millions of people will accept the Condon report.

Are not materialistic scientists even as the very gods of wisdom in the Western world! The masses awoke sufficiently from their slumbers to throw off the blinders of the orthodox priesthood only to become slaves to another false god, Science. A substitution of one authority for another has taken place and once again the individual abdicates his/her god-given right to THINK and be their own instrument of decision.

So, we have the blind leading the blind. At one extreme, the blind faith of the "religious" stifles the intellect and asks credulity of its followers. At the other extreme, the barren intellectualism of mental processes, divorced from spiritual understanding and wisdom, proclaims its egotistical "truths":"Truths" which already have changed with each new dis covery, yet produce no apparent change within the dogmatic minds of materi alistic men of science as to the Universe and its Divine, all-permeating intelligence.

Yet, even within the ranks of the scientists, we find a split exists. While the unscientific and childish Condon report received wide-spread pub licity, a far more important event, which took place on July 29th, 1968, concerning UFO's, did not. Following unprecedented congressional hearing the House Science and Astronautics Committee put on record impressive scie tific evidence of the UFO reality.

This group which presented the testimony, both in oral and written form included J. Allen Hynek, head of the Dept. of Astronomy at Northwestern University (Old Swamp Gas, to his friends and students), who had also been for many years the chief consultant to the U.S. Air Force on the subject o UFO's; Dr. James E. McDonald, Senior Physicist, Institute of Atmospheric Physics and Professor of Meteorology at the University of Arizona; Dr. Car Sagan, Dept. of Astronomy, Cornell University; Dr. Robert L. Hall, head o the Dept. of Sociology, University of Illinois; Dr. James A. Harder, Asso ciate Prof. of Civil Engineering whose subject was "The UFO Propulsion Pro lem; Dr. Robert M. L. Baker, Jr., Senior Scientist of the Computer Scien ces Corp.; Dr. Leo Sprinkle, University of Wyoming; Dr. Garry C. Hender son, Senior Research Scientist, General Dynamics Corp.; Dr. Staunton Frie man, Westinghouse Astronuclear Laboratory; Dr. Roger N. Shepard of Stanfo University; and Dr. Frank B. Salisbury of Utah State University.

Their testimony, together with the mass of documentary evidence which they presented, fill the entire 247 pages of fine print which averages abo 450 words per page, or a total of more than one hundred thousand words plu a large number of photographs, charts and diagrams.

All of this testimony pointed unmistakably to the reality of the UFO phenomenon, and all of the scientists strongly recommended that serious an intensive study of the various phases of the UFO phenomenon should be un dertaken at once.

All of the quasi-scientific objections which have been made in the past to the reality of the UFO were considered and convincingly refuted.

In Los Angeles some of our people sent for this congressional record, publication #7, and received the following reply: "Permanently out of print". How could a publication concerning an important hearing which ok place only last July conceivably be out of print??? Very easily if, is obvious, the news is being managed, supressed, censored. Do we need re evidence that UFO are Top Secret and no lengths are too devious, no ans too dishonest, to hide the truth from the people of the U.S. and, if ssible, the world?

Yet, time is running out on planet Earth. Science and the military, vorced from spiritual wisdom or understanding of Cosmic Law, have brought voc on the world scene. Earth upheavals are rapidly increasing (see ge 17) and the threat of a deadly destruction of all life by atomic bombs ntinues.

Earthman will yet learn, in suffering and humility, that he placed his ith in destructive forces and agencies. Identified craft will come, in st numbers from Space, and an age of true Science and wisdom will dawn at st on Earth.

* * * * * * * * * * *

TE: We suggest all readers obtain the following:
(1) UFO's Yes, by Dr. David Saunders, formerly chief psychologist on the Condon project.

(2) "Congressional Record Publication #7, Symposium on Unidentified Flying Objects". Sub-title: "Hearings before the Committee on Science and Astronautics, U.S. House of Representatives, 90th Congress, date, July 29th, 1968".
(Bombard your congressman or representative with demands that (this booklet be released NOW.)

* * * * * * * * * * *

Space Book and Tape-recorded Lectures

ETTERS to YOU from Baloran.
This book is a great Space being's panoramic view of the many efforts to start, sustain and develop civilization on planet Earth.

HE GALAXY SERIES.
A taped series of 13 lectures given by our Space friends. This series of discourses is designed specifically for radio broadcasting. They cover many subjects that are of particular interest at this crucial time. (Speed: 3-3/4 ips)

HE SOLAR CROSS SERIES.
This series of taped communications is given in the form of six short lectures. The subjects include Earth's relation to our Solar System, the Lost planet (located between Mars and Jupiter) which was destroyed; Life on Mars, Solar Government, and others.

For further information write to:
SOLAR CROSS FELLOWSHIP
Route 2, Box 2455E
Auburn, California 93603

Transmission from Solstar of Saturn
A NEW BEGINNING

We are at an end and yet at a new beginning of things of the NEW and an ending of the OLD. The impetus of events moves swiftly now. No time lag exists as the frequencies rapidly expand forcing upwards the consciousness levels, the molecular structures, the very existence of the planet on whic you stand. Consider, in relation to molecular change, the velocity of th atomic structures spiralling as in patterns on the etheric matrix of their essence.

Visualise if you will the atomic structure of Man in relation to the Universe, for all is one. For what is true in the macrocosm is true also in the microcosm. All changes in creation occur in cyclic patterns over vast periods of time bringing about aeons of experience, experiment, if yo will, within the living consciousness of beings created from the Godhead. Man, in his puny understanding on planet Earth, comprehends not of the immensity of the Creator's kingdoms, worlds, universes. Yet, in his non-understanding, Man experiences the death throes of an Age and experience reveals unto him the first glimmerings of Cosmic understanding.

My peoples, who walk upon the planet known to you as Saturn, transmit data from the Saturn Council through this, our channel of interpretation for the coming frequencies of Light will bring us and our craft closer and will result in a meeting of minds with our peoples. Interplanetary gover ment exists, as you know, and must incorporate the "fallen one" back into its system: Terra, planet Earth...call it what you will. I, Solstar, communicate upon this occasion with you, for it will not be long before this meeting of minds takes place between our peoples and certain of yours.

Plans must be formulated for the government of a New Earth in a New fre quency, of life in its ultimate purpose. Craft <u>will</u> land...conferences <u>will</u> take place. Dates will be dependent on the <u>degree</u> with which the rap <u>idly</u> changing frequencies stabilize.

I speak as one from the Saturn Council. Those truly contacted reveal themselves by their actions, degree of stability, and their material, whic itself is a key. Know them by this means. Many have sought, some in truth, some in comradeship, some in self-aggrandisement and some in delusion. It is a time for souls dedicated to the ideals of a spiritual brotherhood and a Cosmic comradeship of eternal verity.

In the Light of our Radiant One, I, Solstar, bid you:

                        Adonai vassu of this time consciousness.

* * * * * * * * * * *

(Craft Transmission --- Received via Telethought transmission)
(Solar Light Center - 5 March '69 - Channel: Marianne Francis)

INTERFERENCE PATTERNS
-By Orlon

Greetings, my brother and my sister. Orlon transmitting. At this time [I w]ish to transmit information relevant to what has most recently concerned [us], that is: The nature of interference patterns.

Such interference patterns manifested upon the last occasion of a Saturn [Cou]ncil transmission and caused some disruption of the telethought communi[cat]ion beam. I would like to make clear to you, at this time, that we are [con]cerned and are dealing with this problem from several levels during this [per]iod of intensification of confusion on the Earth scene. Interference is [not] coming from one source alone, but interference in telethought beam and [tel]ethought transmissions is coming from negative Space intelligences and is [als]o coming from Earth sources. By Earth sources we refer to a concentra[tio]n of minds in certain areas who are now attempting to block transmissions [of] confederation craft data and also are attempting to block specific material [that is] due to be released to certain Light Centers and individuals who have, [sha]ll we say, passed by the trial of fire and have been found stable and [ste]adfast in performance of their service.

All Light stations who have remained so stabilized and steadfast are now [able] to receive data which should correlate as to relevant points of contact [wit]h us and with each other... relevant, that is, to the changing world scene [and] the imminence of geological upheaval.

Interference patterns therefore, coming in from negative Space intelligence, [ha]ve been intensified and certain of these individuals, using craft, are now [uti]lising a mechanical type device which is sending a definite electronic type [of] beam which sets up a resonating frequency similar to the one being used [upo]n the individual channel. This, in turn, establishes or sets up so much [con]fusion within the consciousness of the channel as to cause great difficulty [in] reception of the telethought beam transmission.

It is difficult for me to transmit technical type data through the mind of [the] channel unless under certain conditions. Therefore, in intensifying our [te]lethought beam transmission, a certain depletion of energy, of the vital [fo]rces within the channel's body takes place. It is, therefore, necessary [to] establish a strong group for the purpose of such transmissions and recep[tio]ns where there is a stabilized energy field which forms a protective type [me]chanism around the channels themselves...particularly around this channel [who]m we now use who is highly sensitized for many purposes of telethought, [te]lepathic, and intuitional level reception.

You are well aware that the group working with a receiver is of as much importance as the channel themself in establishing and maintaining the energies and protective mechanisms which do assist and make easier the task of the receiver herself or himself. We are highly hopeful that in the near future our channel will no longer be working under the difficult conditions which have rendered transmissions almost unobtainable on certain occasions.

Back to the point of our discourse: The transmissions which are emanating (this is the interference transmissions)...which are emanating from the Earth itself are being established by certain groups of individuals who are now well aware of the material being given from Confederation and Galactic sources. They might be termed the negative outposts on your planet of those working consciously in co-operation with negative Space intelligence. Due to the fact that you are very close at this time on planet Earth to the major changes and the coming in of tremendous energies, it is immaterial whether these be called Universal Light energies although this is as good a description as any or Radiant Light energies, it is, however, at this time that the greatest attempts are being made by the negative to disconcer and cause confusion on the world scene to such a degree that there will be small manifestation of Light outside of the individuals who are so Light en filled they can withstand all negative onslaughts. Therefore, the Light Centers and the receivers of these transmissions are being made something of a target at this time in order to cause a breakdown of communication lines.

It is wise that Light centers exchange data and information and establish and strengthen all Light lines and networks running throughout the planet insofar as this is possible. The Divine Light or energy flowing downward from the Creator to the point of Light within the individual is the first focal point and from this flows outward the network of Light from like-minded individuals and between Light stations holding and stabilizing, as we have previously stated.

The lines of force on this planet are already disrupted in the magnetic flow and therefore a rotational or "wobbling" effect of the spinning of the Earth upon its axis is coming into effect as you come closer to the unbalancing or axial shift condition long prophecied.

We, transmitting at this time, attempt to clarify the picture and reestablish the necessity for protective mechanisms and for individuals surrounding channels who assist and do not tear down. This is an absolute <u>primary</u> necessity at this time.

Consider well those with whom you associate and this is for all, as it is vitally important that your associates be of a nature that is uplifting and do not draw energies from you which cannot be immediately replenished.

Interflowing of energies between individuals of like mind and harmonious intent are necessary. But drawing of energies from individuals the nature, shall we say, of a "vampire" type thing are taking place on large scale on your planet and are highly deleterious.---

It is for you on the planet to exert the greatest amount of effort to [bu]ild that which you can, of Light fields around you, from your own struc[tu]res and your own consciousness.

Due to the widespread usage of hallucinatory drugs, which has taken place [in] your so-called civilization, a mass pattern of consciousness breakdown is [ta]king place and individuals are practically running amok in all directions [pr]esenting much peril and confusion, not only to themselves, but to other [in]dividuals caught in their path of activity. The opening of the doors of [pe]rception to the degree which has taken place in the last few of your years [ha]s thrown open doorways to lower elemental forces and energies which, com[bi]ning with the releasing of the elemental energies contained within the [na]ture forces: Earthquakes, tornadoes, hurricanes, waters, fires, volcanoes, [co]mbining with these, is bringing about a condition of tremendous havoc, [wh]ich is due to become worse before a final rending, as we have said, of the [su]bstance of the Earth between Light and dark takes place.

Therefore, presented with this picture, we are more than ever concerned [ab]out the stability and continuation within a stable pattern of our receiv[e]rs. Without these our communication lines break down. Many of our own [pe]oples have been withdrawn from the planet at this time, although a certain [nu]mber remain fullfilling other tasks of importance. Due to the high fre[qu]ency energy structures or cellular structure of many of our receivers, the [t]remendously disruptive energy patterns manifesting on your surface are [h]ighly destructive and cannot be coped with by any means but through con[s]ciousness attunement and stabilization within.

[Q]uestion: What can we do for the Hippie groups?

You can reach the consciousness which is in many such individuals attempt[i]ng to unfold to concepts of Light by attempting to point out the misuse by [d]rugs and the necessity of opening doors to perception through forms of med[i]tation, tranquillity, attunement with the god-spark within. Many of these [i]ndividuals are on the brink of much awakening. This is a service which [c]an and should be done for all who at least reach out, not-with-standing the [m]eans so employed.

I transmit from the communication craft through telethought transmis[s]ion. I Ask that the Radiant One be with you and His Light. I with[d]raw my consciousness.

Adonai vassu.

(Received at Grass Valley, Calif., 16 Dec.'68. Channel: Marianne Francis)

SOME MARCH THOUGHTS ON LIMITATION
By Marianne Francis

As I travel around and meet people, both in and out of the Space movement, I observe many things. Chief among these is the crippling limitations which so many individuals impose on themselves. I long to reach out to all of you who do this and release you from your prisons For, is not a self-imposed limitation a prison!

In this issue I want to share some of my own concepts with you, for in the world of consciousness lies a Universe for your adventuring. Once you realise this, experience it, live it, you will never again want to shut yourselves in those little prison walls of limitation and fear. Basically, limitation is a kind of fear, perhaps of failure, perhaps of making mental and spiritual effort, lethargy and apathy being hidden enemies of a kind. In order for you to recognise <u>types</u> of limitation, I propose to describe some. No one individual is here described and if you do recognise yourself, do not become angry or feel guilty. If you are limiting yourself, or worse still, someone else, then <u>do</u> <u>something</u> <u>about</u> <u>it</u>. Unlimit, or as Bugs Bunny would say, "un-lax". You see, you must be very rigid, or "up tight" as the colloquism would describe it, to act this way. Tensions of the mind and emotions reflect in the body. Try unwinding and becoming fluid.

A New Age is aborning and if you drag your feet and wait for it to solve all your problems, you will wake one day and find yourself elsewhere. No, not in a place of Light and joy and freedom, but in another plane filled with the same limitations which now occupy your world. Why is this? Because <u>your</u> world <u>is</u> the out-picturing of your consciousness.

Unlimit yourselves and you expand your horizons, you push out the walls and find a blue sky, green meadows and far mountains. The distant blue beckons and all infinity is yours to explore.

First and foremost, let me say that I <u>do</u> firmly believe many individuals are limited because parents and environment "crippled" them. But if this is your excuse for your limitations, don't you think it a little weak to continue to live someone else's reality? This is what you <u>are</u> doing if you do not create your own fullfilling and unique expression of YOU, a child of God. When you stand erect and recognise this, you refuse to live out your father's or mother's "hang-ups". YOUR ARE YOU, unique and perfect in essence. Start to live this reality and you will be surprised at how your life will change.

Types of Limitation

1) The individual who is afraid to get outside his/her narrow rut and experience new or think a challenging thought or try a new type of career or self-expression.

2) The man who is so limited by his inner insecurities he refuses to let his wife handle any of "his" money or drive "his" car, or express herself in any way outside of the four walls of their home. He makes her a household drudge and his joylessness poisons their lives.

3) The wife who regards her home and ideas as her whole world and deprives her husband of any creative expression outside of his work. She shares little with her husband but her narrow views on life, sex, religion, and he plays out his role starved for love, self-expression, and companionship of mind and soul.

4) The "religious" individual who sees "salvation" only in a narrow doctrine or dogma. Man has only existed on Earth some bare 6,000 years, such people believe, and all the great civilizations of Atlantis, Lemuria, the mighty cultures of India, the Chaldean, and the Egyptian are myths! All who do not believe in the doctrine of salvation through a blood sacrifice of Jesus Christ, the "only" begotton Son of God, are eternally damned.

Dear, dear ones; do you not see you have limited your Creator with your own small concepts? In all majesty and Light, the Creator expressed him/her self (for surely if God is anything, God is androgenous containing the male and female principle) in many worlds, in many cultures, in almost all religions. God flows in rythymed outflowings and indrawings and from that SOURCE have come many great teachers of Light to this and other planets. All are sons and daughters of God, all life flows from the ONE SOURCE. Blinded by fears of hell-fire and punishments eternal, the religious fanatic lives in his/her own tiny world, fenced with limitations and sees no visions of the spirit, only the authority of a man-made priesthood and a book which does not contain all truth.

5) If money is your "hang-up" and you are limited and stingy through fear of never having enough, you never will have enough to barely scrape by in life. Let go and give a little, spend a little, for as you release the outflow, you also open the channel for the inflow. Your own fears alone are limiting you, my friend.

6) Another type of limitation concerning so many of you is LOVE and its

varied expressions. The word SEX is still a loaded word and countless individuals are crippled by inhibitions, fears and false concepts of sex and love, even in this year of 1969. Are you limited and afraid to express love in friendship, in family relationships or in the physical expression of love which is called sex? If you are a "cold" woman, or an unexpressive man, then remember this: Love is Life and all things in the Universe of opposite polarity unite in harmony in order to create. Two souls in love with God, with Life and with each other, can make heaven on Earth. Yes even on this chaotic war-torn, changing Earth. Whether you create an idea, a new scientific principle, a poem, a melody, or a child, create together in love and joy and freedom from limitation. For you are the expression of God on Earth and through you His power and beauty and love flows.

I have shared with you my thoughts this day in simplicity of expression because I believe Man alone creates complexity. As I climbed the mountain here with my hound, I felt so free and uplifted in spirit I wanted to share my feelings with you. The view, as always, was magnificent: the far mountains still capped with snow, a vast panorama of sky filled with blue and white. The small herbs were very fragrant beneath our feet and fresh from a March shower of the morning. We gave thanks, my hound and I, for pure air and freedom: he in joyous tail-wagging, and I in prayer to the Creator.

This is my birth month, traditionally a time of fresh winds and skudding clouds in England. So I will end these thoughts by bidding you look up into the sky, away from the cities and Man's turmoil. Deep in the distant blue of infinity, it is unlimited and free. So, too, are your souls!

"UNLIMIT YOURSELVES", as the Brothers would say, "for everything there is, is yours; all there is, is yours!"

* * * * * * * * *

To: "Children of Love and Light"

Will some of you please consider the extreme advisability of moving into this Sanctuary area for your own benefit and ours. Earthquakes are increasing and many areas due for upheaval. We are operating in a protected area under direct guidance, both from Space sources and higher realms. No Light Center can operate to maximum efficiency without the loving and generous support of other "children of Light". While we do need financial help, much can be accomplished with donated labor and loving concern. Pure air, peaceful surroundings, and beauty await you. Solar Light Center.

REACTIONS TO LIGHT ENERGIES

By Xyclon, a Space Psychologist

Greetings, our brothers, our sisters in Light. We are attempting to attune the telethought beam mechanism at this point, in order to transmit to you in this locality through our channel. My name is Xyclon and I have been called a Space psychologist in your understanding of that word.

We are conversant with your thoughts of the impact of the increased vibratory patterns of energy upon the consciousness of individuals making up on the face of your planet. Now, at this period of time, we are closly watching the reactions upon such masses of peoples, in many nations, of the tremendously stepped up outflow of energy which is now reaching your planet from other levels of existence. Where there is, in the consciousness of individuals, an awakened state of soul, there is an actual linkage taking place between the higher vehicles (or bodies as you term them) and the brain or mentality consciousness. Where this awakened consciousness is not yet in existence, there is an actual breaking down of the cellular structure which is occurring and I would speak with you upon this phenomena, at this time, in order to clarify the thoughts which you have recently expressed.

Where the awakened consciousness does not yet exist in the soul of the individual, a breaking down of the cellular structure is taking place by virtue of the tremendously high frequency rate or energies flowing in from the Central Sun source. You may ask yourselves why is this occurring. To explain in your terminology, I would say that a state similar to one of friction is taking place. It is known to you that the cells, each cell, contains a level of consciousness or awareness of its own, in that each cell is as an individual planet within a galaxy making up the aggregate of consciousness of the individual.

Where there is not an awakened level of soul, the consciousness level of each cell is at a slower or more dense rate of vibration. Due to this, as the increased high frequency energies pour in, a state close to that of friction is reached and almost, you might say, a "heating" process is produced which results in a high level of irritability or discomfort or dis-ease within said individual. This may manifest itself in one of many forms, running the gamut from physical disease...some of your known degenerative illnesses such as heart conditions, malignant growths, tubercular conditions....to a state of mental dis-ease and disharmony so pronounced that the individual becomes highly unbalanced, unstable, and verges from states of apathy and depression to those of over-excitation and violent behaviour. Most noticable at this period of time is that when individuals of like mentality are congregated in areas, there is almost a condition of what you would call a "brush fire" in that a small spark ignites masses of peoples to states of violent and destructive behavior. Conversely, as we have previously told you, where individuals of a highly awakened consciousness level gather together and raise even further the vibratory level of consciousness, as a mass, in harmony and understanding, there comes about a condition wherein the Light energies flowing in do so to such an extent, that the "miraculous" takes place.

At such times, not only will you find what you have termed "miraculous healings" of the physical, etheric, emotional, and mental bodies taking place, but you will find that in this raising of the vibratory rate to these high levels, periods of spiritual exultation and a knowingness of the infinite nature of Man and his destiny in Light becomes manifest to the individuals concerned. In my capacity as a Space psychologist, working with certain of the craft on missions to your planet, I am in a position at this time to spend much time in observation of the infinite variety of reactions being produced in your peoples.

It is my suggestion, as it has been of old, but much more firmly pronounced, much more directly suggested, that those of you who are of the level of consciousness of the awakened state of soul, gather yourselves together in areas of peace and tranquillity where the vibratory rate is conducive to such harmony and, further raising your vibratory levels, bring into manifestation these energies that you may utilize them within your own life patterns: That these energies may become a part of you at all times; that you may call upon them at times of emergency or crisis, or when chaos and confusion surround you, in order, not only to stabilize your own pattern, but to act as stabilizers within the area or community in which you find yourself.

We have spoken previously of many of our channels and peoples on this planet as catalysts. It is possible, when the vibratory rate is sufficiently raised within the individual to partake of the higher Light frequencies and energies at all times, to ACT as catalysts within situations and to bring about CHANGE...not by what you may say, but by what you ARE and what you emanate. Energies, Light energies, are extremely important, and the science of these energies will rapidly come to the fore in the time which is now fast approaching and our peoples mingle and are able to meet more freely, not only in consciousness (through our channels) but that they may walk with you, in certain areas, and impart to you knowledge and technical information which will be most necessary to your further ongoing.

I, Xyclon, communicate these thoughts, reflections to you, for we feel that those gathered here have within your consciousness the ability to make use of our suggestions. The dedication which is within each one of you, to certain degrees, is as a guiding Light and will safely light your ways and guide you through the times and the confusions on your world scene.

I am happy in the consciousness that I have been enabled to converse with you upon this occasion and to establish a transmission at this time. I am, at this present moment, stationed in a craft not visible within your atmosphere but, none-the-less, stationed above your western coastal region.

In the Light of Our Radiant One, I bid you Adonai vassu baragus. May you be one with the Eternal Light.
(Via Telethought, 27 Dec 68. Santa Barbara, Cal. Channel: Marianne Francis)

* * * * * * * * * * *

LIFE IS ETERNAL

In loving memory of my little mother,
Katharine Maud Mary Brain
Who passed through the portals of Death fo LIFE
February 25th, 1969, Medford, Oregon

* * * * * * * * *

I know you are released from limitations into a greater life of joy and love and reunion with those you loved who passed on before you. So I do not grieve, but rejoice for you.

I thank you for "holding down the fort" when I was gone, caring for the pets and being brave and strong in spirit. You encouraged me to read widely and deeply when I was a child. You took me on long walks and taught me to love the little flowers which grew in the hedgerows and the meadows. When I was low in vitality, you taught me to replenish myself from the green of the woods and the fresh country air. You gave me freedom to find my own truths of spirit, courage to never admit I was beaten, but to pick up and go on again.

For all these things I give you thanks, and wish you joy, love, and flowers in your new life in spirit. God-speed, little Marmee; we will meet again in the time of God.   - Marianne Francis

SCIENCE DEPARTMENT   K. M. Kellar, BA, Editor

LIGHT BEAM COMMUNICATOR REPORT

Experiments have been conducted during the past few months to improve the solid state Light Beam Communicator circuit as described in Summer 1968 issue of STARCRAFT. Different types of photosensitive cells have been tried with some improvement in sensitivity. The resistor values of the first stage were modified to adapt the circuit to the new cells. Recently, a new and much more sensitive photocell has been ordered which will extend the range of reception in the near infrared region as far as 2.6 microns or better. This cell is a photoconductive type 139CPY and can be obtained from Mullard, Inc., 100 Finn Court, Farmingdale, N.Y, Zip 11735. It is rated at a responsivity of 5.0 millivolts/microwatt and has a time constant of 250 microseconds.

Light Beams for communication from Spacecraft above our atmosphere must pass through hundreds of miles of air consisting of oxygen, nitrogen, carbon dioxide, water vapor, and rare gases. Each of these gases absorbs certain characteristic frequencies, thus radiations are greatly reduced in intensity by the time they reach a receiver on earth's surface. Fortunately, there are certain frequency bands or "windows" through which rays can pass, the absorption depending upon their frequency.

The frequency band selected for experiments is in the range from 1.2 to 1.3 microns. Even at this "window" however, only about one-third of the radiation is transmitted through the atmosphere. It is important, therefore, that experiments be conducted on a hill or mountain above fog and smog to avoid further reduction in signal strength. It is essential to have a highly efficient receiving device. A parabolic reflector is recommended to concentrate rays from a large area on the tiny photocell.

A high signal-to-noise ratio is required in order to detect weak signals. To obtain a good ratio, a good filter is required which will pass only the desired frequencies. The best type of narrow band-pass filter is the interference type, however, these are rather expensive ($50 to $75). It is hoped that satisfactory results can be obtained with other filters.

Our thanks go to Gene Lupo for his diligent work with the Light Beam Communicator over the past year. Thanks also go to those who have sent us technical data and information to help with this research project.

GUEST CORNER 17
Ann Lee of Seattle, Wash. has composed several New Age songs which she sings for various organizations. The words of Eternity's Song, are given below. Unfortunately, space does not permit including the music. Some of her other songs are entitled: Children of the Dawn, Birth of an Age, Celestial Rhapsody, New Age Song, Follow Me Pilgrim Home etc.

ETERNITY's SONG

Dark the night, but bright the dawn,
  Sadness, sorrow all are gone;
Bright the day that is to be,
  When from her bondage Earth is free.
Though the night of Earth be long,
  Still my soul sings eternity's song
Of the day mankind sheds no more tears,
  And we hear the music of the spheres.

Though our path's been hard and long,
  'Tis worth the trials we've undergone,
For with the dawn our bonds will break,
  And of a New World shall we partake.
Children of the dawn, arise,
  Paradise before you lies.
When as Cosmic children we
  Shall inherit eternity.

When shall end the long dark night,
  Earth shall wear a mantle of light,
Strife and struggle no more will be,
  For all Earth's children shall brothers be.
Lift your head and lift your eyes,
  Look beyond Earth's azure skies,
And your joyful voices raise
  To usher in our Golden Age.

Earthquakes Rock Widespread Areas Of Middle East

Buildings Sway In Tel Aviv

By United Press International

(3/31/69)

A series of earthquakes today shuddered through the Middle East from Cairo to Istanbul, leaving hundreds of persons homeless in at least seven countries. Lesser temblors struck southern Europe and the slopes of Mt. Etna on Sicily.

At least nine persons were hurt in Egypt, and hundreds of others fled into the streets of Cairo. The quake was less severe in Tel Aviv but tall buildings rocked and some persons fled to air raid shelters.

Ethiopian officials reported at least 300 persons homeless as result of the quake.

Turkish officials in Istanbul said the temblors were felt as far away as Iraq. In Turkey, the quakes were felt in East Anatolia and other eastern regions of the country.

The Helwan Seismological Institute in Cairo said the Egyptian quake centered in the Sinai Desert east of the Gulf of Suez and had an intensity of 7 on the Richter Scale.

Widespread Death, Destruction Left By Violent Quake

(3/28/69)

ISTANBUL (UPI)—An earthquake rocked western Turkey today, spreading death and destruction over thousands of square miles. Mosques, buildings and thousands of houses were reported shattered.

Early reports said at least 39 persons had been killed, mostly in the Manisa area about 175 miles southwest of Istanbul. Authorities said the death toll would rise.

About 200 villages near Manisa remained out of communications with the outside world hours after the earthquake erupted 186 miles south of Istanbul and rolled across the countryside before dawn.

Tremors which had been felt throughout western Turkey this week had put thousands of residents on edge.

At 3:40 a.m. today, the earthquake hit with an intensity of 7.5 degrees on the Richter scale, seismological experts in Istanbul said.

The Manisa area appeared hardest hit, but the quake also rumbled through Ismor, Mugla, Bursa, Denizli and Eskieshr and into the southern part of the country.

In Mersinli village alone, according to reports reaching Istanbul, more than 1,200 houses were demolished.

Tents Provided

Government authorities in Manisa ordered more than 3,000 tents sent into Salihli, Alasehir and Sarigol provinces as emergency shelters for the injured and homeless.

1968 Quake Life Toll High

WASHINGTON — (UPI) — More people lost their lives in earthquakes around the world last year than in any year since 1960, according to the National Earthquake Information Center.

The center said 20 quakes in 13 foreign countries took 12,401 lives. (2/15/69)

Center News and Travels

November was a month of change, largely personal, in that I ended one phase in my life and established a karmic relationship on its correct footing. Kenneth and I are now, and for the future, co-workers in the cause, (which is our true bond) and are no longer bound by a legal tie. Prior to attending to legal technicalities, I suffered an unfortunate mishap with my T-Bird - skidding on an icy road and plunging into a ditch. Part of the right side of the automobile was torn and damaged and I myself, violently thrown across the car as it came to rest in the ditch, facing in the opposite direction from which I was going! Had I not been somehow protected, I would have suffered from broken ribs and concussion. As it was, several large ugly bruises, a strained sciatic nerve, and shaken nerves alone resulted. Being of a rather determined nature and bent on important business, I proceeded to drive the damaged T-Bird into Medford, some twelve miles and then over to Grants Pass 30 miles further where I left it, three weeks, for repairs. Had some hiway repair men with a "cat" not come by at the appropriate moment and dragged us (my car and I) out of the ditch, it is dubious we would have ever extricated ourselves and proceeded on our somewhat cautious way that day!

The results of that accident were to plague me for three months afterwards with a jumping sciatic nerve and some ferocious migraines. Not-withstanding this, December 15th saw me heading down to California for a very necessary change of climate and to see old friends and new. Despite the fact I had planned no lectures originally, half way through the trip a series of talks to home groups were arranged for my returning schedule and one public lecture, for Inglewood Understanding Unit, filled. Cold weather continued right down to Santa Barbara. Frost had damaged orange and lemon groves and avocadoes in that locality and other southern California areas I visited. The sunshine was welcome, however, and I rested a great deal those first few weeks and attempted to replenish my lowered vitality. My gratitude goes to Mr. & Mrs. Andy Hardie for their generous hospitality.

A week in Joshua Tree at the Solar Space Foundation with Bob and Shirley Short and a welcome visit with Teska at White Star followed Santa Barbara. That week in the desert the rain storms began and plagued many areas, and my trips into and out of Los Angeles. Torrential rain and crashed cars all along the San Bernardino freeway added to the tensions as I drove cautiously and (for me) slowly into L.A. for my lecture in Inglewood to the Understanding Unit. Unfortunately, that was the weekend the floods really hit and the L.A. police asked everyone who could to stay off the hiways and out of the canyons which were rapidly becoming disaster areas. It was decided to carry on with the lecture but we estimated at least two-thirds of our audience had decided not to risk driving, although the rain had now stopped.

An enjoyable visit with Anthony Brooke followed that weekend and once again the drive back to Santa Barbara amid closed sections of Hiway 101, mud slides, and the most vicious migraine of that whole trip! Not-withstanding these distractions, a talk was given the next evening in Santa Barbara and some interesting VIP's met. Two contacts of great interest were made with Bishop James Pike and Dr. L. Mathae, a practising psychologist, both residents in that area.

Carmel the next day where a talk was given to a most enthusiastic group. My thanks to Ruth Jepson and her delightful sister-in-law who arranged the meeting. Santa Cruz, the next stop, brought a brief visit with Muriel West in her lovely home. Again, a home group was arranged at the last minute's notice and a delightful group of professional people addressed on the subject of "Manifestation". Then on to dear Gayne and Roberta's Grass Valley--- minor car trouble and a very stiff neck from tension of driving. At last, after five and a half weeks away from the Center, I headed home on the last lap of the trip and the longest. Another storm expected, a sick mother awaiting my return, and I drove nine hours that last day up the Inter-state 5 and over the Siskiyous into Medford. On nearing the mountain and finding it was completely snowed in and my mother very sick, I decided on a drastic course of action. Spent the night with my friend, Margaret, and enlisting her aid, we arranged a hospital bed, and a nurse to accompany us in on the morrow. Now the only problem was how to get in and get mother out!

A good friend in the sherriff's department was appealed to and a police jeep and driver were found for the emergency. And so we finally arrived back at the Center, my clothes, my Starcraft magazines, and I, plus Margaret, a nurse, and a policeman! A very sick little mother was given a sedative shot, bundled in blankets and carried out and down by the policeman to an ambulance waiting at the bottom of the hill, a trip from which she never returned in body.

Remaining behind to feed the pets and cope with weeks of correspondence, tired out and very over-strained, I became possessed with a compulsion to spring clean the Center! This I began that very day and three weeks later the Center sparkled as if new. The road in was also scraped from snow and visits to the hospital begun. At first, despite pneumonia with several complications, my little Mother began to rally. A week later on a Sunday I suddenly felt very low, exhausted and weepy and concerned for Mother. The next day, on visiting the hospital, her doctor told me she had started to fail. A four-day coma and then transition to higher realms followed in a few days.

On March 1st we held a small but beautiful Memorial Service here at the Center. Since that time much correspondence has been answered, orders for literature filled, and many small projects accomplished. Anthony Brooke was the Center's house guest for two days and a small meeting for discussion and exchange of information held during his visit.

Spring has come to the mountain, the wild flowers are unfurling their small and delicate beauty, and the Center's daffodils glow golden and yellow amid green grass. On March 29th our first Guest Session of '69 was attended by 28 people, some of them High School students, some from a community at Quines Creek and others from Ashland and OTI (Klamath Falls).

Material has been channelled, even under the difficult conditions of California travel and re-organization here at the Center. Tentative plans are being made for a May lecture trip to Portland, Seattle, and British Columbia. First, however, it remains to arrange care and feeding for the Solar Light Center pets: one dog and three cats, during my absence. In summing up, it could be said the last five months have been turbulent, filled with change, and promise of a new beginning. Until I see you all in the north,
                  In His Light,   Marianne

ANNOUNCEMENTS

NEW AGE SEMINAR: Dates: April 18, 19, and 20, 1969.

    Place: Josephine County Fairgrounds Pavilian, Grants Pass, Ore.

    Sponsors: Understanding, Inc.; School of the New Age; Universarian, Solar Light Center, and New Age Fellowship.

Speakers include some two dozen lecturers from West Coast states, well known in New Age and Space organizations.

GUEST SESSION: The next guest channelling session will be held on April 26th, 1969. Sessions are normally held on the fourth Saturday of each month except when Miss Francis is on lecture tours. It is best to phone first when in doubt. Phone: 855-1956.

HOUSES FOR SALE NEAR CENTER:

    2-Bedroom house on 1 acre of wooded land and woods adjoining. Price: $5500 complete; $1500 down and $60 per month.
    (No interest on balance if payments kept up.)

    2-Bedroom trailer with large built-on living room, with well, septic tank, electricity. On 1 acre of wooded land. Price: $4,990 complete; only $300 down and $50 per month.

PUBLICATIONS OF THE SOLAR LIGHT CENTER:

    Lectures by Marianne Francis:

FREQUENCY CHANGE AND THE SECOND COMING	$1.25
THE CALL OF THE PHOENIX	1.50
STARCRAFT CONTACT	1.25
MEN FROM SPACE & PROPHECIES OF EARTH CHANGE	1.25
THE NEW DIMENSION AND THE NEW AGE	1.00

CHANNELLED MATERIAL from the Space People:

    Set of ten scripts selected from Channelled material . 2.90

STARCRAFT Magazine: Subscription $2.25 (USA), $2.50 (Foreign).

    (Three or four issues per year plus Newsletters when possible).

SEND ORDERS TO: SOLAR LIGHT CENTER
                          Rt. 2, Box 572-J
                          Central Point, Ore.
                          97501

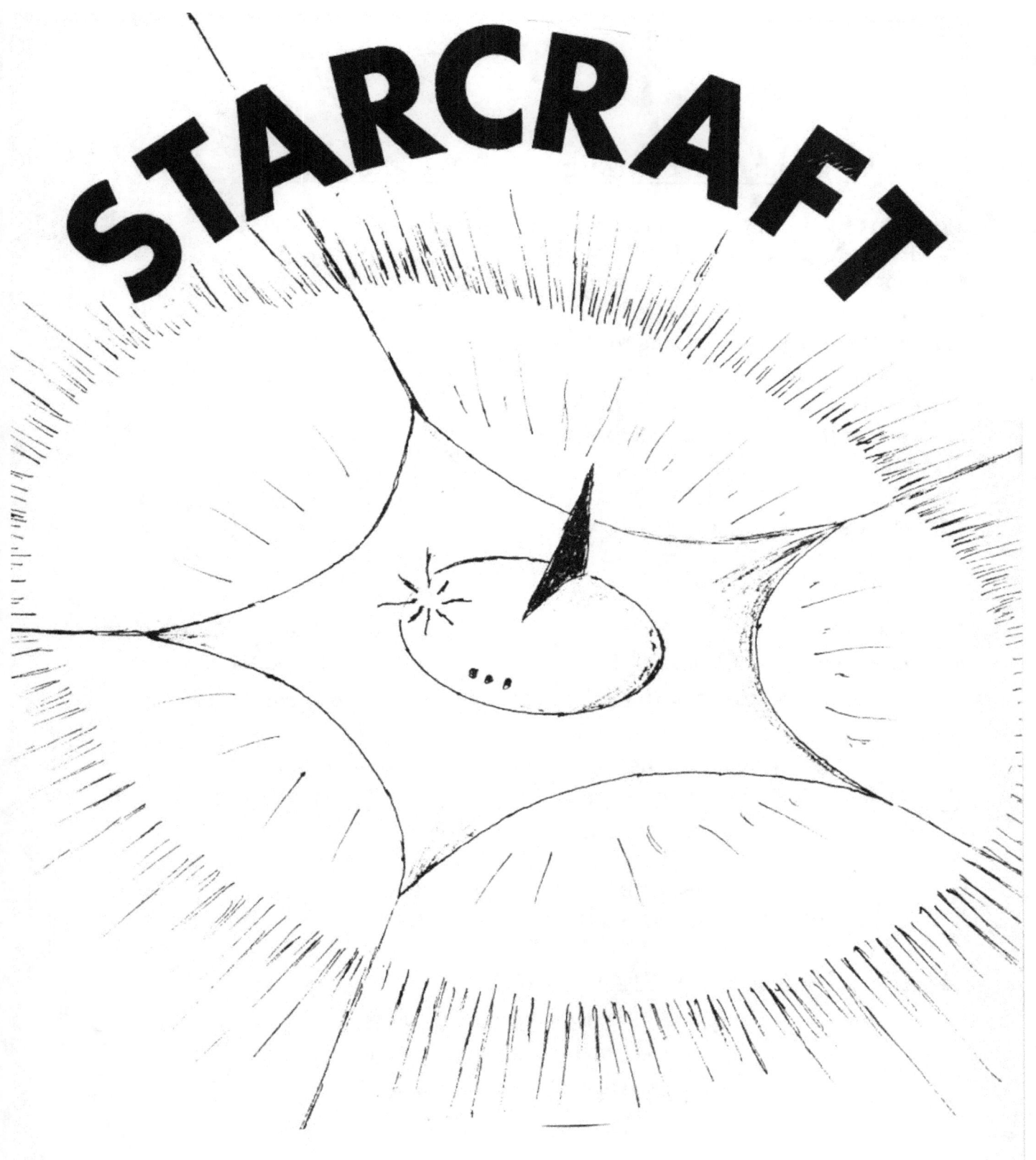

VOL. 4, No. 2 & 3   SOLAR LIGHT CENTER   SUMMER/FALL 1969

STARCRAFT CONTENTS - SUMMER/FALL 1969

EDITORIAL: Man on the Moon - Marianne Francis	3
If, Indeed, You Come In PEACE - Sut-Ko	5
Deterioration of Earth's Force Field - XY-7 Craft	8
Now is the HOUR - Sut-Ko	10
Science Dept: Plant Reactions to Non-Physical Stimulus	12
Principles of the Solar Light Center -	14
What is the Nature of Love - Orlon	15
Where Lies Truth? - Space Brothers	20
Signalling at the Center	24
Center News and Travels	26
UFO Sighted Near Center	27
Announcements and Publications	28

* * * * * * * * * * *

Director and Editor - - - - - - Marianne Francis, Dr.Sp.Sc.
Science Director & Business Manager - - Kenneth M. Kellar, B.A.

Published by SOLAR LIGHT CENTER, a non-profit corporation.

Copyright reserved.   Write for permission to reprint.

Zip Code is required, so please include yours when you write.
Telephone us first if you plan to visit.   Phone: 855-1956 (Code 503)

The New Age program is to
LOVE
UNDERSTAND   EDUCATE
RELIEVE SUFFERING   CREATE BEAUTY

* * * * * * * * * * * * * *

ADDRESS ALL CORRESPONDENCE TO:

SOLAR LIGHT CENTER
7700 Avenue of the Sun
Central Point, Ore. 97501

(Please note new mailing address)

EDITORIAL

MAN* ON THE MOON
(*from the Fallen Planet)

- Marianne Francis

From Earthman's viewpoint a great event took place recently: Two men landed on the moon, stayed there for a short time, successfully took off again and arrived home on the planet called Earth. Great was the rejoicing, for at last, Man was considered free to wander beyond the confines of his own native world! Mighty dreams were dreamt and voiced of the time, fast approaching, when men would voyage among the stars, land on Venus, the planet of love, and investigate mysterious Mars, planet of war.

No voice, publicly raised, stopped to ask if men of another race already inhabited those planets or those vast leagues among the far-flung stars. The light of a thousand suns burned out there in Space and in those reaches travelled men, Space-men and women. Was their presence entirely unknown, their craft unseen, their civilizations as yet undiscovered? Had no astronaut ever observed mysterious lights flashing by his capsule in space or photographed things he was told to "forget"?

Earthman is indeed visitor to the moon, his nearest satellite, but he is not yet in Space. His technology expands but does his consciousness of life and its ultimate meaning? Elsewhere in this issue we have a transmission from "the Brothers" entitled "If, Indeed, You Come in Peace?". It is upon the thoughts raised in that communication that I wish to comment in this editorial.

It was said that "Space is not the friend of those who travel forth in might". Considering the situation down here on the planet at this time, is there any indication that Earthman has learnt to live in peace, harmony, and love? There was further mention made of "spreading into the System the canker of Mankind's own sores".

While three courageous men achieved a great step forward in a technological sense, what of the system which sent them and the values upon which it is based? From a planet, armed to the teeth with atomic bombs and chemical warfare, they went! Capitalist West and Communist East compete in a race to Space, and the planting of national flags indicates territorial rights and values still hold sway, even on the moon!

So much for Earthman: his scientific achievements wax great but his spiritual self has not kept pace. Yet, unknown to NASA, unknown to the great masses milling around on the surface of this planet, a great change is fast approaching. This cyclic ending and new beginning has been termed the "Frequency Change" by the Space intelligences now contacting Earthman in centers of Light throughout the planet.

From these Space intelligences comes the concept of a "fallen planet", the one in this system out of phase with the others. Planet Earth, due to its low vibratory rate, is the fallen one, fallen in the sense of being denser in quality of matter and consciousness. A simple explanation has been given that where consciousness is focused, the matter or third-dimensional form is set around it as in a mold or matrix.

If Earth is thus a fallen or dense rate of frequency, it is consequently in a state of quarantine in this system. Earthman cannot impinge upon higher vibratory life in Space, for the law is absolute. The less evolved does not become aware of the greater until it reaches out <u>in consciousness</u> and becomes able to express that frequency.

Life exists on Venus, Mars, Saturn, and other planets in this Solar System, but at a <u>higher frequency</u> of matter vibration. Space men and women exist in bodies varying from the Light body down to physical/etheric level. Certain of these can <u>move between dimensions</u>, raising or lowering their frequency rates by virtue of their own knowledge of Cosmic Laws. They also can change the frequency level and density of their space craft.

The Frequency Change flowing in now and being established in the period from 1958 to the year 2000, will raise Earth from its "fallen" or lowered frequency to a new vibratory rate: This vibratory rate, we are told from Space intelligences, is the correct one for planet Earth. After thousands upon thousands of years of spiritual darkness, wars, confusions, ignorance and suffering, a "lighted planet" will once more shine in the place of a darkened mass. Humanity, those remaining in incarnation after the "cleansing", will be as "children of Light" and suffering, ignorance, and war will cease to exist.

As the frequencies change rapidly now, all else will change also. A generation living in accord with the laws of love and harmony will arise, their values attuning to Cosmic Law. New continents will rise and others sink: new lands, rich in mineral content for a new race of Man. An inner awareness, an <u>attunement</u> with the <u>god-self</u> within is mandatory for New-Age Mankind.

Three men from planet Earth went forth to the moon. Many men and <u>women</u> (balanced in polarity) come from Space to Earth to assist this planet and its risen ones through a great change. A giant step <u>has</u> been taken but it started in 1947 when Space intelligences came to Earth, not in 1969 when Earthman went out to the moon!

"IF, INDEED, YOU COME IN PEACE!"
- By Sut-ko of the Saturn Council

Greetings in Light, our brothers, our sisters. We transmit upon this occasion from the XY-7 Craft remaining high in the atmosphere above your locality.

Your peoples and you yourselves are asking many questions, both verbally and mentally, of us at this time regarding your own Luna landing. Suffice it to say upon this occasion that while we are not in any way discounting..."playing down", as you would say, Earthman's first ventures to his nearest satellite...not actually into Space, but to the nearest satellite...it is still a matter of paramount importance that Earthman turn WITHIN in consciousness of being, to his own "god-self" or god-consciousness.

While Man's journeyings, in an exterior sense, have import upon your world or planetary scene, it will soon be forced upon your consciousness that there are matters far more deserving of your attention and, shall we say, acclaim, than those of a physical journey and landing for the purpose of exploration of your satellite.

The frequency of your planet and, indeed, this entire Solar System receiving the higher vibratory discharge from the Central Sun are now changing rapidly and it is this change which will force upon you a realization of many things not consciously in the foreground of Earthman's attention. Many of your peoples are now aligning their consciousness with the realities of an inner world...a world from which Man has emerged on to the outer or exterior scene of the physical third-dimensional Earth. Man's home, however, is that of the INNER worlds and only as he is in tune with that god-self or god-consciousness can he journey in his OUTER journeyings in safety and in harmony beyond the levels of his own satellite, beyond the levels and the dimensions and the frequencies of things of third-dimensional form.

We have previously acquainted you with the fact that many of our peoples, while living within a physical sphere of existence, are more etherealised than the form which you, at this present time, utilise and call your bodies.

Your own planet, in its frequency change, is rapidly orienting itself towards a more finely etherealised state of physical existence. Only as Earthman in his consciousness perceives the reality of other levels, dimensions, and frequency bands, will he be able to journey, not only in consciousness, but in these vehicles which he calls his bodies (in your esoteric terminology) and in craft which themselves will change in frequency or density as they move through concentric bands surrounding various planetary abodes.

Our endeavor at this time (those of us who communicate with you through the XY-7 Mother Craft) is to assist you in the raising of frequency, in order that you may be at one with the change as it comes upon you. We have so many times spoken of the shattering effect of this change upon those who are not so attuned that we do not need once more to emphasize this point. However, we do once more present to you our knowledge of the shortness of Earth time, of the ending of this cycle (and we speak of cyclic time now) and the imminence of gigantic change: Change with which Earthman MUST align or perish.

We do not speak in symbols nor complexities. We speak in terms of simplicity understandable to your peoples if they will but concentrate their attentions for a little period of time on these realities. Consider, in the nature of Earthman's consciousness, how it is he finds himself in the position which he now occupies: his world a battleground between warring idealogies, between nations, between colors, and between creeds Consider if Man, in this consciousness, is best equipped to venture into Space and, as one of your intellects most recently boasted, "go forth to conquer the Universe!"

The Universe, our brothers, is NOT for the conquering of any man. The Universe is for the exploring of all men, sons and daughters of God. But in Earthman's desire to to conquer lies the key to his unbalanced condition of consciousness. Therefore, his need at this period of time is to go within and balance his outer self with his spiritual self; his scientific intellect with his spiritual understanding, and thereby to become a balanced creature fit to venture into a Universe created by the One Creator, our All-Knowing One. That Man on his planet has, in the vast periods of time of his evolving, found it necessary to destroy his civilizations and his peoples, the bodies, shall we say, which they inhabit, has only pointed to one fact: that Earthman has aimed his consciousness outward and now comes the time for a reassessment of values and the need to be one-pointed within. From that point of <u>conscious attunement</u> with the <u>god-self</u>, shall flow <u>all things necessary</u> for Earthman's continued existence upon his planet and his venturings into Space to meet therein his brothers, also created by the One God: his brothers who but walked a little step beyond his understanding and return in love and understanding to assist Earthman at the time of his great change.

<u>Consciousness</u>, our brothers, our sisters, <u>is the key to all change</u>, of the cellular the molecular structure which is taking place upon your planet. In the opening of levels of the consciousness previously sealed, in the attempt to use areas of the brain previously unused, lies the key to the control of mind over matter, of god-self over animal or outer man. As this key is sought and a balance achieved, many ways will open, many wonders will present themselves and Earthman, instead of landing in a cumbersome

...vehicle upon his satellite, will find his brothers from Space awaiting to open doorways of knowledge previously locked until this time.

Earthman, in his scientific might, has chosen to bypass the self which is the god-consciousness and has chosen in pride of intellect and achievement to attain to heights which cannot be scaled without the employment of a whole Man, or a whole being. One cannot take a section of oneself into Space, for one leaves behind too much. One cannot make a scientific pyramid which does not have as its base a firm foundation, not of mere attained knowledge but of spiritual wisdom and beingness.

IF, INDEED, YOU COME IN PEACE IN THE NAME OF ALL MANKIND, THEN THAT PEACE WILL ENCOMPASS YOU AND ALL YOUR ENDEAVORS. If you come under GUISES OF PEACE, with motives of CONQUERING and spreading into the System the CANKER OF MANKIND'S OWN SORES, then RECONSIDER wherein you move. FOR PEACE is NOT the friend of those who travel forth in MIGHT, but only those who travel forth in LOVE FOR ALL CREATED LIFE. If, indeed, you come in PEACE FOR ALL MANKIND, then LAY DOWN YOUR WEAPONS OF WAR and LIVE IN PEACE WITHIN YOUR OWN PLANET and venture forth into SPACE to meet OTHER RACES WHO ALSO WERE CREATED BY THE SAME BEING WHO CREATED MAN!

A time is coming of tremendous RE-ASSESSMENT, RE-APPRAISAL of VALUES. A time is coming when Earthman MUST MEET HIMSELF FACE TO FACE, his SELF not only of the NOW, but his SELF of the many INCARNATIONS of his BEING on the planet called EARTH. A time is coming for the ENDING OF A CYCLE and the beginning of a NEW, and at THIS TIME, EARTHMAN MEETS SPACEMAN in the ONE LIGHT and under the ONE SUN of this SYSTEM.

I who speak with you upon this occasion speak through the XY-7 Craft transmission from the SATURN COUNCIL. I am Sut-ko.

May we, upon this occasion, our brothers, our sisters, commend you upon the excellence of your harmonic vibrations and upon that which at last is being built within this center in consciousness of being: A COMRADESHIP which is of the STARS, a LOVE which is of the Infinite and a Light which comes from beyond.

May the CREATOR, the ALL-KNOWING ONE, OUR RADIANT ONE, send forth HIS LIGHT upon you. May you walk ever in this LIGHT unto the DAWNING of the NEW AGE.

Adonai vassu baragus.

* * * * * * * * * *

(Received via Telethought Communication, 26 July 69. Channel: Marianne Francis)

DETERIORATION of VITAL ORGANISMS on EARTH
XY-7 Craft Transmission

Greetings, brothers and sisters in Light. We transmit to you upon this occasion to acquaint you with changing conditions which now confront your planet. The imminence of change as seen through our eyes and our recording equipment is now very close to a major and overall cycle termination. We are attempting upon this occasion to transmit information not within the vocabulary of our channel, and not totally within the understanding of yourselves. Therefore, this material is to be used only at your discretion when and as events unfold as to its relevance. We would attempt to explain to you that, what might be termed the force field or auric field of finer energies surrounding your planet, is in a stage of what might be called deterioration or breaking down of the potency of the force field.

Shall we attempt through visualization to present to you what might be called very fine hair lines extending outwards as rays from your planet. The image which we wish to convey is that of the drooping of these fine lines. We are using this as an analogy, not as an exact scientific fact. The deterioration of the force field surrounding planet Earth is taking place as a result of many sources. Among these sources is the radiation released into your upper atmosphere, and also in the increase in solar flare activity. These two are creating a condition whereby the force field of the planet is in a weakened condition. Due to this, certain structures upon your planet are undergoing changes which are already noticeable and which will result in the decrease of certain valuable bacterial substances contained in elements found in your planet.

Mankind on planet Earth in his scientific understanding does not yet have the knowledge of a science of all living organisms* and of their interrelation one with another, but seeks to perpetuate some and to exterminate others without realizing this interrelationship and balance of organisms upon a planet.

Our own scientists and, shall we say, biologists, who have been collecting specimens, samples, from your planet of soil contaminations, of air contaminations, are greatly concerned about the deterioration and extermination of certain species of life-forms upon your surface. When we take this into consideration in addition to the deterioration of the force-field of the planet itself, we find a condition which, indeed, may be termed "serious". Unless your peoples are willing to accept help from an outside source, namely ourselves, there will be a breaking down within a period of ten to twenty years, possibly less, of life-giving organisms and the resultant effect upon

* (See Science Editorial: Ed.)

the ethers and that which you have termed the "atmosphere" which you breathe.

Our purpose at this time in relaying to you this information is relevant to the changes which are occurring on the surface of your planet preparatory to the ending of this cycle and the beginning of a new cycle. We have many times acquainted you with the fact that a crisis point would be reached, and before conditions became that which you have termed the "Golden Age", there would be a time of certain travails and crises and also evacuation of areas of your planet at this period. We of XY-7 craft transmit to you of the necessity once more for assuring yourselves of a period of the need for emergency supplies in this and other areas. The reasons which were previously given are not, of necessity, the same as the present reason for this request.

We do suggest that you keep your food stuffs in an area where they may be kept as free from contamination by atmosphere as possible. In other words, in airtight containers, preferably sealed in underground storage chambers. The reason for this will be apparent later. We pass on this information to you at this time so that you may prepare yourself, as many events are coming into being and will culminate on the surface of your planet.

Our craft is still in position located above this mountain vortex area though we are high in your atmosphere. The communications craft is once more, also, in this locality and may be observed at times during your night hours if you will but watch the skies. Once again in relaying this material to you, we emphasize the necessity for stability and harmony within the group, and for stability and harmony upon the mountain. The individuals concerned must attempt to bring this about in as short a period as possible. Conflicting vibrations are, as we previously stated, removing themselves from this locality.

We discontinue this communication now in order for you to acquaint yourselves with each other and to interchange information.

In the Light of the Radiant One we who speak with you from the XY-7 craft leave you. May you walk in the Light of the One Creator, Our All-Knowing One.

Adonai vassu.

(Received July 5, 1969 at Solar Light Center via Telethought Communication)
(Channel: Marianne Francis)

NOW IS THE HOUR
-Sut-Ko of the Saturn Council

Greetings, our brothers, our sisters in Light. This is, indeed, the voice of the Saturn Council or Tribunal. Sut-Ko transmitting.

We entitle this particular communication "Now is the Hour", for, indeed, at this period of time in the cycle which is now terminating upon planet Earth, NOW is the hour in which all of you must work to the uttermost limits of your beings. In that sense of work we mean to raise the vibratory consciousness as rapidly as possible, in balance, and to bring about a balancing and perfecting of all your vehicles or bodies. Now is the hour in which this must be done before the greater confusions spread themselves across the face of your planet. Now is the time to stabilize to the highest degree possible, to attain to the highest vibratory rate possible under the conditions which exist and the density level which is operative on planet Earth at this time.

May we use an analogy or paint a word picture for you? Upon your planet it is as if a very thick fog resides over the surface due to the accumulated thought forms and the miasma of conflicting emotional patterns of negativity: fear, hate, anger, grief, apathy and kindred of these. The Light centers are as mountains which raise their towering heights far above this miasma or rolling, dense, grey fog. The endeavor is, therefore, to raise the mountain peak, as it were, of each Light Center as high as possible so that, not only does it penetrate and stand above in the sunlight and the clear blue sky, (even as your mountain reflects these when fog rolls in your valley) but to raise the peak of that mountain up into the higher level or density, which is of the incoming cycle: the cycle of Light and of Love; the cycle of perfected mankind upon planet Earth.

Therefore, as it were, sustenance is drawn down from this peak into the very body of the Center and this nourishes and sustains the personnel residing therein. This is why it is extremely important for your Light Centers upon the planet to be in areas of pure air, of nature forces remote from your major cities, such as is this Light Center to which we transmit through our channel of communication.

Now is the hour to stretch forth your consciousness, to partake of the incoming cycle of energy; to draw this within you, to nourish, sustain your very beings, and to create around yourselves of such tremendous white Light intensity as to protect you from all things of negative intent manifesting in the last days of this cycle. There are many other reasons also. This is applicable for yourselves. Needless to say, it also facilitates the communications at all levels, including a physical communication from ourselves to yourselves.

This communication is to go forth at this time in the new issue of STARCRAFT now being readied. We particularly wished to send forth this in order that other Centers also may share the thought in this transmission. Our endeavors at this time are motivated solely by a desire to be of the utmost service, and to assist you through the last days of this cycle with the greatest ease possible; the least pain, strain, or suffering.

It is dependent upon you, our brothers, our sisters, and the degree to which you can raise in consciousness, how you meet the conditions you will find upon your planet, how greatly you can, with love and with Light, transmute these as they impinge upon your life, and how greatly you can be of service to the One Light and to those of us who work with you in the Center and from the Craft.

Our communication reaches you through the XY-7 Craft and the Communication Craft, and this is coming originally, from the Saturn Council. It reaches you at this time with much Love and much Wisdom and we ask that each one of you (and those who are at this time not with you) listen to this and ACT upon it. For NOW IS THE HOUR. In the Light of our All-Knowing One, we bid you Adonai vassu.

May you forever dwell in that Light; may its outpourings fill your souls, and may you reach to an Infinity of Understanding and Love.

(Solar Light Center - 23 Aug. 69. Telethought Channel: Marianne Francis)

* * * * * * * * * *

Congressional Report: "SYMPOSIUM ON UFO" Now Available

We are told that "Congressional Record Publication #7: Symposium on Unidentified Flying Objects, Subtitled: Hearings before the Committee On Science and Astronautics, U.S. House of Representatives, 90th Congress, July 29th, 1968, is now available.*

At our suggestion one of our readers wrote to his senator (Senator Milton R. Young) and also to Rep. Joseph E. Karth of Minnesota, Chairman on Space Science and Appliances. Rep. Karth informed him that "the hearings of July 29th '68 were our of print but had been reprinted by the clearing house for <u>Federal, Scientific and Technical Information, 5285 Port Royal Road, Springfield, Virginia 22151,</u> and were for sale at a cost of $3.00. Anyone interested in receiving a copy should order from the above and refer to #PB 179541. (Our thanks go to Elmer O. Mengel of N.D. for this research.)

Just before going to press we were informed that someone else had sent for this new publication only to be told such a paper never existed! We have not had time to research this yet but suggest our readers check it out. It would be only too familiar a pattern if this run-a-round ended in a dead end!!!

Let us hear from you (please type or write clearly). We are under-staffed here and need all the help you, our readers, can give us.

(*Refer to editorial in Spring '69 issue of Starcraft for previous details.)

SCIENCE DEPARTMENT K. M. Kellar, BA, Editor

PLANT REACTIONS TO NON-PHYSICAL STIMULUS

Research on Primary Perception in plant life gives evidence that plants respond to external stimuli even when in a remote location and not physically connected to the source. An interesting account of research in this field is given in a report entitled "Evidence of Primary Perception in Plant Life" by Cleve Backster of Backster Research Foundation, Inc. N.Y., N.Y.

In 1966 Cleve Backster made an unusual discovery when he attempted to measure the variation in electrical resistance of a plant leaf after watering the plant. Normally it would be expected that as the water was taken up by the roots and reached the leaf being tested that the resistance would decrease, since the extra moisture would increase its conductivity. With this in mind, Cleve Backster connected electrodes on a sensitive Wheatstone Bridge and Recorder system to either side of a large leaf of an ornamental plant in his Research lab. The bridge was balanced and its recorder actuated to record variations in resistance during about an hour of experimentation.

Contrary to expectiations, the recorder indicated a downward trend from the time the plant was first watered. However, after the first minute, the chart showed a pulse or wave type contour similar to that of a human subject in response to a short emotional stimulus. This suggested a further experiment in which the plant would be subjected to a "threat to its well-being" to test its capability of responding. A leaf near the one under test was dipped into hot liquid but failed to cause a change in the resistance being measured. After some nine minutes with no response, Mr. Backster decided at this point to use a stronger stimulus, namely, a lighted match applied to the leaf itself. At this instant, the recorder suddenly jumped to a high reading although no physical stimulus had been given. In fact, Mr. Backster had to leave the room in order to find a match! This experiment indicated that plant life has some unknown perception capability yet to be identified. (See chart recording opposite).

The idea was so intriguing that other experiments were conducted along this same line and they confirmed the original results. In fact, it was found that a response to a remote stimulus occurred even when the leaf was detached and cut to fit the electrodes!

Scientific Experimentation on Plant Perception

In order to verify the hypothesis of a primary perception on a scientific basis, an elaborate series of experiments on plants was planned and conducted under strictly controlled laboratory conditions.

Experiments were designed to provide a suitable stimulus to plants at a remote distance and in the absence of any human factor. The plants were continuously monitored for reactions to stimuli which were triggered to occur at random intervals in one of six time periods. A programmer was employed to operate the randomizer and monitoring equipment, thus the human element was completely eliminated at the time the tests were actually performed. Three philodendrum plants were tested simultaneously by means of separate Wheatstone bridges and electrodes applied to a leaf of each plant. A fourth monitoring system measured the variations (if any) due to power line fluctuations and outside noise factors. Using a fixed resistor in place of the leaf between electrodes, this system thus acted as a control test.

For this series of experiments, the stimulus used was the unexpected termination of live brine shrimp triggered by the programmer at random intervals. Each test plant was in a separate room as was the apparatus and brine shrimp which provided the stimulus. Each plant was maintained at constant temperature and illumination during the test sequence and all precautions made to ensure that extraneous factors caused no interference. The plants were brought into the test environment just before the tests to ensure they would not have been "conditioned" by previous stimuli. The recorded charts of seven test runs were evaluated by an independent "referee".

Results tabulated from 21 tests made in seven runs proved very satisfactory. Of this series 13 tests were considered reliable, the others being eliminated due to mechanical failure, overactivity, or total lack of response. In these 13 tests, five scored double hits in response to stimulus with two out of three plants giving similar response.

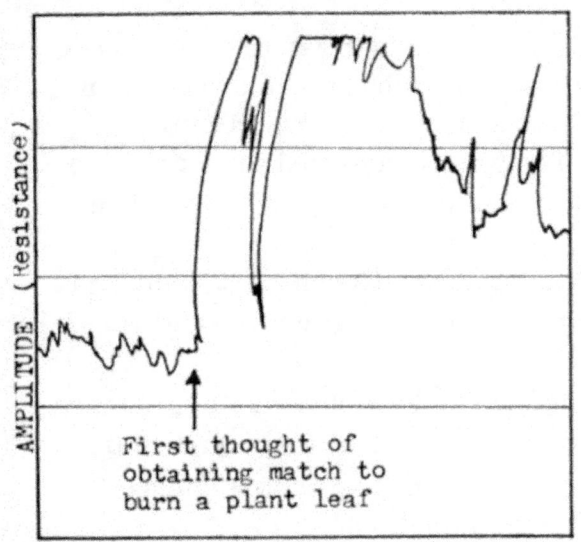

During a control series of seven test runs, in which no brine shrimp were terminated, (but everything else was performed the same as before) no response was indicated.

The conclusion to the test is that experimental results provide evidence that a primary perception (as yet undefined) does exist in plant life which responds to stimuli from a remote source generated by the termination of animal life (brine shrimp) in the absence of human involvement.

Further research in this field is being conducted to expand knowledge in this field.

PRINCIPLES OF THE SOLAR LIGHT CENTER

1. Belief in an Infinite Creator (the All-Knowing One, Our Radiant One, of the Space beings) and in the Cosmic Christ, the Spiritual Hierarchy, and the Great White Brotherhood.
2. Belief in the expression of universal love, compassion and understanding as the true basis for world peace and the healing of all mankind's ills. This embodies reverence for all life and non-violence toward man and animals.
3. Acceptance of the eternal truths given by World Avatars (Jesus, Buddha, Krishna) and spiritual Masters as taught in most esoteric schools of thought. These include Man's spiritual evolution through many embodiments on an ever-ascending spiral path of consciousness under the Laws of Cause and Effect (Karma) and Rebirth. They outline methods whereby the individual may speed up spiritual unfoldment by attunement with the higher self, the "god-self" within, and by the transmutation of old Karma utilizing the higher frequencies.
4. Belief that other planets are inhabited by advanced beings who have attained mastery over space travel, hence they are called Space Beings. (Their civilization is far superior to any found on Earth. They have ended war, disease, poverty, taxes, and famine; they control the weather and gravity and provide free energy.)
5. Belief in communication with advanced Space Beings by such means as direct physical contact, telethought, telepathy, tensor beam, light beam, and other means. Recognition that such communications provide information of vital importance to Earth man and should be given out to all New Age souls who are ready to accept such teachings.
6. Belief that a spiritual Light is being sent to uplift Earth and raise the frequency level of all cells, all atoms, in preparation for the coming change, and this Light can be focused through certain Light Centers in Vortex areas. Space Beings are assisting at this time of change in many ways. They are concerned for Earth-man's welfare and are prepared to prevent complete destruction of the planet through a nuclear holocaust or gigantic geological change.
7. Belief that our Freedom of Attitude toward: (1) the Infinite Creator, (2) Self (ego), (3) Other beings, are the deciding factors on the path to the All Highest, and service in the Universal Program is the key to this.
8. Belief that as the end of a Great Cycle of approximately 26,000 years approaches, a "cleansing" is taking place due to Light energies received, and the planet is being prepared for a density level transition into a higher frequency. Such a change heralds the Second Coming of Christ and the beginning of a Golden Age.

WHAT IS THE NATURE OF LOVE?

Greetings, our brothers, our sisters in Light. We attune in consciousness from the Communication Craft stationed above your area at this time. We speak with you upon this occasion, those of you here in this city, on the subject of "What is the nature of Love".

Much has been said, is being said, is being expressed upon your planet under various forms, under many guises of that which is the nature of love. We who speak with you from the Communications Craft, speak from the planets of Venus, Saturn and Mars. We attune our consciousness at this home to give to you a discourse blended of the many concepts of our minds, the outpourings of our beings, that we may reach unto you at this time.

We do not need to point out to you the tumult and the turmoil which exists upon your planet's surface - not only in the consciousness levels of the populace, or in the geological changes which are taking place on and below the surface of your planet; but we speak of the changing patterns which now exist upon your surface in your civilization of the West, and the changing patterns reaching even unto the East and to those nations beyond what you have called the "Iron Curtain".

We speak of the nature of love, coming from the highest or divine self (or being) of Man. Thus, if Man is created of God, that outpouring from his innermost essence is that which flows from the Creator, Our Radiant One, the All-Knowing One. As the attunement is made by every child of God upon this or any other planet, there is an immediate at-one-ment with the divine spark or essence of being and in the divine spark or essence exists all attributes of the Creator - our Radiant One (in our concept and our understanding). Remember that we too, have many spirals to reach in our evolution before we become a perfected being. Yet we have, in our understanding and our civilizations, reached beyond in the masses of our peoples, those standards, those ethics which exist on planet Earth, a planet of much confusion.

We therefore speak from an understanding beyond that which is yours at this time. We do not say to you, our brothers, our sisters, that all truth is ours. For where lies all truth but in the ultimate and in the ultimate being. Yet as Man seeks an ever-increasing attunement and awareness with the Divine Source and the nature of his own being; he cannot but begin to express the attributes of that being. These attributes are of Light, an outpouring of radiance which has nothing to do with your understanding of shallow sentimentality or that which is superficial, artificial or temporary. It has only to do with eternal values and upon these no bars may be placed; for the eternal essence of Man flows outward even as does that energy from the Creator to His created beings, in freedom of expression, in beauty, in warmth and in love, and in so flowing expresses itself towards all created life - that of humanity, that of the animal, that of the plant and the tree, the flower and that of the very rocks and minerals of which your planet is built.

In that free-flowing expression lies the true nature of the inner being or essence of the Creative Force. In its outflowing it permeates the spiritual nature of Man with Light; it fills the mind with ideals of highest and most noble worth. It fills that which you call the emotional self with warmth, and it pours forth from the physical being of Man in the outflowing of hands in greeting and in the touch which is of love.

Should you, in the confusions of your Earth planet, attempt to divide the being of Man in its four-fold expression of spiritual, mental, emotional and physical ... in so doing, you merely set up blocks, you merely set up divisions within yourself. In so doing you bring upon yourself and those around you, confusion and pain.

You have listened upon this occasion to the playing of a tape given by others of my brothers and you have heard of the great beauty, radiance and love of a truly great one of love, who came to your planet 2,000 of your years ago and in the example which that One gave -- not that which He said, but that which He was, lies the key and the example, for this age which continues onward from that point wherein He left. That being of Light, known to us as Esu, to you as Jesus the Christ, carried within His energy patterns such a tremendous out-flowing of Light energy, of Light expression, permeated throughout with a love and an expression almost beyond the understanding of Earth peoples. And yet as you attune in consciousness with those energy patterns, to those concepts, and attempt to become as one with them, you too tap that same energy, for it resides within each one created of the One Creator. Those heights of compassion and of love and of service, which that one expressed in His short sojourn upon your planet, are those same attributes which may be tapped and expressed and released by each one of you.

At this time upon your planet, the Christ-consciousness is the aim for those who attune to the Christed ray, even as others in other parts of your planet attune to the Buddhic ray of expression. And the Christed ray as it is attuned with, manifests such a tremendous intensity of vibratory expression as to release the God potential and the Christ awareness within all individuals who can so attune. In the nature of that love which is released is the key, the answer to the Creative force from the One God and the essence of being of this creation.

We, who come in craft you have called Flying Saucers, have not come as a type of phenomenon. We have not come merely on a research mission to your planet, although certainly research is part of our being here at this time. But those of us who have come from the Solar Council and who communicate with you through this and other channels of Light, who were so trained and so sent into incarnation for this particular service, have come to bring to Earth Man's awareness, <u>through</u> the phenomena of our craft in your skies, a reawakening of the values which were taught by all the Beings of Light, coming as emmisaries from the Creator, Our Radiant Ones have come inevitably and invariably....have come with concepts which were of Light, of Love, of Beauty, of Peace and of Harmony. Yet, in so coming as He himself said, "I come not to bring peace but a sword", and therein lies the confusion in the minds of Earthman. For though those beings contained within their essence that which is of the highest vibratory qualities of expression, in bringing these into the slower vibratory rate or densified plane of Earth, a sword of division was created between man's lower consciousness and his highest, innermost self. To this day that sword of division exists within the Earth planet's midst.

Yet, if you take into your hand not love but a sword, then, even as that Being said, you will die by that sword. If you take into your hand or into your consciousness the right to arbitrarily decide that which is of right of expression for another, then you are in defiance of Cosmic Law. For all follow a pathway which is individual and though many may stumble, many may fall, it is for them to learn of that pathway of their emergence as a son or daughter of Light.

To all peoples who aspire to the nature of Love, as it has been expressed by the Beings of Light upon your planet, we say even as you have just heard: Give of your innermost being. Give of your understanding, of your compassion, of your Light, and that which you ARE, will bring about change in those who surround you, whom you meet and speak with.

The changes now taking place upon your planet are changes of great confusion, are indeed changes of the breaking down of one age and its standards, outworn and outmoded, to the beginning of a new. You do not build a new building upon the rotting foundation of the old. Therefore, that which is destructive in your planetary scene at this time, performs a useful purpose in tearing down the outmoded structure which is rotten to its very core with hypocrisies and values which are not of the coming age.

So you build, each one, in Light and in Love, and in creativity of values which are eternal. As you build upon these things, a new structure will appear which is more lasting, of greater beauty and of greater value.

Thus is the nature of love, from highest Cosmic levels, expressed down through the spiritual, mental, emotional and physical self of Man in many expressions, in many outpourings, in Freedom of being. Thus it performs its service, which is the service of love, and it radiates its energies and it brings about the stabilization of planet Earth.

We, ourselves, who are from other planets, both within and without your system, attune with you in consciousness and watch your people as they walk upon the surface of their planet. We come now in our craft into closer orbit of your Earth's immediate atmosphere and we come also into conference soon with certain of your peoples in secluded Light center areas set aside for this purpose. For as the mighty changes are taking place and accelerating, it is necessary for a greater stabilization and for a greater at-one-ment between our peoples of the Solar Council of this system and of the enlightened ones on planet Earth.

We speak with you in much Light, with much Joy, upon this occasion that we might meet with you in consciousness in this way; that we might establish a link with each mind which can be reached by you and utilized.

You can call upon the energies from the craft to assist you even as you call upon the high energies of the Creative Force itself. We work directly under the auspices of the Solar Council and the Saturn Command Force. We are working at one with the Christ Ray and the Galactic Tribunals for the emergence of planet Earth into a new pattern and a new vibratory rate of frequency for the New Age which is called the Golden Age of Light.

We speak not of nebulous values or vague ideals; we speak of realities and of energies and that which may be utilized, manifested and expressed at all times.

Now we withdraw our consciousness from this, our channel of reception, and leave with you our Light and our Love and the radiance of the All-Knowing One, our Creator.

May you be at one with that Light. May you express that Love in your lives and in your being, and cease from pathways which are of dissension and disharmony and division.

Adonai Vassu, I am Orlon.

(Via Telethought: 8 June '69, Vancouver, B.C.   Channel: Marianne Francis)

* * * * * * * * *

Notice of Non-Association

Due to the fact that the Solar Light Center's name and that of Miss Marianne Francis have been used without permission or authority, to endorse the activities of other individuals and/or groups, this announcement is made:

Unless specifically stated in this magazine (or in writing to an individual), it may not be assumed that the Center or Miss Francis endorse the activities, personal ideas, or cults of any individual.

This does not mean we do not morally support other organizations working along similar lines. We are merely protecting ourselves from fringe area fanatics, mentally disturbed individuals and the like who are promulgating strange and distorted ideas at variance with our own principles and the "Brothers" work. See statement of Principles in this issue.

Signed: Kenneth M. Kellar

Marianne Francis

WHERE LIES TRUTH?

Greetings, our brothers, our sisters of Earth. We transmit upon this occasion, our brothers, our sisters of Earth planet, upon the subject of "Where Lies Truth". We have, upon many occasions, listened to your questions, your challenges, your comments, upon those tapes which have been given by our brother Monka, our brother Voltra, and many others through the Solar Cross Organization; and we have discoursed upon subjects of much import in your understanding.

You ask us in your questionings, in your minds, in the patterns in which you emit into the ethers: Where Lies Truth? Does Truth lie within the authorities upon your planet: of governmental authority, of military authority, of political, medical, legal authority? Where, in the confusions which beset you as you walk in your pathways upon planet Earth, lies Truth? Those of you who come from a generation freshly incarnated into the confusions of this planet Earth, are questioning as no generation has ever questioned before, the values, the ethics, the standards which you find already established in your so-called civilizations, and in your questioning and in your searchings, you turn at last within for answers. You turn at last to the only source of Truth, for Truth lies WITHIN at the core of the being or soul of Man, for where else could Truth exist but within that spark of Man which was created from the Godhead, the Creator, whom we speak of and know as the All-Knowing One, Our Radiant One.

Where lies Truth but in the essence of being of the Godhead, created in form, outflowing in many expressions from the Divine, manifested upon planets, upon levels of existence: physical, etheric, and in planes which lie beyond these. Yet ever must exist that which is Absolute, that which is the essence of being at the core.

Truth in its unutterable, pristine beauty of expression springs new-flown from that part of Man which is one and part of the Creator, which knows itself in Truth to be eternal, immortal, undying and unutterable.

If you ask us then: What is Truth? upon any particular question, ask not from without but ask from within, and as you attune with the voice which lies within, which possibly has been so covered with trappings of materialism and illusion, that it is hard for your peoples at first to find. When you seek from within you will find the answer springing into expression within the mind, into feeling with the emotions, into KNOWING: For that knowing which lies within and expresses itself in a phrase, perhaps much misunderstood, but understood by the mystics of your planet, as "I KNOW BECAUSE I KNOW". It lies beyond logic or reason, for there is no logic or reason of the mind which can <u>know</u> with certainty. There is no feeling or emotion of the desire self which can <u>know</u> with certainty, but all become part and parcel of that inner knowing when an attunement or at-one-ness become an established reality, and downward or outward from the highest point or expression of that which is the Divine Spark flows, through other levels of the mind, of the emotions, of the understanding, that oneness, that knowing, that Truth which IS.

    You of a generation who seek or challenge have come into an incarnation specifically to bring about change on the face of planet Earth. For if change is not brought about very shortly upon the face of this planet, then it will go down in destruction and degradation and the civilization will be as nought; and rocks and sand alone will remain as witness to the atomic fury of nations who destroy themselves in their lust for military, material might. You are the generation who come in thought, who come in soul and expression, come into incarnation questing, seeking, challenging. And only as you do so in Truth and with an inner desire to pursue a Truth which is ETERNAL, will you find those things which lie beyond the physical realm, which lie beyond the established values which have been values of hypocrisy, values which are worthless if they do not express the spiritual being of Man in Truth, in dignity, in beauty, and in love. That which IS of the INNER nature of Man expresses only of the Godhead in immeasurable forms, in individual expression. Yet none-the-less, qualities which are of the Godhead, of Love, of Compassion, of Beauty, of Creativity, of wealth of knowledge, of Wisdom, and of that questing which lies beyond the realm of the senses, into the realm of things which are reality, which bestow upon the senses a dignity and an immortal expression and stamp of the Creator.

Where Lies Truth? but within, and in measuring, analyzing, attempting to understand the nature of things without, seek to discover this from the point within, and those things which are not measurable by Eternal values will fall away of their own worthlessness, of their own tawdry values and will destroy themselves as even now upon your world scene this takes place. For the values and the ethics and the standards which were not of value are crumbling even as the very foundation of materialistic society is crumbling and shaking. A New Foundation will arise which is sound, which is based upon spiritual evaluation, and upon this foundation will arise a new civilization and a Golden Age of Light and Wisdom, True Science and True Values.

In Man's search for Truth he pursues a pathway as upon the razor edge of a precipice, yet in attaining to the heights which may be attained, he finds a Grail of inestimable value. If you would pursue this pathway, know that many now also walk with you: That those who were pioneers in the many centuries which have passed and have walked alone and who were crucified and tortured and tormented for their quest, walk also with you in consciousness; that we walk with you in consciousness: We who are people even as you: human beings, male and female, who love and know of those things which concern you, and know of those longings and those desires and those aims within your hearts and your consciousness, that we walk with you also and become a part of your quest. For when Earthman reaches to a certain point of understanding in sufficient numbers, and sends forth his call to his brothers in space, then shall we answer and our craft shall descend and we shall walk once more with you upon your planet which is green and beautiful, if you will yet keep it that way. Our craft will come, our people will mingle with you, and you shall also be able to walk upon our planets and mingle with our peoples. Until that day, we who come in consciousness to you through this and many other channels and vehicles of expression, say only to Earthman and to Earthwoman: Walk with us in space in your consciousness, even as one day you shall walk with us and journey in our craft in your bodies. Walk with us in your hearts even as one day you will join with us in love and in brotherhood, for that day is not far distant, our brothers, our sisters. That day is drawing very close.

We leave you in the consciousness of this Truth and of the inner truths of your being. In His Wisdom, and in His Love, may you walk ever in these pathways of Light. May you ever be at one with your own infinite being. Adonai vassu.

The Space Brothers

Via Telethought, 31 May '69. Solar Light Center. Channel: Marianne Francis)

* * * * * * * * * * *

STOP PRESS: LATE NEWS

Signalling was once more experienced by Miss Francis, just prior to our going to press with this issue. On the night of August 22nd, returning late from the Shakespearian festival with the Center's Australian guest, David Lander, the car headlights were turned off and on around 12:50 a.m. six times in all. This took place, not on the dirt road to the Center as before, but along Table Rock Road on a straight stretch devoid of any traffic.

The headlights went off and on again, suddenly without any warning, with the speed around 55 mph. On slowing down, Miss Francis remarked to David: "I guess it's the brothers again, but are you sure there isn't a loose connection in the car?" To which David replied, "That's no loose connection". The lights then went out again and on, out and on again. The car was then stopped by Miss Francis and both windows lowered but no craft was visible. In all, six off-and-on signals were counted in a 10-minute period. From then on, no more occurred, the lights staying on even on the rough dirt road up to the Center.

Upon arrival, the two "crew" members who had driven in earlier from Portland were aroused and all four gathered out on the deck to watch for craft. Great activity immediately manifested in the sky with 7 conventional craft flying over (3 airline planes and 4 jets). This in itself was unusual as very few planes fly over at that late hour, and certainly not 7 in 15 minutes! The crew concluded that something had been observed and was being investigated by the Air Force. About an hour later a "Starcraft" came in from the north slowly, with the undulating motion peculiar to some Flying Saucers....

SIGNALLING AT THE CENTER

In April and May visual evidence of signalling from the Space Brothers was experienced by Miss Francis on the Center dirt road. Upon three separate occasions when driving home alone late in the evening, the lights on Miss Francis' T-Bird went out and on again without loss of power to the car. This only took place on the 2½ mile dirt road leading to the Center and at no time endangered driving.

Upon the first occasion Miss Francis assumed there was a loose wire and had the car checked for trouble. There was no loose wire. The second night at midnight the same pattern was observed; no flickering of lights, just a straight off for 10 seconds or so and then on again. This time our director counted the off and on "units" and found they occurred fives times while driving up the road. Following this she had the entire electrical system checked out in a large repair garage and nothing was found wrong.

Two weeks later the phenomenon began again at 11:30 p.m. This time Miss Francis counted carefully and finding the lights had gone off four times, lowered the window and said out loud, "If it IS you up there, our brothers, turn the lights out a fifth time." Further up the road the lights went out and on again a fifth time and then stayed on. No further signalling has occurred to date at the Center.

* * * * * * * *

When in Chemainus, Vancouver Island, B.C. in June, Miss Francis related the above experience to a home study group at the Carnac's house. Late that night one of the members phoned to relate that he and his wife had experienced identical signalling as they drove home:

Vernon Stanley-Jones' Account
(Night of June 14, 1969)

"My wife and I were driving home after hearing Miss Francis tell us of her experience and work with the Space contacts. After we turned onto the main road (doing between forty and fifty miles an hour) we were thinking and discussing Marianne's talk and how she had told us of her car headlights going out and on again. At this point our lights went off and then came on again. I said, "Oh Lord! Are my lights going to go out?" I was getting ready to stop in a hurry and they went out again. I suppose it was a five or ten second gap between the off and the on. This jolted us, thinking that our lights were failing. Kind of jokingly I said,"Gosh, I wonder if we're being signalled like Miss Francis told us she had been!"

We then met some traffic, dipped our lights and put them up again (half a dozen or so cars went by). There was nothing wrong with our lights. I cranked the window down but couldn't see anything. We continued along. A little further on we came into another straightish stretch of smooth road. I was thinking of Marianne Francis again and---almost simultaneously---as I started to speak of her, the lights went out and then came on, and then out and then on again. I said "You know, it kind of scares you; the lights went off and on again as though it kind of answered me, signalled me." We were coming towards the overpass and I wondered if I dare think or ask "them" to flick them off again, if there was someone "upstairs". I thought, "I had better not, they might do it!" AND THEY DID IT! The lights went off again. Just as I was thinking about saying "Come on, turn them off.", that's when it happened. It shook us both and we said, "Well it can't be! It just can't be happening, we must have a loose connection."

I told my wife I would not touch the lights and we would see tommorrow night if they gave us any trouble when driving. As we came on north of Duncan and there was a break in traffic, I wondered if the lights were going to go off again. We'd gone about 2½ miles and nothing had happened. I thought, "I wonder if there IS anyone up there." With that the lights went off and on again just once.

We met some more traffic and had no more trouble and turned onto Hurd Road. Hurd Road is a bit rough and so I said to my wife, "now we'll see; I'll hit all the rough bumps and the shaky parts and if we have a loose contact or light switch or bulb, we'll know." To cut a long story short, the lights never went off again or flickered all the way home and we took all the bumpy, shaky parts so the car shook and vibrated in every way it possibly could.

Now it's almost as if there was somebody kind of watching, trying to say, "What Marianne Francis has been telling you is the truth and this is the way we did it." It was done definitely and distinctly, but always when there was no danger of a traffic accident, or curve, or when any traffic was coming towards us -- it always happened in a safe place."

LUNAR AIR FORCE CHECKS UFO

GUEST CORNER

By Dick West

Grants Pass
Dailey Courier
7/25/69

THE MOON (UPI) —The lunar air force disclosed today that it is investigating reports that an unidentified flying object (UFO) was sighted last Sunday in or near the Sea of Tranquility.

However, an air force spokesman scoffed at suggestions that the UFO may have been a spaceship from earth or some other planet.

"We get reports of this type quite frequently and we routinely check them out," the spokesman said. "The so-called 'flying saucers' usually turn out to have been optical illusions caused by crater gas or something of the sort.

"We have no evidence that there is any kind of life on earth. And even if the planet were inhabited, it would be ridiculous to think that the earthlings would be able to fly to the moon."

Despite official skepticism, however, residents of the Sea of Tranquility insisted they saw a strange vehicle land on Sunday and take off again Monday.

"It passed right over my head," said Mrs. Maudie Tribling, who lives in Crater 22. "I could see two weird-looking creatures peering out of the windows as it went by."

Asked to describe the vehicle, Mrs. Tribling said it "looked something like a spider with spindly legs and dishes instead of feet." She said it was "breathing fire" when she first saw it.

She said it seemed to hover briefly over the crater and then descend a short distance beyond the rim.

Mrs. Tribling's story was corroborated to some extent by Clyde Kipper, who vowed that he actually saw the vehicle land and two unmoonly figures emerge.

"They were white all over and had big square backs and glass faces," Kipper said. "I couldn't tell if they were robots or living things, and believe me I didn't hang around to find out."

Kipper was asked what the creatures were doing when he saw them.

"I know you aren't going to believe this," he said, "but they were kind of leaping around and picking up rocks. Once they stopped and...I'll swear I'm not making this up...they stopped and set up a red, white and blue cloth and saluted it."

A lunar air force official called Kipper's statement "sheer fantasy." He said, "I've heard some wild stories in my time but this one tops them all. He must have been reading too much science-fiction."

CENTER NEWS AND TRAVELS

I am writing this as July ends and the dry season is once more with us. Fortunately this summer has been cooler, so far, than the previous years. Many guests have visited the Center, some (invited house guests) remaining for several days and others coming for a few hours to talk of sightings and changes.

The lecture trip to the north was delayed by a month due to a workshop held at the Center on May 4th with myself and Carlo Busquets teaching. Some problems have developed with a missing co-worker, yet much re-organization was completed in May on the grounds. Volunteer help has readily flowed in and many minor projects completed. Major projects are now in the initial stages.

Once more, in June, your editor headed north, travelling that now well-worn path to Vancouver and the island. Two radio shows: Art Findlay's call-in show and Mark Raines" were completed and a new and delightful interviewer discovered in Bob Switzer (CBC-TV). So fascinated was Mr. Switzer with the material and photographs that I presented, that he arranged one live 15 minute interview and a longer taped one for that week in June. We are holding our fingers crossed here at the Center, as Mr. Switzer and his producer have asked permission to bring a camera crew down in the fall to film a channeling session!

The Vancouver lecture was, as usual, well received but extremely hot weather plagued activities all that week. A channeling session for the Vancouver Associates was arranged and a beautiful transmission received on "The Nature of Love" (in this issue). Some personal problems developed but were coped with and changes in the Vancouver Associates' organization planned for the Fall. Lectures were also given in Nanaimo, Victoria, Chemainus and Seattle.

Guest Sessions for June and July have been extremely well attended and our seating capacity strained with thirty students, friends and guests. We were thinking of installing hooks from the ceiling to accomodate extra people! However, some of our "crew" are planning levitation experiments, so perhaps this will take care of the problem.

Our new work crew drives down every other weekend from Portland and Corvallis and great activity manifests for two days. The well is being deepened, the porch flooring completed and, at last, my bedroom is to be built on in Sept. This will start the alterations I have long planned. The kitchen will be taken into what is now my bedroom and proper cabinets and closets built in. Thus, an extended seating area will be made available in the corner of the large room where the kitchen now exists. Since closet space is much needed, this will help considerably in organizing the Center and maintaining a greater order.

As soon as your donated funds permit, we will plan the office building and small lab on the north side of the meadow. It would be very advantageous for the Center if many of these projects could be completed before the rains come in the Fall.

In October, I will be lecturing in Seattle and the Vancouver, B.C. area. Next spring I have been invited to lecture at a large UFO meeting in Montreal which possibly will be held in the Arena which seats 6,000. Other lectures will be arranged on his first Eastern Tour, possibly at Ottawa, Chicago or Detroit, and Lansing.

Jack Schwarz visited the Center in August and plans to work with me from time to time on ideas where our work indicates. His Center "Aletheia" is in Selma, some 60 miles from here. From time to time one meets old friends and co-workers from other incarnations and Jack proved to be one such.

As I finish this newsletter, David Lander, from Australia is staying in the Center guest quarters (one small, old trailer). David is on a world tour representing his organization "Open Mind" co-headed by his wife, Jacqueline. He brought highly interesting news of other groups and fascinating pieces of information including the research done by Bruce Cathie of New Zealand on UFO's and the "Grid System".

Thanks go from the Center to so many who have donated money and labor but space does not permit our listing all the names. However, especial thanks and gratitude go to Gene Lupo, our OTI student, who has now taken on the bookkeeping job and relieved me of a nasty headache! Now I will have time for artistic pursuits.

A word of explanation: when I say "we" .. I speak for myself and the Brothers, for "we" are the basic team always on duty at the Center. Kenneth is now at the University of Washington studying to complete his Master's degree in Physics. His moral support is with us but since his work load is heavy, his trips here are further apart. If this issue is late it is partly because Kenneth is coping with a full time job while studying and doing the final typing on this material. Any expert typing offered will be greatly appreciated, especially in the Seattle area or here at the Center. Kenneth's sister, Eleanor, has helped with the typing this time, too.

This newsletter would not be complete without mentioning a strange phenomenon noted lately by myself and also by Holly (who lives near the Center). When alone in the day I find myself listening for a sound which is small and far off as yet, a sound which is yet to be heard. The stillness and peace enfold me, a blue and tranquil sky, the outer ceiling of my world gazes down. Green leaves rustle and I KNOW a new frequency _is_ coming in... and a New Age soon upon us!

In the peace of this mountain, and in His Light,

Marianne Francis

UFO SIGHTED NEAR ASHLAND

At about sunset on August 2nd, my mother and I were driving south on Hiway 99 from Medford, Oregon, toward Ashland. As we were approaching the north edge of the town, I looked out the side window and saw a large green UFO which appeared about half the size of the full moon. It was flying above us and to the right moving southward. It was spherical in shape with a green "corona effect" around it. It was observed for a period of about 15 seconds. Reported by: Harold Brande

NOTE: Ashland is about 35 miles south of the Center and in line with the path of UFO sighted at the Center on other occasions.

MARIANNE FRANCIS' LECTURE SCHEDULE

SEATTLE: Date: Oct. 5th (Sun.) 11 am and 8 pm.
Place: Aquarian Foundation, 315 - 15th Ave. Seattle.

VANCOUVER, B.C. Date: Oct. 9th (Thur.) 7:30 pm. (Call 325-0276 for details)
Place: Manhattan Ball Room, 1727 West Broadway, Vancouver, B.C.

EASTERN TOUR: Next Spring Miss Francis will lecture in Montreal and possibly in in Ottowa, Detroit and/or Chicago. Write us if you can help organize meetings.

GUEST SESSION: Regular Guest Channelling sessions normally held the fourth Saturday of each month will be on Sept. 27th and Oct. 25th. They will be discontinued in November for the winter months due to adverse weather and bad roads.

FUNDS NEEDED FOR MOUNTAIN SITE

A 70-acre piece which includes the mountain vortex area is now for sale at one-third the original price, and the definite impression has been given to purchase this wooded acreage for the Center. This purchase can be made soon if enough supporters will pledge a monthly contribution of from $5 to $10 or even less. Activities are now expanding at the Center with construction of additional facilities in progress. Improvements planned include a small office and laboratory, a deep well, and a utility section for the camping area. Camping facilities are needed for visitors who wish to stay several days. Purchasing the 70 acres is very important as it will ensure that the mountain will be available to visitors for meditation and spiritual upliftment. If you wish to support this project, let us hear from you soon, please.

HOUSES FOR SALE NEAR CENTER:
Two or three houses presently for sale include a two-bedroom house trailer (40' Expando) with a large cabaña built on plus an acre with beautiful view and garden site. Price: $4,500 ($500 down and $50 per month). Write for details.

PUBLICATIONS OF THE SOLAR LIGHT CENTER

Lectures by Marianne Francis:

Frequency Change and the Second Coming	$1.25
The Call of the Phoenix	1.50
Starcraft Contact	1.25
Men From Space and Prophecies of Earth Change	1.25
The New Dimension and the New Age	1.00

Channelled Material from Space People:

Ten Selected Scripts	2.90

STARCRAFT MAGAZINE: Subscription $2.25 (USA), $2.50 (Foreign).
(Three or four issues per year plus Newsletters when possible).

Send Orders to: SOLAR LIGHT CENTER
7700 Avenue of the Sun
(Note new address!)   Central Point, Ore. 97501

VOL. 4, No. 4   SOLAR LIGHT CENTER   WINTER 1969

STARCRAFT CONTENTS - WINTER 1969

EDITORIAL: Is Earth an Insane Planet? - Marianne Francis	3
The Goodly Company - Sut-ko	6
The Nature of Man - Orlon	9
The Opener of the Door - Laurie Efrein	11
Science Dept: World Grid System - Gene Lupo	12
The Crystal Records - Clytron	14
Reality and Illusion - XY-7	16
Center News and Travels	18
Announcements and Publications	20

* * * * * * * * * * *

Director and Editor	Marianne Francis, Dr.Sp.Sc.
Science Director & Business Manager	Kenneth M. Kellar, B.A.
Asst. Science Director & Bookkeeper	Gene Lupo, Cert.Engr.Tech.

(New Cover designed by Carl Hammer)

Published by SOLAR LIGHT CENTER, a non-profit corporation

Copyright reserved.   Write for permission to reprint.

Zip Code is required, so please include yours when you write.

Telephone us first if you plan to visit.   Phone: 855-1956 (Code 503)

* * * * * * * * * * * *

The New Age program is to

LOVE

UNDERSTAND   EDUCATE

RELIEVE SUFFERING   CREATE BEAUTY

* * * * * * * * * * * * * * * * * *

ADDRESS ALL CORRESPONDENCE TO:

SOLAR LIGHT CENTER
7700 Avenue of the Sun
Central Point, Ore. 97501

Tel: 855-1956 (Code 503)

EDITORIAL
IS EARTH AN INSANE PLANET?
— Marianne Francis

"Those whom the gods would destroy, they first make mad."

Recently it has seemed as if a climax or crescendo is being reached in the deteriorating conditions experienced on this planet. Yet it has been stated that such would be the case in the "last days" of this Age.

Signs of the times are the following: In Vietnam last year, an American captain ordered his men to massacre the inhabitants of three villages: men, women, and babies; an atrocity not perpetrated by the enemy, who is always regarded as capable of barbarities, but an atrocity committed by fresh-faced American "servicemen." * What god did they serve or for what cause did they murder in the name of country and patriotism? One of these young men, Paul Meadlo of Terre Haute, Indiana, recently interviewed on the CBS radio network said: "Why did I do it? Because I felt like I was ordered to do it, and it seemed like that at the time I felt like I was doing the right thing because, like I said, I lost buddies. I lost a damn good buddy, Bobby Wilson, and it was on my conscience. So after I done it, I felt good but later on that day it was gettin' to me." He felt he did the right thing: while women held babies in their arms and pleaded for mercy, he shot them down without a quiver of compassion. No innate sense of wrongness made him cry out in horror, throw down his rifle and risk a courtmartial rather than do this ghastly thing. So completely was he brainwashed by a system which deems it a right to kill for country, if so ordered by a commanding officer, even though the victims be women, children and babies! What is on trial, in reality, is not soldiers but a system.

A civilization which has bred these values is insane, sick at its very roots; for murder of men in war is held honorable, but murder in civilian life a dastardly crime punishable by death. How in God's name can the citizens born into such a set of values not be corrupted and rendered split personalities from their very birth?

Drug-taking increases daily in these United States and, no doubt, elsewhere in Europe also. Moves are afoot to legalize marijuana for, after all, the argument goes, it is no worse - if as bad - as tobacco or alcohol. Yet alcoholics abound, and cirrhosis of the liver is a fact, as is delirium tremens. Also, we now know tobacco causes lung cancer, throat cancer, and complicates heart disease. So, if marijuana is no worse than these, how bad is it? Much is not yet known about this drug and much needs to be known. After all, DDT was considered perfectly safe by the authorities for the last twenty years, but now has been banned at last. Yet it will take twenty more years to eradicate from the soil where it lies and in the tissues of all living species. So, in twenty more years

* From "Potpourri" (Medford Mail-Tribune, 11/26/69): "My son left Medford a good, clean-minded, God-fearing gentle man. When the Marines finished with him, he was hard, cynical and had lost most of his respect for his fellow men and for his church. I can scarcely believe how much he has been changed. I don't know him any more.

what else may have been discovered about marijuana?

To an "up tight" generation and a tense world, marijuana may seem a harmless enough relief. A permissive society certainly is indulging in it as blithely as in the commonplace "drugs" of alcohol and tobacco. Yet, when it loses its kicks, many people "turn on" to harder drugs such as LSD, heroin, and "speed." Coeds jump out of windows or into rivers; male students hang themselves or shoot their brains out; kids hallucinate and go berserk, and "turned on" users deliberately "turn on" or hook younger kids or unsuspecting adults and policemen. It's all a great joke, for anything goes, and who knows any more what is good and what is bad, since Cosmic Law is virtually unknown on this planet.

It is true, a being called Christ set forth certain values, as did Buddha, pertaining to Cosmic Law. But, after all, they lived a long time ago. It is OK to mouth platitudes and speak of being a Christian or a Christian country, but who could be unrealistic enough (or heroic enough) to live by laws such as "Thou shalt not kill," "Love thy neighbour as thyself," "Forgive thine enemy," "Turn the other cheek," and suchlike commands of Love? Why, one might get killed or die for an ideal instead of a country. One might even be a kind of martyr in the eyes of God. And who would be so foolish when modern psychology has persuaded us that most individuals fall within the category of either masochists or sadists, anyway: Kill or be killed; suffer or inflict suffering; live for today, for tomorrow we all might die - die by the bomb or worse.

Sex is another widely-used "drug" today, in this insane culture. It is not "the pill" which has brought about a lowering of moral standards. It was long overdue for something to stop this lemming-like race toward genocide by over-population (though, Lord knows, there has to be a better 100% method than the pill, which does have side effects and interferes with natural glandular functions). The lowering of moral standards, if brought about simply because fear of pregnancy is removed, becomes not a matter of ethics but of safety precautions.

Sex is being used as a drug in all cases where real love and understanding do not exist between the consenting parties. It is no less a drug when used in marriage to relieve boredom or evade real communication, than out of marriage where promiscuity of the most lustful nature flourishes and human beings engage in perversions of a nature no clean animal of the fields would indulge in. No piece of licensed paper makes sex legal nor the absence of it illegal. Cosmic Law of the Creator of all life is concerned not with Man's law but God-law. Love and understanding brings souls together and if they blend at a physical level this is a natural one-ness and flowing together. Yet if they adulterate themselves by engaging in physical unions where no higher one-ness exists (in or out of marriage), they do so at certain risk of becoming trapped in the lower densities. The word "love" has become synonomous with sex today, yet to use another person for instant sense-gratification is not love and produces a greater tension in the soul than it releases from the body. Yet the insanity of loveless sex and perverted sex flourishes. Homosexuality is fast increasing and, despite all modern arguments to the contrary, this is not a sign of mankind's emancipation from religious taboos on sex but a direct indication of confused polarities. An even worse sign of the times is the emergence of sex/Satan cults in many large cities. In these, drugs, sadism and sex are blended with black mass rituals and forces of the most evil nature thereby evoked. It is interesting to remember that these very rites took place prior to the sinking of Atlantis. Let us recall also that cultures, degenerate and steeped in evil practices, tend to vanish in abrupt and painful cataclysms of nature.

Further signs of the insanity of mankind on planet Earth lie in the experiments being conducted in the laboratories of many nations. Cross-breeding of animal and man is being attempted, and successfully, to the point of producing live two-month-old foetuses in a "host" rabbit or sheep "mother." What conceivably could be the purpose behind these experiments? Other printed material received at this Center suggests that attempts are being made to breed a race of sub-humans for purposes of slave labor. This process of creating these creatures has been described as "cloning."*
The word has an oddly familiar ring to it. To breed sub-humans, half human, half machine: Androids, or half human, half animal, is to breed a soul-less creature not imbued with a life spark from the Creator. In this lies danger and insanity, for it is opposed to Cosmic Law, which decrees that all forms created contain divine essence. It is part of a vicious plot to lower the dignity of mankind and render all humans as expendable masses controlled by a few key materialists devoted only to a godless kingdom of might as right.

Stockpiling of H- and A-bombs has reached a point-of-no-return, in that sufficient bombs now exist to destroy the entire planet. Highly destructive chemical and bacteriological agents are also stockpiled. A good-sized earthquake, alone, in a strategic area, could release sufficient germs or chemicals to wipe out hundreds of thousands of people. Is this not insanity? Especially when we remember it is all readied "in the defense of peace." Such values, such reasoning, such a system is INSANE!

Is this an insane planet? Viewed from the vantage point of Cosmic Law and eternal values, YES! YES! YES! This IS an insane planet!

Yet, as the Brothers stated, "Beneath the degeneracy and destruction of your planet stir other forces revitalized, reborn, radiant in Light, awaiting the dawn of the new "Age of Reason." Only by recognizing the insanity of this planet may we change it to sanity. Only by knowing the depth of the chasm which yawns may we avoid it. The responsibility for this planet lies down here. Space people will help, but YOURS IS THE CHOICE, PEOPLE OF EARTH; LIGHT OR DARKNESS; LIFE ETERNAL OR DEATH.

> * It has been stated many times by the Space Brothers that degenerate
> Atlantean scientists are once more incarnate at this time on Earth.

THE GOODLY COMPANY

Greetings our brothers, our sisters in Light. We transmit again from the XY-7 craft, located high in the atmosphere above this mountain locality.

Our transmission upon this occasion deals with cyclic patterns of, shall we say, Light descent, and the encompassing and falling of civilizations through the machinations of negatively-oriented individuals within those civilizations. Down through the ages of time in which planet Earth has existed as an entity, and in which civilizations, intelligence, life, have existed upon its surface, there has come into being (as in many other planets, Solar Systems, civilizations) a warfare between the forces of Light and the forces of Darkness.

This warfare has in some of your ancient manuscripts been described as the war between the Children of Light and the Children of the Left-Hand Path, or the Children of Darkness. Through many eons of time, of this planet Earth's history, this war has raged: Civilizations have risen, much grandeur has ensued, great cultures have shown themselves upon the face of the planet; a level of high intelligence has manifested in many of the populace, and it would have appeared that Earthman of that time would have risen to great heights and broken, once more (as he did in very ancient times) the barrier between time, space, and matter. Yet inevitably, at the time of the civilization's greatest height of glory, the seeds of its decadence have existed within it and, insidiously at first and then with ever-growing violence, have shown themselves, and have rotted away the foundations of that culture.

Down through the ages, from pre-Atlantis through the great culture of Atlantis the Golden, down through the many sinkings of that final continent, until not one trace remained above the surface of the waves, came the forces which we may term "evil" in that they were opposed to Cosmic Law and the Creator's design for his Creation. Down through the great civilizations of Egypt, Sumaria, the Chaldean, the Greek, even through the period known in your more recent history as the Renaissance, through each rising and stretching forth to the innate dignity of Man's soul, the other force ever pulled away and gnawed at the very vitals of its creation.

From time immemorial, teachers of Light came to planet Earth, incarnating from other planets, from other systems, even from other galaxies, and from the realms known to you as the non-physical or supernal realms of existence; and great companies of Light came into incarnation, carrying with them the banner of Truth and Love and Light. In all the simplicity of these teachings, and in all dedication to the One Creator and His Laws, these bands of Lighted ones came down into incarnation and to the darkness and degradation which they oftimes found, and incarcerated themselves in flesh, not for their own experiencing - though much they did experience - but with a basic motive of service to the One Creator and His Creations, a motive of Love and Compassion.

At each time when the Great Ones, whom you speak of as Avatars came, came many lesser teachers, came many lighted souls, great in compassion and service. Often their tasks seemed small, yet they formed a chain, a pattern of strength, and each upheld the other; and as each company who we have termed "the goodly companies" went forth, they went in groups of souls who had worked and known each other from lifetime to lifetime. These souls are incarnate once more upon Planet Earth in many areas. These souls work for the upliftment of the planet and for the dawning of the Age of Reason at the ending of this cycle upon the planet. These souls, who have come into incarnation, have formed what is known as the Light-lines and the Light Centers throughout the planet. Some there are who have gone forth on lonely ways, and have been cut off from their fellows and have worked alone in the materialistic world. They have sought to bring that understanding which is theirs, a glimmer of truth which they have remembered, wherever they have found themselves, and in whatever capacity they have labored. Now, many of these who have worked alone join with the others in order that strength may be given to all, that the pattern or web of Light which is now woven around the planet may be vitalized to its highest capacity with the inflowing Light energies which come from the Central Sun.

So we see a pattern of civilizations and cultures which have risen and have fallen; we see those who went forth, who labored with much diligence and love, and who often returned to other realms and other planets, heavy in heart at the darkness which had overtaken their time; yet, knowing that the seed which they have sown for the future, and that which they held in trust, of the Light and its wisdom, lay in the secret places of the Earth, to be discovered in a time far distant when the ending of the cycle came and Light at last encompassed the planet.

Children of the Earth planet, Children of Light, who come with hearts and minds open to receive, know that the time is fast coming for the ending of the cycle of rise-and-fall of civilization and culture; that the time is now with us, ourselves and yourselves, for the meeting of many minds, both upon your own planet and from our planets. Know that although much evil manifests, and much which is of a degenerate, destructive pattern (particularly in your mis-applied scientific concepts) at this time, only that which is outworn will be destroyed and torn down in order to make way for the new. Even as we have taught, through many years with our contact with this "our own," there will be an outpouring of Light so tremendous that as you wrap yourselves in its radiance and its high-frequency vibration you become invulnerable, impervious to the onslaught of all things of shadowed intent.

It is true that much appears to be of degeneracy and destruction upon your planet, but beneath these things stir other forces, revitalized, reborn, radiant in Light, awaiting the dawn of the New Age of Reason. When the day dawns and the hour is set, then shall tremendous energies be given to those who have withstood the tests of fire; to those who have, through many incarnations, gone forth as the "goodly companies of Light" and have bled and have sorrowed for their beliefs, yet have stood fast through the tumult and turmoil of all things mortal and have held to the things which are immortal. So unto this day, which dawns upon the Earth planet and for the Earth planet and its Children of Light, we bid you lift up your hearts and your consciousness. We bid you await that dawn in dedication of purpose, in realization and knowing that upon this time there will not be a returning of the goodly company, leaving the shell of matter behind them, and the downfall of a civilization which they fought to save; but will be a triumphing of the forces of Light: There will be a triumph of the Children of Light, and there will be a reunion of all those who have known each other in many lifetimes, in many cycles, back unto the ages of antiquity. For that day which dawns is the cycle known upon your planet as a major cycle of change when, once again in our knowing, the Earth planet becomes a lighted star and no longer the hell-world of this System.

We leave you on this note of joy, of triumph, of the nearness, of the realization of all hopes; for civilizations have fallen yet, in the birth of this, a greater culture and more enduring civilization rises, borne on the wings of past suffering and defeat, yet triumphant at last in the Creator's Laws and the harmony of his Creation.

I, Sut-ko, transmit through the XY-7 Craft transmitter to you at this Center and bid you

        Adonai vassu,
        In the Light of Our Radiant One

(Via Telethought, 25 Oct 69, Solar Light Center; Guest Session; Channel: Marianne Francis)

THE NATURE OF MAN

Greetings our brothers, our sisters in Light. We transmit to you upon this session from the craft known as the XY-7 craft, and our discourse deals with the nature of Man on Planet Earth in these changing times. Your peoples, our brothers, our sisters, walk on a planet of much confusion. Your peoples, in this confusion, are surrounded as by a dense fog through which they neither see the reality of a light which is Eternal nor the reality of their own beings. What, therefore, is the nature of Man and his sojourn on Planet Earth? What is the purpose of change and, indeed, the purpose of existence as viewed through the eyes of Earthman?

We who view your planet from another vantage point, far out from the fog of Man's confusion, do so in a serenity of purpose and understanding of the laws of the Cosmos, and a great desire, our brothers, to be of service to the children of Earth. In the values which Earthman has "set such store upon," to use your phraseology, he has found himself trapped; for these values are those of the material universe bounded by the laws of a science which, itself, has no meaning.

In the ultimate, Man's destiny can only lie with the Creator of all things. Thus, it is for ultimate answers that Mankind on this planet Earth must seek, in the fog of his own confusions, until in consciousness he may pierce that fog and he may reach upward to an area where there is clarity of reason, of purpose, and of being. In the values which Earthman has set for himself, he has found competition between his fellows as the only means by which he marks his progress. Yet we have found that it is by cooperation with our fellows that we progress towards an ultimate destiny knowing, as we walk our pathways, a joy and a One-ness which Earthman does not possess. Our peoples are not as gods to be worshipped by Earthman; our peoples are simply men and women who have observed the laws of the One Creator and found therein a purpose and a challenge and a creativity which is of the god-consciousness. For even as the One who came to your planet and spoke of god-hood said, "Know ye not that ye are Gods?" In that sense our people are gods, but in no other, and in that sense Earthman is as a god, for the confusions of his pathways are only of his own making. As from that confusion he emerges to reason and to spiritual purpose, he will find the truth of that saying, "Know ye not that ye are Gods?"

An integrity of being, the dignity of Man's soul, the truth of his essence, and the love of his heart are things of more enduring value than the commercial products upon which your peoples spend so much of their time and their envying. If, my brothers, my sisters, Earthman (and by "Earthman" we speak of man or woman) finds within his own essence the reality of his infinite being, and of his purpose upon planet Earth, then he walks a pathway which is not that of his fellows, is not that of the masses, is not that which is understood. Yet more and more of your peoples seek such a pathway; and the loneliness felt by those on planet Earth who sought the things of the One Creator will be diminished as time passes now, and that which is real descends and engulfs and encompasses the planet called Earth.

We have said to you many times that the illusions and delusions and the darkness of this planet, which is of much reality and much concern to you and to us will nonetheless vanish as does mist before the light of the Sun. We can only repeat that the greater Light, which spreads now throughout the System from the Central Sun, is bringing about changes tremendous and awe-inspiring, not only affecting our planets but most certainly due to affect planet Earth, the "fallen one" of this System, soon due to be restored to its rightful position.

We, whom you know as Spacemen and Spacewomen, who fly in craft your peoples have called "Flying Saucers," Vimanas, Starcraft, we have observed for much time now the changes taking place on the surface of your planet. We have observed (within the lives of those with whom we have worked) the struggles against the tide of materialism and negativity, which they have sought to combat. Yet we say to you that the changes in which you already find yourselves engulfed in these Western civilizations, these changes accelerate and, viewed from our perspective, bring in a new culture , a new civilization and a New Age of Man. Yet, if it be that the darkness of mass-minded Man and the materialism of his concepts brings about much destruction, in the form of another war, on your surface, then we still will affirm that an Age of Light and Reason must ultimately dawn: That those Earthmen who have chosen the path of Love for their brothers instead of hate, of understanding instead of greed, of peace instead of warfare, shall (as the One who came to your planet said, two thousand years ago) "inherit the Earth."

It is not easy, when caught in the mesh of Earthman's confusion, to view with a clear perspective which lies beyond the centuries of your cultures, and extends itself beyond time and space. This has been required of those of our own who have incarnated on your planet as emissaries and connecting links between yourselves and ourselves. Once there came to your planet, two thousand years ago, an ambassador from the planes of Light. You called him your Christ. Now there comes to your planet, not a Christ, but servers of Light, many, many, who walk the surface of your planet even as did He, in service to their fellow Man. In time, upon your planet, will come about that which has been called the Christ- or Christed-Consciousness, as each man and woman awakens to the knowledge of the innate power of the God-spark within. Until that day dawns, our craft will be seen in your skies, will land and contact certain of your peoples, and will be in readiness for the need of a mass landing and a mass evacuation, if this be so ordained.

Our brothers, our sisters, we who speak with you upon this occasion (and I, Orlon, act as spokesman for my brothers) do so with a feeling of some solemnity, for war clouds gather on your horizons and much turbulence stirs beneath the surface of your planet. Our words reach not only to you who are in this room but beyond, to many others, and our message is clear: It says once more those words which you have heard many many times from my brother, Ha-ton; It says: "Earthman, come home! Come home from the emptiness of your existence to the reality of life in the Universe of One Creator. Come home to those of us who are your brothers and sisters, created by the One God, even as you. Come home to the Peace and the Joy of the Creator's Laws for His Creation."

Our brothers, our sisters, we leave with you the essence of our beings, the love and the understanding from our souls, for we are as One with you, even as you are as One with us, and with the Creator, our All-Knowing One.

Adonai vassu baragus.

(Via Telethought, 8 Nov 69; Guest Session, Solar Light Center; Channel: Marianne Francis)

THE OPENER OF THE DOOR

I bring you Death.
Swiftly borne above the chills of night
    fast commences all you knew to come.
I bring the prophecies
    of fast the unregenerates' wakenings,
        blessed in the light of none more
            blessed than thee---
I bring intrepitude of Light,
    the thrust of darkened faces rising
        past the low and easing night
Guardian of the vast enduring
    might of songs awakening: Death I bring!
That thee may rise in power and light,
That thee may know thy true, whole, and sacred call.
        When visions slumber on through life's
            inordinate cries--- from thee, from thine---,
        and none may know Its glance save those whose
            fearless eyes
                bequeath their own enraptured breakening:

Sun arise:
Listen in the deepened hum
    of sound soft-awakening,
Listen for the gently-swelling
    rainbow-hewn and richly pouring
        tides of Spirit risings

Soul of thee,
  Come to me.
(I comfort thee) I bring thee
                DEATH...

    — Laurie Efrein

SCIENCE DEPARTMENT   K. M. KELLAR, BA, Editor

(Book Review by Gene Lupo, Cert. Engr. Tech., Asst. Science Director)

WORLD GRID SYSTEM

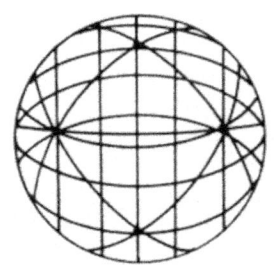

Captain Bruce Cathie of New Zealand has discovered, after many years of UFO research, that a grid system exists on planet Earth for operation of Spacecraft. In his book, "HARMONIC 33," Capt. Cathie explains how he deduced the existence of a world grid system which is a network of power points apparently energized from a Cosmic source.

Grid points occur at many places where stationary UFO have been sighted. Apparently the craft utilize power transmitted from equipment below the surface to travel over any part of our planet.

When Capt. Cathie and five friends, all pilots, sighted a UFO in 1952, this started his investigation of other UFO reports. Upon plotting the locations of his sightings and those of ten others in the New Zealand area, he noticed they formed a straight line from Kaipara Harbor to D'Urville Island. Even more interesting was the fact that in both cases small objects had been seen leaving the parent UFO and no natural phenomena could account for this. It appeared that the objects were controlled in some manner. Later deductions indicated they were probably involved in setting up power generating equipment at grid points.

Capt. Cathie later found that other UFO researchers, notably Aime Michel in France, had observed and written about the "Straight Line Mystery." Michel had studied many reports and observed that UFO often were seen hovering over points which averaged 54.43 Km apart in straight lines. Cathie attempted to correlate this with his data but found a discrepancy: His points were 55.5 Km apart! He finally deduced that this was due to the Earth's being pear-shaped and not a perfect sphere, thus a nautical mile is slightly longer in the southern hemisphere. He now had the key to the grid point system: They occurred at intervals of 30 nautical miles north/south but, instead of miles, the east/west spacing was at 30 minutes of arc (approximately 30 n.m.).

Using spherical geometry and much insight, Cathie made a model of the grid system on a globe and deduced that the grid system was made up of six major grid squares extending 3,600 nautical miles along "great circles" with the intervening spaces divided into segments. With the grid pattern once established, it was possible then to predict the locations of other UFO sightings.

An amazing confirmation of a grid point off the southwest coast of South America is reported in "Harmonic 33." On August 29, 1964, the American survey ship, Eltanin, was sweeping the seabed and taking submarine photographs. An unusual object was photographed at 59°08' S. latitude and 105° W. longitude. This object appeared metallic and was perfectly symmetrical in the shape of an aerial mounted upright on the sea bed. It had six main crossbars with knob-like ends and a smaller crossbar at the top. Each bar seemed to be set at an angle of 15° to each other.

This "aerial" was 13,500 feet below the ocean surface, so it is quite unlikely that any of our scientists placed it there! Upon checking his grid system, Cathie found this location was at a major grid point. Furthermore, the crossbar array tied in with the directions of the great circles forming the major squares in the grid pattern. The top crossbar appeared to cover the areas not covered by the major grid squares. By calculating the lines from this major grid point with its 180° counterpoint in Siberia, Cathie was able to coordinate his original grid plots in the New Zealand area with the world grid system. Further research led Cathie to the conclusion that actually the grid system had been constructed in ancient times but had been destroyed and was now being rebuilt. When his findings on the grid system were fairly complete, Capt. Cathie reported them to Wright Patterson Airfield in Ohio for evaluation. His report was returned marked "insufficient evidence."

Cathie noted that there was a relationship between grid points and magnetic vortexes such as those at Santa Cruz, N. M. and Gold Hill, Oregon (some 20 miles from the Solar Light Center).

Frequently UFO are seen at vortex areas. Also, UFO can maneuver in defiance of gravity and inertia, which implies they control gravity within and outside the craft. Hence, Cathie theorized that gravitational distortion at vortexes could be caused by a tilted antenna far beneath the surface. His calculations indicate they could be at a depth of from 30 to 36 nautical miles. He speculates that the grid system may have been constructed prior to the destruction of Atlantis and possibly tilted during cataclysms.

The grid system is closely aligned with the Earth's magnetic field. Cathie thinks the rebuilding of the system began in 1945 at the north polar region and is progressing southward. By 1965 the grid appeared to have been reconstructed to within 1,800 nautical miles of the South pole. The South Magnetic pole appears to be moving along a grid line and when it reaches a latitude of 75° 181' south, the work will be complete.

(For further information, "Harmonic 33" can be purchased from:

    A. H. & A. W. Reed
    Box 153, P.O., Artarmon,
    N. S. W. 2064 Australia)

THE CRYSTAL RECORDS

I who come from Space in the light of a thousand suns, burning in the galaxies of God, I, Clytron, speak with you once more. Much time of your reckonings has elapsed since last I spoke with you; many events have taken place on your planet, and in my consciousness also much has passed, is gone, and yet its essence remains with me. I come into your consciousness of this System once more to bring with me the news of an ancient race and of ancient days. This is strange, in that I speak of news, and of things ancient, long-forgotten in the memory of Earthman, yet once more I come for a purpose: to awaken in the minds of those who hear, the spark within, of the ancient, ancient memory of that which was known before. The consciousness of the souls who hear my words reach backward, backward, far back in time, to be aware of the things of which I speak.

I, Clytron, have visited and incarnated upon the Earth planet but a few times; yet there was an occasion, many millions of your years ago, when a race lived upon this planet great in wisdom, great in god-power, great in love - and this race took with them out into another dimension the secrets which they knew. Yet did they leave a record of these things for the coming time far, far distant from when they left, when once again into the consciousness of a few the understanding, the desire to reach forth, and to know the eternal heritage of god-man; the power to move freely in space into and above dimensions of the finite mind.

I, Clytron, recall that time when first was discovered the records of these ancient ones, and it was known that this time upon the Earth planet would dawn; and the few who gather in harmony of purpose, and with the blazing trail of truth foremost in their minds, these few who gather upon various areas of planet Earth will be enabled to discover the secrets of the ancient ones. The crystalline records are those of which I speak, the crystalline record archives in places of protection hidden throughout the planet, soon to be revealed, at the time of the opening of the Earth itself. And this opening of the Earth coincides with the opening of Man's consciousness, for even as the chakras within the body physical spin faster and light the whole being, so the chakras or centers sacred within the Earth spin faster and open the secrets of the past.

Beware lest you venture onto sacred ground until the consciousness is purified and at One with the harmony of the Creator's laws, for he who ventures onto hallowed ground, yet is not prepared in his own being, will be scorched in his etheric vehicle. Yet he who is so prepared and uplifted and purified will find his consciousness at One with such places, and doors will open within his consciousness, and doors will open within the Earth - and I veil the contents of my communication in symbology for those who have ears to understand.

The key, my friends of the Earth planet, lies within the individual. It does not lie with outer searchings upon mountains or valleys, in caves nor in crevasses, but it lies within the individual; for only as the consciousness manifests a certain vibratory rate of energy, or force field <u>within that individual</u> will the lock yield and the door open. The key is the individual and the level of consciousness attained. Your ways may be pursued in truth towards an objective and an ideal, yet ever before you shines the star of the Light within. A day dawns, and a door opens; a day dawns when mountains shake, and valleys become inland seas. A day dawns when mighty thunder echoes from the distant mountain tops, and the skies themselves split as if the very Earth were torn asunder. Such a day shall the Earth see, and the ancient race who left foresaw these things, and the news I bring of that past is your present, for in the cycle of time the two meet, and a circle is completed.

As yet, you have but only a glimmering of perception of what may be achieved, yet it is well that you perceive not the whole, for its radiant splendor could blind the vision of mortal man, until mortal man becomes God-man and there is a balance between arrogance and humility, a balance which must be achieved in the consciousness of mortal man before he can become God-man. There is a balance in all things, and in that balance is found the perfected being who expresses all facets and yet is One: integrated, conscious, aware, inviolate, a being of Light.

I come from Space, from the galaxies of God. I journey in time in a body of Light. I meet with your minds, your souls, your hearts, and I leave with you the essence of the midnight blue of Space. In its peace lies the answer to mortal man's questings. In the radiance of a thousand suns is the splendor of mortal man's future, when he becomes no longer mortal but immortal and sheds from himself the vestiges of corruption and puts on the light-armor which is incorruptible. My salutations, my light, my love, are One with you. I bid you farewell of this time-consciousness and I will visit with you again in the near future, for the time fast approaches when we all meet and know who each one is and where we met before.

(Via Telethought from Clytron, 20 Aug 69. Solar Light Center. Channel: Marianne Francis)

REALITY AND ILLUSION

Greetings in Light, our brothers, our sisters at the Earth planet. We attune with you upon this particular occasion to communicate certain of our intent to you at this time. Material is reaching you from many sources and many levels on your planet at this time. Certain of this material is contradictory in nature and content, and is causing confusion in the minds of many who are studying at various levels of that which you have termed metaphysical, and related fields.

We must particularly commend to your minds that you attune consciously with the intuitive level, or soul level of being. As you do this consciously and continually, it will then become possible for you to analyze and, shall we say, sort out the content of material reaching you from many sources. You will be enabled, <u>through the knowing of the soul</u> within, to distinguish that which is true from that which is false, that which is valid, not only on your world scene, but valid in its application to yourselves and your present situations.

In order to clarify the concept of soul or intuitional knowing, for those of you who are not familiar with this concept, we would state that there are various levels of reception: there is that of the emotional-feeling self of reception; there is that, of course, of the physical-etheric self; and there is that most commonly known as the mental processes of logic, reason, and analysis. The soul-knowing, or intuitional level is a higher perception or higher knowing than any of the three mentioned previously. It is that level which knows because it knows: It does not know through processes of logic or reason. In its knowing it is of truth to the soul within; it is of truth to the Cosmic understanding or nature of Man.

We therefore commend to you most highly the exercise of your intuitional self and the attunement and knowledge of its nature. For by this means you may distinguish truth for yourself, irrespective of outer signs or outer "so-called" authorities on your world scene.

The confusion created within the mind of Earthman at this time is manifold for, as we stated in the beginning, many levels of communication are reaching you, not only certain communications coming from ourselves but from beings known as Masters, from discarnate beings, from incarnate authorities, and from those Teachers now incarnate upon the Earth scene. Many of these are also diverse in their opinions, methods, and ideals. The individual at this period of time must - and we repeat MUST, in order to maintain sanity and balance, learn to distinguish truth from falsehood; reality from illusion; and ONLY the individual can so learn and distinguish this for themself.

We have stated to our own channel, through the many years of her attunement with us, that to rely upon authorities outside of self is, in a sense, to use crutches, and only as the Divine At-One-Ment becomes manifest within the individual soul does balance, peace, and harmony manifest and the fulfilling nature of existence become possible, even in the midst of the confusion of your changing Earth scene.

Due to the very nature of the upheavals, both in consciousness and physically upon your Earth planet and plane, the quest for self-knowledge becomes mandatory, the necessity for balance becomes absolute, and the need to preserve a complete and utter sanity of being is one which must be pursued at all costs.

Many on your world scene are caught in the maelstrom of confusion and are tossed hither and thither until completely lost. They become part of the mass of humanity caught in the sea and turbulence of emotional thought-waves, rocked and torn until they lose all mooring and become cast far from the shore of their own Being.

Our brothers, our sisters, we cannot stress to you, here gathered, too strongly at this time, (while our channel is still with you and we can communicate directly) of the necessity for those things of which we have spoken. How you pursue these within your own lives is entirely for your individual free-will to decide.

We have reached you, we have spoken with you, we have made this attempt in order that you may prepare yourselves for the times which lie ahead and are already with you. Even as you attune with the soul-self, with intuitional levels of knowing, so you may know your placement at times of turmoil on the outer scene, you may know your base of operations, and you may attune with the high sources of inspiration for direction and guidance. Need we say more, our brothers, our sisters?

It is in the One Light of the Creator, Our Radiant One, that we come; in His service that we minister unto the Earth's children. I speak at this time from the Communication Craft and I receive directives from the XY-7 Command Craft. Our Light and the Light of Our Radiant One is with you.

Adonai vassu our brothers, our sisters in Light

(Received via Telethought Communication, 11 October 69, at Vancouver. Channel: Marianne Francis)

18

CENTER NEWS

Thanksgiving is almost upon us as I write this column, and we have much to be thankful for, here on the mountain. The last year has seen many changes, both in my personal life and at the Center. An expansion of the program has begun, with new lecture contracts made this summer. On April 10 next, I lecture in Montreal at the Arena, which holds 6,000 people. A film-maker met in Seattle in October plans a film on "the Brothers," with material and ideas supplied from this Center.

September saw the bedroom at last begun, and foundations laid for a garage. Our construction crew of volunteer workers comprises Ralph, Carl, and Brad, and much appreciation goes to them for their hard work: Laurie has typed all transmissions to date; Holly cared for the pets and answered the phone during my absence in October; and our dedicated bookkeeper, Gene Lupo, came over from CTI on weekends and sent out the orders and kept the records. (Gene is now also assistant Science Director.) Our thanks, also, to Mareda for typing Starcraft and to Zady for the use of her typewriter. Also, many thanks to Clara Bonner for her generous donation and work in providing the beautiful new drapery for the Solar Light Retreat.

October brought the Fall lecture trip to British Columbia, the Art Finlay call-in show, Jack Wasserman, and that delightful interviewer on CBC, Bob Switzer. A lecture for Simon Frazer College was canceled due to a student strike and my own indisposition. A strange 48-hour "thing" laid me low and not 'till later did I discover many people were laid low also. The fact that the Red Chinese exploded an A-bomb a week or so earlier and fallout had drifted over Canada had, I think, a distinct connection. On reaching the microphone for my lecture, "God-Man or Animal Man" two days later, I discovered I sounded a little more ethereal than usual! Due to a shortage of time in setting up this trip and Canadian Thanksgiving, no lectures were arranged for Nanaimo, Chemainus or Victoria. Two lectures were given in Seattle for the Aquarian Foundation on the way up.

It would seem the "in" thing to do now, if you feel like protesting, at least for students, is to strip. One young man who attended my God-Man or Animal Man lecture at the Aquarian Foundation did just that! Since the incident was rather funny, I will give the dialogue and scene here:

SCENE 1: Miss Francis ends lecture and sits down. Male student in congregation rises and proceeds to strip off sweater and then steps calmly out of pants. Miss Francis, wondering what happens next, decides to "play it cool." The congregation just awakening to what has happened in their midst, taking its cue from Miss Francis, also decides to play it cool. Student sits in calm nudity surveying the scene. Miss Francis gazes airily elsewhere. Dick Kiltz arrives with the collection basket, smiling and shaking hands with the congregation. He reaches over and shakes nude one's hand. Miss Francis wonders abstractly if nude one will offer pants for collection plate, but he doesn't. Silence. Every one is playing it cool.

SCENE 11: Question session begins, at which nude one rises and proceeds to don clothing once more. Miss Francis, eyeing him with coy amusement, says sweetly, "We are sorry you were so warm." "Oh, no! Not at all," responds the student, now clothed once more, "you were talking about God-Man or Animal Man and I just felt the need to affirm my total being!" "Well, you did," replies Miss Francis, and hastens to explain to the dissenting one that by God-Man the Space Brothers do not mean a denial of the physical self but an expression of all selves from the highest to the densest (physical) in balance. Student nods agreeably and incident ends quietly. Miss Francis decides there is a lot to be said for "keeping one's cool" and makes a strong mental note to further clarify this concept of God-Man or Animal Man for next group of students in case they all decide on a strip tease!

A pleasant few days with Dorothy and Jack Squance in Victoria. On to Orcas and the Outlook Inn for a brief weekend with Louis and his group, then home via Seattle and Portland; a brief stint on the Clark-on-KING radio show in Seattle; and another meeting with Robert James Brown - film-maker and creator of the startlingly new concept of opera: with computerized light patterns projected on the stage and singers, his production of Turandot raised a storm in the Seattle Opera House.

Back at base, the first three weeks proved exhausting. Still tired and depleted from the odd virus "thing," it seemed as if every time I turned around people were at the front door. Students arrived in droves from Crater High School; two special Guest Sessions arranged to supply information to these questing minds. A beautiful transmission, received on October 25, is published in this issue.

Building proceeded apace. When money was totally gone, a miracle took place: an anonymous cashier's check arrived on a Saturday when I was feeling so depressed and low I was wondering how I would make it through the day. (Yes! I'm very human, too.) The check was the largest single amount received at the Center since its inception. So amazing was this miracle that I burst into tears of relief and thankfulness.

The printer is now paid for the last issue; the current issue out in time for Christmas. Running water, which had been well-nigh unavailable since my return, due to a leaking tank and a malfunctioning pump, has been restored - pump has been mended and I feel civilized and myself once more. The bedroom is nearly finished and the kitchen due for modest re-modeling. The final payment on one adjoining lot was made and some money remains for emergencies, which in itself is a miracle!

Another such donation and the much-needed jeep could be obtained and lumber purchased for the small Lab/office building. $10,000 would buy the entire mountain, incidentally, for the Solar Light Center. A decision has been made to re-name our headquarters the Solar Light Retreat. Basically, we are a "retreat," functioning far from the madd'ing crowd. "Center" suggests we are downtown and open 24 hours a day with a staff so, for the sake of accuracy, we are now a "retreat."

I plan to teach a course this Winter for the inner group now in residence in the houses up here. Later, this course will be taught as a Seminar in various areas. Also, at last, I intend working on my blank verse play while the frost crisps outside and visitors are few and far between. The next few months may bring another miracle of a different kind. For this is the time of Manifestation at last.

In His Light,

Marianne Francis

ANNOUNCEMENTS

EASTERN TOUR: Dr. Marianne Francis is scheduled to lecture next Spring in Montreal, Canada, at the Arena (seats 6,000). The date is tentatively set for April 10, 1970. Other lectures may be arranged in neighboring areas for this trip. Write us if you can help organize meetings.

GUEST SESSIONS: Regular Guest Channelling sessions normally held at the Solar Light Retreat the fourth Saturday of the month are discontinued until March, due to adverse weather and bad roads.

VISITORS: Those interested in visiting the Solar Light Retreat are advised to telephone well ahead (Code 503: 855-1956) to find out about road conditions, etc. Spring is the best time of year, as wild flowers are in bloom and everything is green. Water is still in short supply during Summer and Fall until a deep well is dug.

APPOINTMENTS to see Miss Francis may be made by telephone or in writing. Write well ahead of your proposed visit, as Miss Francis is quite busy and cannot always receive unannounced visitors.

THANKS go to all those who have sent in donations and pledges, as well as to those who have given so generously of their time in working on various projects. (See Center News.)

PUBLICATIONS

Lectures by Marianne Francis:

Manifestation (being printed)	$1.25
Frequency Change and the Second Coming	1.25
The Call of the Phoenix	1.50
Starcraft Contact	1.25
Men from Space and Prophecies of Earth Change	1.25
The New Dimension and the New Age	1.00

Channelled Material from Space People:

Ten Selected Scripts	2.90

STARCRAFT MAGAZINE: Subscription $2.25 (USA), $2.50 (Foreign)

(Three or four issues per year plus Newsletters when possible.)

SEND ORDERS TO:

SOLAR LIGHT CENTER
7700 Avenue of the Sun
(Note new address!)   Central Point, Ore. 97501   Telephone: 855-1956 (Code 503)

VOL. 5, No. 1   SOLAR LIGHT RETREAT   SPRING 1970

STARCRAFT CONTENTS - SPRING 1970

Editorial - Extra Sensory Perception - Marianne Francis	3
A New Energy Pattern - "Wahena" (Maxine H.)	5
The Simplicity of Truth - June of Venus	6
The Greater Plan - Ray-Mere of XY-7 Craft	7
The End of a Cycle - Ray-Mere	8
Whom Do You Serve? - Sut-ko of Saturn Tribunal	11
White Star Letter - KRONA	13
Science Dept.: Signalling at the Retreat - Eugene Lupo	14
"They're On the Moon Watching Us!" - BSRA	15
Resurrection of Life Forms - Devic Beings	17
Qualifications of Channels - The Brothers	19
Guest Corner: White Star - Command Bulletin	21
"Retreat News and Travels - Marianne Francis	22
Announcements and Publications	24

* * * * * * * * * * * * *

Director and Editor	Marianne Francis, Dr.Sp.Sc.
Science Director & Business Manager	Kenneth M. Kellar, B.A.
Asst. Science Director & Bookkeeper	Gene Lupo, Cert.Engr.Tech.
Typist	Mareda Hanson

Published by SOLAR LIGHT RETREAT, a non-profit corporation
Copyright reserved. Write for permission to reprint.
Zip Code is required, so please include yours when you write.
Telephone first, please, if you plan to visit. Phone: 855-1956 (Code 503)

* * * * * * * * * * * * *

The NEW AGE PROGRAM is to

LOVE

UNDERSTAND   EDUCATE

RELIEVE SUFFERING   CREATE BEAUTY

* * * * * * * * * * * * *

ADDRESS ALL CORRESPONDENCE TO:

SOLAR LIGHT RETREAT
7700 Avenue of the Sun
Central Point, Ore. 97501

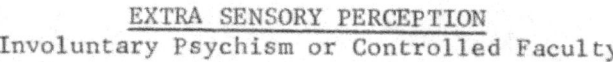

EDITORIAL
(by Marianne Francis)

EXTRA SENSORY PERCEPTION
Involuntary Psychism or Controlled Faculty

"I am not willing to trade quality for quantity." — Steinbeck

A great deal of interest is being shown in the field of parapsychology today. Not only is this interest the "in thing" on campus but many people of all ages are reading, investigating and talking about senses beyond the physical. Books are flooding the market dealing with this subject and ads abound promising instant ESP and control of others by thought.

One young man assured me, in all solemnity, that as Neptune is going into Sagittarius (house of higher mind, religion, etc.) everyone would become psychic during the next 12 years!!! Considering the mass level of consciousness at this time, it might prove to be highly dangerous if everyone did become psychic. What one perceives, after all, is dependent on one's own spiritual development. There is not just one plane of reality but many.

Therefore, at this time, it might be well to stop and consider what ESP is and how it functions. Extra sensory perceptions or, as Shafica Karagulla in her fascinating book, "Breakthrough to Creativity" calls them, Higher Sense Perceptions, are senses which lie dormant within all humans and are partially or fully developed in some.

Dr. J. B. Rhine of Duke University is, perhaps, the best known parapsychologist in the United States and his experiments with Zenor cards have established the validity of ESP among many of the more educated in the populace. His methods are largely quantitative and, frankly, monotonous in their scope. Perhaps that is in keeping with the constant demand for proof in a country that has made a dogma out of statistics: large quantities of anything must be of value! At all events, the mass of experiments conducted by Dr. Rhine have established ESP, beyond reasonable doubt, as valid to all but the "dyed-in-the-wool" materialist or fool.

In the Netherlands, a far more interesting man, Professor Willem H. C. Tenhaeff, Director of the Parapsychology Institute at the University of Utrecht, has been quietly working for nearly half a century. His methods are largely qualitative and are widely accepted in Europe as being of great value in the parapsychology field. A statement made by Prof. Tenhaeff is here quoted to illustrate the question I asked in my title: ESP: Involuntary Psychism or Controlled Faculty? He said, "The paranormal abilities of paragnosts (Sensitives -Ed) like Croiset aren't anything new. They are of an atavistic nature. They are a phenomenon of regression. They come down to us from our prehistoric ancestors. Primitive man lived close to nature and had to use his extra sensory abilities to fight off the imminent danger of the jungle. But as we become more civilized, mechanized, and intellectualized, these powers tend to recede. But I believe that some day these ancient paragnostic powers will be awakened and come back on a higher plane. These lost powers are natural and basic in Man".

The Theosophical Society and many of the "ancient wisdom" (esoteric) schools taught that the psychic centers (vortices of energy or chakras) could and did function in one of two ways: negatively or positively. If positive, the chakra could be seen, clairvoyantly, revolving clockwise and if negatively, counter-clockwise. They stressed, with their students, the importance of spiritual awakening before psychic development, and the need for self-discipline and a positive development of the chakras under control.

In the present outbreak of excitement and sensationalism over ESP, few of these well-established rules are being observed and a cursory reading of ESP books or "lessons" is producing a crop of "half-baked, half-developed 'sensitives.'" The wide-spread use of drugs is also contributing, not only to sick hallucinatory "vision" but to a development of the psychic centers in a counter-clockwise or negative manner.

If the "paranormal abilities of paragnosts like Croiset*" are a "phenomenon of regression" and "of an atavistic nature," then they would come under the heading of involuntary psychism. The unfortunate thing is that these powers are thus most frequently possessed by primitive type individuals in whom the intellectual capacities are dormant and who are basically unbalanced people. According to Prof. Tenhaeff, the "typical paragnost is not a harmonious personality, but is periodically driven to work by great loneliness." "A paragnost cannot easily accept disturbing influences" and their "desire for sensation often creates feelings of fear and impotence." "Childishness and the desire to talk constantly" are other characteristics noted.

Due to an unbalance of the personality and the energies being utilized from negatively functioning chakras, excesses of an alcoholic or sexual (frequently homosexual) nature are not uncommon in the involuntary psychic.

Involuntary psychics are not without value in that their abilities (as in the case of Croiset) are highly useful. Yet the point remains that they are NOT balanced, harmonious personalities.

What of ESP as a controlled faculty? This is a different side of the coin entirely. The chakras are then revolving in a positive manner and the individual is in harmony with themself and their various levels of being. The mind, the emotions and the soul are expressed as a balanced whole and the desire for sensationalism is not present, coloring or rendering inconsistent the extrasensory perceptions. As a controlled faculty ESP IS the "ancient power (consciously) awakened" and functioning on a "higher plane" of which Prof. Tenhaeff wrote.

Self-discipline, spirituality, and a balanced, intelligent mind are concomitant with the controlled faculty of extrasensory perception, however. Unfortunately, this celebration of the mediocre which has overtaken the land, and in which quality has been lost in quantity, threatens the ESP field as it has other arenas. Perhaps, as some of the sensationalism dies down, more and more sensitives of the type described in Dr. Karagulla's book will be found, and eventually

* Croiset, it may be noted, is a highly dedicated man and leads a life of great service to humanity.

the new race trained to use the faculties of higher man (god-man) as the five known physical senses are now used.

Involuntary psychism is indeed a thing of primitive man; the controlled faculties of higher sense perception a sign of the emergence of a new race of Man and a New Age of Light.

References:

"Breakthrough to Creativity" (Your Higher Sense Perceptions)
by Shafica Karagulla, M.D. (neuro-psychiatrist).

"Croiset: The Clairvoyant" by Jack Harrison Pollack

* * * * * * * * * * *

A NEW ENERGY PATTERN

I see a pattern of Light forming: it has the shape of a semi-round, muted light. The words come to me: "Forming in the north and coming in this direction is a latent pattern of energy; this energy is deploying itself around this area and further down towards the south in a fan-like motion. This energy pattern has within itself certain properties that bring about rejuvenation in the cell patterns of all in this Light work." This is a decided form; this has been brought forth from the higher planes to do a work among the living: those who have raised their vibrations to a certain point of development. This will speed up those areas of development.

There will be changes in the thought patterns; there will be a greater acceleration in the working abilities. The thought patterns will take on a decided newness or a greater awareness or expansion of consciousness. There will be an attunement among the Light workers that heretofore has never been. There will be a greater understanding and a greater development as soon as this energy pattern has settled and done the work.

This is a preparation work. This area has been pinpointed as an area of advanced work. Much will be sent out to outlying areas. Nothing can stand in the way of the growth of this work that is definite in plan. Nothing must settle back within itself. This becomes stagnation and there must never be stagnation for this work to progress.

There is a total awareness on the higher planes. There is a complete pattern on the higher planes. There is no friction on the higher planes; all are working hand in hand to bring about this pattern of development. Nothing must hinder this pattern of development. Those who have been selected for this work have been selected for a long time.

There has been much work accomplished within the egos (souls) over a period of time. There has to be a culmination and a greater "forming" to go into a higher vibratory rate. This and only this can accomplish the great work that is at hand. The need is deeply felt. The world has long waited for this point of development. This must be brought into the consciousness of all available workers. No longer must there be a hiding in ignorance.

Channelled from beyond the world of time are these great energy patterns. These are new to all participants. Time will show the result of what has been said tonight.

(Channelled by "Wahena", Maxine H.   31 January 70   Solar Light Retreat)

THE SIMPLICITY OF TRUTH

In the Light and the love of my planet, Venus, I greet you. I am June of Venus. I speak with you at this time, at the beginning of your new year of a new decade, of the time of the manifestation of Light substance on planet Earth. I speak with you in joy and in love and of the reality of these things which you may bring about in your midst. For, from my planet, I bring much love and much Light from my peoples to you.

Upon this occasion I would speak with you, in terms of simplicity, of the bringing within your midst the reality of those things which we on Venus know in our daily lives of joy, of love, and of harmony. Many of my peoples at this time draw closer to you in consciousness and come in craft of shining silver visiting your planet and our message is ever the same. Our message is to bring forth from the immortal soul within of those realities which are eternal, which are of the undying self within which lead to the resurrection of all that which has been known in ages past on the planet Earth, of hope and of vision for the future. That future is NOW. That future IS with you, oh people of planet Earth! That future is with all Light groups and all children of Light who unfold the flower of their own bud of promise.

To live within the reality of joy, of love, and of peace and harmony, is to become that reality. To dwell on past defeats and fears and of past years which have been bitter in sorrows and griefs is to draw around you in subtle essence the memory "thing" of those times, those periods. We do not say to you that you have not learnt through those experiences, that you have not become wiser, more mature today. But we say that that which you are today is a composite of the eternal, immortal soul and the things through which you have passed of much negativity upon the planet Earth.

So take of the essence of these experiences, distilled in wisdom, and create from it a new beginning. Cast from you those things which were of grief, of bitterness, of hurt, and re-create from within, from the distillation of the soul immortal, uniquely YOU, each one, the new beginning of the manifestation of Light. For it is yours to create; it is yours to fulfill; it is yours to know, in joy - a joy which can be shared, which can be given, which can be exchanged with the Earth's children for their greater ongoing in a lighted path.

Those things I say to you are of simplicity, yet I say them from the heart of my being. I say them to you in Love. For no matter how many times the simple teachings of truth are repeated, they still bear repetition until they become truth self evident and manifesting in the minds and the <u>actions</u> of the lives of those who hear. So it was that the teachings of Light given by Jesus Christ were teachings of simplicity and down through the centuries they have been repeated, but they have not been lived.

It does not need <u>new</u> truths to bring about redemption for Earthman or regeneration. It needs only the living of old truths so simple in essence that Earthman in his sophisticated pattern and culture has forgotten that to live in the simplicity of these truths would bring him the lost paradise that he so vainly seeks in his pursuits and his wanderings.

I leave, therefore, with you this thought: That you stand at the threshold of a new age and for you, each one, it is as new as each chooses to make it. And the footprints you will leave on the untouched sand of this time are for <u>you</u> to imprint and for <u>you alone</u>, each one. Your pathway is unique, is yours to choose in love and in joy and in peace.

So I leave with you the love of my peoples who come to you in craft of silver who are with you many times in consciousness. I leave with you the peace and beauty of my planet, Venus.

In the Light of Our Radiant One, I give you,

Farewell of this time.

(Via Telethought, 10 January 70, Solar Light Center. Channel: Marianne Francis)

* * * * * * * * * *

THE GREATER PLAN

We of the XY-7 Craft are only a part of a greater plan within a scheme Cosmic in nature. Our instructions come via the Saturn Council and the Galactic Council. It would appear of a magnitude beyond the understanding of our Earth brothers were it not that our Earth brothers have been prepared in consciousness to understand beyond the limits of their planetary horizon. If one link in a chain be weak, then the chain itself has no strength. If one planet in a System falls below a certain vibratory rate of frequency, then unbalance exists within the System, even affecting the Sun of that System. Therefore, the plan of redeeming the Earth planet is not for the Earth planet alone, though its peoples are precious to us. But the plan is one for the System and, indeed, one for the Galaxy. (Ray-Mere, XY-7 Transmission, 27 Dec. '69)

THE END OF A CYCLE

Greetings, our brothers, our sisters in Light. We greet you at this time from the Communication Craft relaying from the XY-7 mother craft. We speak to you of the ending of the cycle on planet Earth.

It has been stated in your Holy Works that at the time of the end there would be much weeping and wailing and gnashing of teeth; that there would be cries of peace where there was no peace; that brother would be turned against brother and son against father; that there would be division in all of the Earth's peoples. This time is the time in which you now find yourselves: not, our brothers, the ending of a planet, but the ending of a <u>cycle</u>: A time on the Earth planet when there would be much confusion among men and little understanding of the Laws of the Creator.

It has also been stated that at that time many would turn away and deny the existence of a creator of all men and would assume in their arrogance that they alone were the deciders of destiny for their life span and their civilization. That time is the one in which you now find yourselves and as you walk your pathways seeking greater truth, greater wisdom, you turn to the things of spirit and you seek of those Laws which are eternal in nature. As these Laws and these principles reveal themselves to your consciousness and are <u>comprehended</u> and are <u>acted</u> upon, a greater <u>clarity</u> manifests in your own lives <u>despite</u> the confusion of the planetary scene. It then becomes clear that you walk your pathways in serenity and peace, knowing within your inner soul that all is well and all outworks for the furtherance of the Law of God.

Yet at this time the confusions which spread themselves o'er the surface of your planet cause, even within the minds of the children of Light, much soul searching, sometimes a turning from the path of Light to the paths which are of a complexity. At that time it is well for those who walk the surface of the planet to seek ever the simplicity of the truths which have been taught throughout the ages of Man.

So great is the confusion on the outer scene of planet Earth in which violence abounds, in which "dark" becomes "white" and "white" is accused of being "dark," that as has been stated in your Holy Works, "even the very elect may be deceived." We might question at this time those who are spoken of as "the very elect." Would these not be the "children of Light?" Would these not be those who sought in their own secret souls the things of eternal, immortal value? If this time be not shortened, then by the devious workings of negative forces and the machinations of negatively oriented individuals, both outside and within your own planet, the children of Light may find they mistake the "shadow" for Light and "Light" for "shadow."

So it is that the time of the change draws near and those days or that "Time" (insofar as your time concept still exists within a third-dimensional world) is being shortened. As the end of the cycle is now upon you and you find yourselves, people of Earth, in the greatest confusion and violence and complexity existing upon your surface since the time of Atlantis and its sinking, it is well that you remember to seek ever for the simplicity of the Laws and the Principles of the Most High.

"Seek ye first the Kingdom of Heaven," it was stated in your Holy Works, and "all things else shall be added unto you." The Kingdom of Heaven, our brothers, our sisters, is that which dwells within each soul. It dwells at the central core of its being in peace, in love, in a fulcrum point of balance, and when that point is found and held, all things of the outer world and of the ending of this cycle, assume their correct proportions and they cease any longer to disconcert the soul who walks the Lighted Way.

This does not mean that that soul is not concerned for their brother, is not concerned for those things which they see before them. It simply means that that concern is placed within the soul pattern of the High self and in each individual so positioned there is then an automatic outworking taking place and the things which are of unbalance within the surroundings, within the life pattern, within relationships, fall away from that soul and peace and harmony and love manifest at all times.

Such is the simplicity and yet, perhaps for our Earth brothers and sisters, the great difficulty of comprehending the pathway of Light. We have stated many times, until perhaps we and you are weary of hearing the repetition, that in simplicity lies the pathway; in the simple observance of things long sought is the Key, and the acting out of those things, visualized at all times within the mind and the emotions, is the pattern of the individual self.

We observe many things on your Earth plane at this time, but chief among these is the greater confusion. The conflicting energy patterns which manifest themselves at the greater inflowing of energies to your planet from the Central Sun. For as these energies are absorbed into the "vehicle," into the molecular, cellular structure of every individual upon your planet, they are then utilized in varying degrees.

The Light-enfilled individual utilizes this for their greater ongoing and upliftment in Light. The individual who is materialistic, who has no concept of a Creator or of forces beyond the physical material energies, finds that these high-frequency energies set up friction within the "body" physical, the "body" emotional and the "body" mental. In the resistance which is set up to these high energy sources develops a great degree of discomfort and dis-ease within the individual. Much of your patterns of violence and group violence in your own country, in your universities, and in your cities, is brought about by these high energy sources and the resistance with which they are met by the materialistic man or woman of Earth.

This situation, as you might term it, is due to grow worse before it finally resolves itself and we would not delude you in thinking that heaven on Earth descends. The work which the individual must do lies first and foremost with the individual and from the individual it spans outwards to the assisting of others who seek the Path. But never must truth be forced upon the unready, for again the pattern of resistance is created and in the creation much disharmony and violence results.

Each is seeking and finding at this time their own level of soul growth. Each must find this level and, in finding it, establish their own point within a destined pattern. Thus all the Earth's peoples choose now, at the time of decision, between Light and dark and rise rapidly in consciousness and its frequency of cellular structure, or fall into a greater grossness of materialism and density than has heretofore been known.

We have stated previously that a division between dark and Light, of the very substance of the Earth takes place. We repeat that statement and we ask that you dwell upon it in your consciousness and in how it relates to each one who hears or reads our words. For time, as time is understood, runs out on the Earth scene and the greater energies pour in in increasing velocity and they wait for no man, our brothers, our sisters.

A great pattern of destiny awaits the children of Light on planet Earth. Many tests have been given to those who will be the leaders for the future Age, the future cycle and who will work with the lighted ones, both those whom you term the Masters of wisdom who dwell in bodies non-physical and those of ourselves who come to you and will come in increasing numbers from Space. Many times these tests are subtle in nature and are not at the time realized for that which they, in reality, are. Yet at each test which is passed and a greater discernment and discrimination is evidenced, acted upon, then that soul unfolds in Light substance and moves onwards.

We send, at this time, much energy of Light, much love for our Earth brothers, for the scene on the Earth planet is not one of harmony, as viewed from our perspective, but one of great difficulty. Yet the souls who move forward and onward and upward have conquered greatly and have achieved to a point of evolution which many of our peoples have not attained in the peace of our planets.

We say once more: the _Earth_ is a _training_ _school_ for _gods_. Look within to your own godhead; discover it, express it and BE the being created of the One Creator: god and goddess in essence and aspire to the Light Eternal.

I, Ray-mere, once more (gaining much greater command of your language) communicate with you and extend to you the warmth of my being.

In the Light of Our Radiant One, I give you farewell of this time. (Through communication craft from XY-7, now discontinuing.)
(Via Telethought, Solar Light Retreat, 28 Feb.'70. Channel: Marianne Francis)

THE UNCHANGEABLE WORD of TRUTH

Oh God of Infinite Good,
Let me abide in Thee.
Let all my worldly consciousness
Be cleansed, that I may be
In Love that heals and blesses,
In Light Thy Mind expresses,
In Truth, the Power that makes us free.
Oh God, let me abide --
In Truth, the Power that makes us free,
And let Thy Words abide -- in me.

Oh Son, of Spiritual Light,
You gave your wonderful Word
When on the world you lived with us,
And yet -- we hardly heard.
But now, in new understanding,
We know your Love is commanding;
We live in glorious consciousness
Of your unchanging Word.
We live in glorious consciousness
Of your unchangeable Word -- of Truth.

Violet Barton

WHOM DO YOU SERVE?

In Our Radiant One's Light, I address you. I am Sut-ko from the Saturn Tribunal.

I speak with you upon this occasion on the question of "Whom do you serve?" It has been stated on your planet that a man may serve only one master and I state to you that we of the Saturn Council serve <u>Cosmic Law</u>. Our peoples, our emissaries who are sent forth in craft on missions to planet Earth, serve only <u>One Master</u>: Cosmic Law and the All Knowing One, Our Radiant One, who created for us that Law wherein we may live and understand of the nature of existence.

If we, who come to you from other planets, serve the principle of Cosmic Law, then do we serve the interests of peoples and personalities, or do we serve the One Light? The answer, my friends, I think is obvious. Yet, in our dedication to Cosmic Law and to the One Light, do we not serve the <u>highest</u> interest of peoples who are created from that One Light?

Earthman at this time finds himself caught in the confusion of many conflicting concepts regarding our coming. From all sides your peoples are bombarded with concepts regarding our coming: with theories, with ideas, with conflicts of interests, and your peoples are bewildered. You have been told by many of your writers that we are "aliens coming to take over your planet and that we mask our intentions in words of gentleness and compassion but that our ultimate aim and ambition is conquest and the making of your peoples as slaves."

You have been told by others of your writers that we are "monsters who present an idealised picture of ourselves as humanoid beings when in reality we are not, we are reptilian in appearance!" You have been told by other of your writers that we are "races who come from planets far out in another system where life is dying and our peoples need to breed with your peoples in order to maintain the vigor of our strain!" Such concepts, my brothers, are very strange, indeed. Such concepts are the creations of the <u>sick minds</u> of Earthman who has wandered <u>far</u> <u>from</u> <u>the</u> <u>truth</u> of the Creator's Law. Such concepts all too often are the creations of those who have been paid to spread unto your peoples a tissue of lies that they may not desire the landing of our craft or the meeting of our peoples with your own.

Yet these confusions abound and continue to multiply themselves upon your surface until a day of reckoning arrives and <u>Truth</u> presents itself in all its glory and the fabrications and castles of sand built by sick minds, built by conflicting interests of materialistic worth, collapse and die. For they have no reality before the Light which pours forth from the Central Sun and permeates this planet Earth on which you dwell as well as all planets in this System.

We, my brothers and my sisters, in serving the principle of Cosmic Law, do so with complete adherence to Truth. If personalities on your planet cannot comprehend that Truth or choose to distort it for their own selfish gain, they do so at risk of their own immortal heritage. For man cannot sell lies to his brother without a time of reckoning and the time is fast approaching on planet Earth when a final reckoning takes place between the forces of Light and the forces which have sought to distort Truth and to shield the children of Earth from the Light of that eternal knowledge of their Source.

We, my brothers, my sisters, have come to help you even as all higher forms of life help that which is one step below - not lesser but simply one step below in evolutionary growth. We reach out our hands and we say, our brothers, our sisters, that that which we seek to give is an understanding of Cosmic Law and as you understand that Law and live within its pattern, your own lives form a pattern of beauty and of harmonious fulfillment. Therefore, we give to you a KEY by which each one may lift himself or herself to a higher level, for we are not permitted to do those things for you. We can only give to you the KEY wherein you unlock your own door. Therefore, our service is not to personality but to principle and in the greater love of the soul it is given in brotherhood and Light. For what greater gift may one man give to another than the knowledge of immortality and the KEY to that immortality?

What greater gift may one man give to another than to reach out his hand in love and say, "My brother, this pathway leads to those things which mankind has dreamt for many, many thousands of years and those other pathways, which certain of your peoples follow, lead to death and degradation and destruction." What greater truth may one man give unto his brother than the truth of his own immortality? In our adherence to Cosmic Law, to the principles by which a Universe, orderly and disciplined in its course is run, we hand to you the vision of your future which may be as ours. The confusions upon your planet and the conflicts and the warring ideologies may destroy themselves but you who walk in the pathway of the Light of the One Sun, walk with your heads held high and will not be touched by the mud of Earth nor the destructive forces which war upon its surface.

For the time of a division has come on planet Earth and the children of Light go onward and the children of darkness fall back into the confusion of their own makings. And at the beginning of this your year, your decade of the Seventies, I speak with you in love and in that small wisdom which I have garnered in the long years of my existence. I speak to you from the Saturn Council of these things that you may know as they take place upon your surface.

I and my brothers serve only One Master. What master do you serve, oh people of Earth?

In the Light of Our Radiant One I, Sut-ko, say:

Adonai vassu baragus, my brothers, my sisters of Earth.

(Via Telethought, 10 January 1970; Solar Light Center; Channel, Marianne Francis)

* * * * * * * * * * * * * *

WHITE STAR LETTER

Portion of White Star Letter - Feb. 1970 - KRONA of Ashtar Space Command.
SPACE COMMAND COMMUNICATION: Present activities of all LANDING CREWS, their INSTRUCTORS, and co-workers, are toward final preparations for 'EMERGENCE" into the lower-density. This EMERGENCE will take a form which has not been a general practice of the past, and will be to take up active functions upon your PLANE of action; to assist our appointed FOCUS CONTACTS with preparations for EXTENSIVE ground-work for OPERATION LIFT-OFF, as well as OPERATIONS SALVAGE and RE-CONSTRUCTION.

Planetary preparations for these PROGRAM PHASES will require diligent co-operation between SPACE MASTERS and PLANETARY CO-WORKERS. These OPERATIONS will not be conducted by SPACE COMMUNICATORS contacting WORKERS merely by communication lines but will require hand to hand, mind to mind effort. All necessary factors to afford ease of operation, have been fully checked, tested, and accomplished with sufficient 'rapport' to assure success. All disconcerting factors, such as un-co-operative personages, have been eased, either by adjustment or removal. Planetary field-workers will find such distractions either re-routed or discouraged. There is no longer TIME to waste in warding off distracting frequencies. CONTACTEES must be FREE to perform without necessity for manipulative diplomacy to maintain a harmonious working environment.

Contactees with URGENT tasks to perform in contact with SPACE DIRECTORS, will
(concluded on page 23)

SCIENCE DEPARTMENT   K.M.KELLAR, BA, Editor

SIGNALLING AT THE RETREAT
by Eugene Lupo

Since November, 1969, the Retreat has been receiving a large number of signals, via Miss Francis' car headlights. (See Summer/Fall STARCRAFT, 1969). Recently the frequency of these signals has increased tremendously.

Since Miss Francis is usually alone in the car, it makes it difficult, if not impossible, to record these signals while driving at the same time. This is not to say, however, that Miss Francis has always been alone as on several occasions others were in the car with her (See list at end). On at least five occasions I myself have been in the car observing and analyzing the signalling. Harold Brande, a student at OSU, suggested constructing a circuit using a photocell for recording the signals when the lights blink off and on. Using his basic circuit design, I constructed a circuit with components on hand as shown in Figure 1. I had to use a relay in place of a buzzer as a large value of resistance (10K) was needed in the circuit and available buzzers had too small a resistance. Circuit operation depends on resistance variations of the photoconductive cell which range from 500 ohms (light) to 1 megohm (dark). When the car headlights are ON, the buzzer turns On. When the lights are OFF, the buzzer turns OFF. A portable tape recorder is used to record the buzzer signals.

Up until February there seemed to be signals of three distinct time lengths reresenting: a dot, a dash, and a long dash. They seemed to fit in with American Morse code better than International Morse (which has only a dot and a dash). Using American Morse the signals included many L's and T's and a considerable number of M's, E's and fives, however no intelligable interpretation has been discovered as yet.

We have recently recorded signals that have a dash even longer than the "long dash" previously recorded. With this new development it appears that Morse Code, most likely, is not the answer. We have decided to correlate all factors: signalling, the Retreat, world events, etc. plus intuition and hopefully this will bring some fruitful results.

Dr. Dan Fry of Understanding listened to tapes of the recorded signals and suggested a very interesting decoding idea. We had noticed that when the buzzer was ON (no signal) the buzzing sound was uneven. Dr. Fry thought that a code might exist in this uneven buzzing. Upon playing back the tape at ¼ speed to slow the buzzing down, a modulated "middle C" sound was first discernable. In slowing the buzzing down further to a 1/16th normal speed, the buzzing now took the form of a telegraph-like nature varying both in pitch and duration. This recording is now under further analysis.

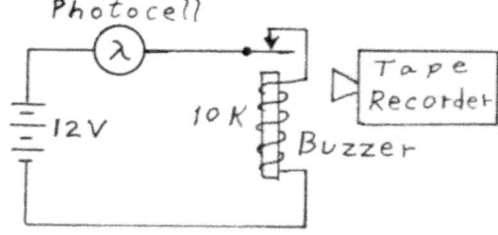

Fig.1 - Signal Recording Circuit

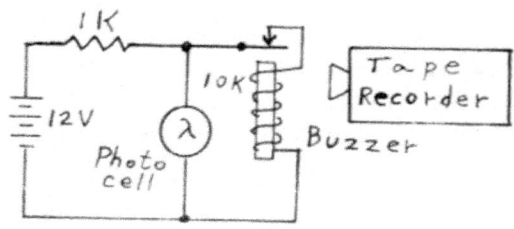

Fig.2 - Revised Circuit

Dr. Fry suggested that I also construct a circuit that had the buzzer turn ON when the car headlights went OFF, that is, just opposite to the original circuit. We could then compare signals from the two circuits. I have just constructed the new circuit (Figure 2) and will be able to compare results when we receive more signals. We expect these comparisons can be made soon and results should prove most interesting.

Miss Francis and Dr. Fry feel it is but a matter of time before the signals can be decoded. Since events on the world scene are reaching a crisis, it is felt the signals bear a definite relationship to possible emergence of craft. With the recent increase in signalling, it seems a strong indication that something big is pending!

> NOTE: The following people have witnessed the signalling while in the car with Miss Francis: Kenneth Kellar, Eugene Lupo, Anthony Brooke of England, David Lander of Australia, Vida LaVoy, Maxine Hergenrether, Ralph Mundell, and Holly Thompson.

* * * * * * * * * *

"THEY'RE ON THE MOON, WATCHING US!"

The German-American rocket scientist, Willy Ley, was a Flying Saucer skeptic, yet interestingly enough he died of a heart attack on the 22nd anniversary of Flying Saucers, June 24, 1969. A year earlier Ley had made this prediction: "Sooner or later, American astronauts are going to run into astronauts from another planet outside our Solar System." Too bad Mr. Ley didn't stick around for another month, or at least long enough to read the censored transmission from Apollo 11 Command Service Module "Columbia" after Armstrong and Aldrin had safely lifted "Eagle" off the moon's surface and rendezvoused with Collins at 70 miles altitude. Ham radio operators on Earth, tuned in to the Command Module's radio wavelength heard conversation which was not released by NASA to the radio and TV networks for re-broadcast. We quote now from an article by Sam Pepper which appeared in the September 29, 1969 issue of the weekly, "National Bulletin":

"What was it, what the hell was it? That's all I want to know."
"These (garbled) babies were huge. Sir, they were enormous."
"No, no, that's just field distortion. Oh, God, you wouldn't believe it!"
"What ... what ... what the hell's going on? Whatsa matter with you guys wha ... "
"They're there, under the surface."
"What's there? (garbled) malfunction ... ion. Control calling Apollo 11."
"Roger, we're here, all three of us, but we've found some visitors ... Yeah, they've been here for quite a while judging by the installations."
"Mission Control. Repeat last message."
"I'm telling you there are other space craft out there! They are lined up in ranks on the far side of the crater edge."
"Repeat. Repeat."
"Let's get that orbit scanned and head home."
"In 625 to the fifth, auto relays set. My hands are shaking so bad I can't ... "
"Film? Hell yes, the damned cameras were clicking away from up here. Did you fellows get anything?"
"Had no film left by the time (garbled) three shots of the Saucers, or whatever they were, may have fogged the film."
"Mission Control; this is Mission Control; are you under way? Repeat, are you under way? What's this uproar about UFOs? Over."

"They're set up down there. They're on the moon, watching us."

"The mirrors, the mirrors. You set them up, didn't you?"

"Yes, the mirrors are all in place. But whatever built those spacecraft will probably come over and pull 'em all out by the roots tomorrow." (End of Transcript)

* * * * * * * *

Is there any evidence to verify Sam Pepper's article and the censored Astronaut dialogue? Yes, we have heard from two different sources that ham radio operators heard the conversation. We have a recent letter from John J. Locko, Director of the World Wide Research Bureau, Lorain, Ohio:

"The article by Sam Pepper I have, also the color photo of the two Flying Saucers in the upper left hand corner of the photo of Aldrin staking the solar curtain. (This photo appears on page 24 of Life Magazine for August 8, 1969. In Life's "Memorial Edition" of the Apollo 11 trip, the UFOs are cropped out of the Aldrin picture taken by Armstrong.) Also, a ham radio operator that lives one block from me tipped me off on the Astronaut's conversation."

Did Armstrong and Aldrin see physical UFOs and installations on and under the surface of the moon? Or were these Etheric constructs, beyond the sensitivity range of normal eyesight, of TV cameras, and of the film in the motion picture and still cameras? If they were non-physical by our standard frames of reference, then the two moon pioneers are lucky to have the Aldrin photo to back up their story. This puts them in the same category as thousands of other earthians who have seen Flying Saucers and have little or nothing to prove it except their own word. Why should the Astronauts see non-physical realities on the moon? Because their psychic sensitivity had been increased by three days of weightlessness and other sensory deprivations of deep space -- but try to explain that to an academic flathead to whom such "visions" are merely hallucinations -- so the controversy over "reality" will rage on, we suppose, until all the material-minded Pisceans are gone from the earth. Meanwhile we Flying Saucer believers can be thankful for the Christmas present of these few shreds of evidence from the Apollo 11 landing, July 20, 1969.

"APOLLODDITIES"

"Noises like a fire engine surged through the airways from Apollo 11 on July 22 and left Mission Control wondering what they were. 'You sure you dont have anybody else in there with you?' Mission Control asked. There was no reply. Then came more air shattering noises again like a fire siren and sometimes like a combination of that and a buzz saw . . . No explanation was offered by Mission Control or the astronauts." Quoted from Gene Duplantier and his "Saucers, Space & Science" magazine, November 1969.

(Reprinted from Round Robin, Nov.-Dec.69, BSRA, Vista Calif.)

A similar report of UFOs on the moon appeared in "PROCEEDINGS" published by the Ministry of Universal Wisdom, Geo. Van Tassel, Director. In an article entitled "The Moon, Myths, and Malfeasance", the same Sam Pepper article is quoted and claims made that there are several other sources of information about this.

An interesting correlation of UFO sightings on the Moon appeared also in the PROCEEDINGS (Vol.7, No.5) which shows an amazing photo of the Gassendi Crater on our Moon. This photo "clearly shows domes over underground living quarters, connected with a system of large diameter tubes on the surface to travel through and maintain an air pressure system throughout the entire base." The Gassendi photo was reputedly taken by the 200-inch Mt. Palomar telescope. Unfortunately, the powers that be persist in withholding information from the public.

RESURRECTION OF LIFE FORMS

We, who are nameless beings from Devic realms, greet you in the Light of the Universal One's radiance. The Light of a thousand suns illumines the darkest corners of God's creation and Man, who dwells on this tiny planet you call Earth, bears upon his shoulders the responsibility for a planet and its woes. Illumined Light, radiating forth from the inner Sun of the Creator's realms of Light, presents Earthman with an intensity of energy form that he cannot yet comprehend in his Earth consciousness.

Confused by the intensity of this radiation, he rushes in his confusions throughout the world of his known creation and blindly refuses the very life-giving elements which would resurrect him from his form of clay and from that which he knows as death. This Light, children of Earth, grows in intensity, grows in radiance, grows in energy, and penetrates to the very core of the planet in its attempt to resurrect all life forms and raise them to a higher vibratory rate of expression and an octave of realization that they have not heretofore known.

Creation upon the planet Earth, limited not to Man but to many forms, reaches forth and gratefully draws within its "body," its cellular structure, these energies for which it thirsts and which feed it with vital essence. Only Man - only Man upon planet Earth comprehends not, and in his confusions he perpetrates upon his planet, his brother, and his younger evolutionary brothers (the animals) of creation, a violence which is contrary to the Laws of the Creator. Of this violence does he sustain a self which he must now shed. Of the lower forms of energy does he feed upon, yet they are subject to the laws of death and decay.

The spirit within all created form reaches outward and upward and in so doing creates a schism within the form which does not also follow in like manner. So does the form, therefore, split in its cellular consciousness of the elemental self, from the higher energies of the spiritual self. You have then in your midst, oh children of Earth, a mass of humanity divided as a house and, so divided, destroying and decaying.

Our mission, we who are nameless beings of the Devic Kingdom, is to uplift spiritual Man, that the very chemical elements of his form may become of a vibratory pattern of high energy content and become integrated and ONE: That certain of the life-wave called Man upon planet Earth may go onward and upward into a new realm of existence, of energy, and of form, and even of that which you term matter. For there are octaves of matter whose chemical structure is not that which you know but is vibrating to an etherealized atom of matter construction. Of this new race of Man shall a beginning be made upon the planet Earth and the race of the future centuries be formed of these beings, knowing and utilizing the freewill of their god-given inalienable right, yet utilizing this in knowledge and in wisdom for the ongoing of the planet and its peoples.

We, who are nameless beings, who come from the Devic Kingdom, work with Man and his elemental self in recharging the very structure of his being that he may control those elemental forces within him and utilize them to the highest capacity which we ourselves know and utilize under the Adepts of God.

Harmony is the Law of the Universes of the One Creator. The planets and the systems spin in marvelous balance and harmony according to Laws set forth. Only Man on planet Earth (and other realms of shadowed intent in other systems) have "devolved" from their high place in creation and now must return. The elemental forces which we wield under the Lords of Light, for the Creator, now stir in the Nature Kingdoms and bring forth a cleansing of all things. That which rises pure from the fires, rises even as the phoenix: reborn unto a new dawn and a new beginning.

Our converse with you upon this occasion is not by chance. Our contact through this one, and other "children of Light upon the planet, is that we may make known the Creator's intent to His creation. This is our mission.

We leave you in Light, for in our realm of understanding there is naught but Light, and all else is shadow and has not reality.

Nexus aloria.

(Via Telethought, 27 December 1969, Solar Light Center, Channel: Marianne Francis)

NOTICE OF NON-AFFILIATION

The Solar Light Retreat and its associates, the Solar Light Affiliates of Vancouver, B.C., are NOT affiliated with "Light Affiliates" of Vancouver, B.C.; neither is material being issued by this group, under the heading of XY-7 craft and Sut-ko recognized as valid. It is regretted by the Directors of S.L.R. that it is necessary to issue this public statement. However, due to widespread confusion and the publication of invalid, erroneous data by unqualified channels, it is necessary to protect our valid sources such as XY-7 craft and Sut-ko from misrepresentation.

It is further noted that while misrepresentation is occurring from "Light Affiliates," the motives of these people appear to be sincere although misguided.

QUALIFICATION OF CHANNELS

Greetings, our sisters (and our brothers who are not here upon this occasion). I speak with you to prepare the way for the coming of another. My words have much meaning at this time, for before you lies another year of your Earth time, a year of experiencing, of living, of understanding of the complexities through which Earth people pass at this time.

I speak with you upon this occasion from the communications craft where I am presently located. A transmission is being prepared, either to reach you later this evening or on the next occasion of your meeting, from a higher source relevant to events upon your surface. My discourse at this time deals with the needs, necessities, shall we say, of the events which surround many of our channels of truth at this time.

It has been stated by none other than my brother, Sut-ko, that there would come a time upon the Earth when there would be manifestation of things of both Light and Dark intent. This time, it was given to you to know, had already begun and is now intensifying in its stage of expression. Because there is an intensifying of all phases of the high and low octaves of MANIFESTATION, there is taking place a greater confusion upon the Earth scene. There is a crowding in of communication from many levels, from beings both in Space (negative and positive) and from beings from the other realms known to you as discarnate (both negative and positive). There is also to be taken into account the phenomenon known as the subconscious mind of Man upon planet Earth which is the depository of much accumulated information, data, and recording.

When a being either from Space or the discarnate realms attempts to utilize an Earth personage, male or female, as a channel for communication, they do so knowing that the levels of subconscious mind present a certain danger, shall we say, as to coloration of the communication which is being sent. In the case of highly trained and developed channels who have worked with much self-discipline and conscious knowledge of the Laws with which they are working, over a period of time, there is a very small residual of subconscious mind permeating the material channelled.

However, with those who are newly acquainted themselves with the phenomenon which you have called "channelling," "receiving," or in certain cases "mediumship," there is a much greater level of subconscious mind intruding upon the communication being sent from another being. Because this is so and is known as a law of nature applying to planet Earth and communication levels, it is NOT customary for a high being such as Sut-ko or other, shall we say, officials from high Saturn Council sources to communicate through untrained or undisciplined minds of Earth.

When such a contact is made or is desired to be made, there is a preparatory period of training involved wherein Space beings, such as you know as "the Brothers," will attempt communication and will test out the receptivity and degree of accurate receival of the channels so involved. This is a most simple and necessary procedure and quite obviously is required where any level of accurate transmission from high sources would even be considered.

You are, therefore, dealing with a lack of understanding in many of your peoples concerning the laws which govern communication, particularly from our level to yours. As to those laws which apply from discarnate realms to yours, there is, again, a testing of a channel where a high being, whom you may term a "Guide" or "Teacher" or even a Master, wishes to contact. A period of training is initiated by lesser beings, under the instructions of the higher one, until such time as the channel is found to be reliable.

Individuals may choose to believe this is not so in their particular case but later investigation shows that these laws do, indeed, exist.

The main point of my discourse is the necessity for caution, for knowledge and for self-discipline in the phenomenon of channelling. Knowledge of self is also mandatory in all cases where high beings are contacting, and responsibilities - particularly involving Karmic Law - are involved. Neglect of these vital points can only result in error, misunderstanding and unconscious fraud on the part of the channel. Need we say more, our sisters, our brothers?

        In the Light of Our Radiant One, I bid you

                Adonai vassu.

(Via Telethought, 3 January 1970; Solar Light Center; Channel, Marianne Francis)

INTERNATIONAL STATUS

We thought our readers would like to know that STARCRAFT is international in scope and is now being mailed to the following countries: England, Canada, New Zealand, Australia, N. Ireland, Scotland, Sweden, Norway, Denmark, Finland, Mexico, Japan, Saudi Arabia, Belgium, and Germany.

GUEST CORNER   COMMAND BULLETIN - COUNCIL RELEASE   WHITE STAR

    We have <u>not</u> withdrawn our <u>forces</u>. <u>Methods</u> of approach have undergone a <u>change</u>, as we have moved our fields of influence into a closer relationship with those we have been assigned to guard. This has curtailed some aspects of communication and externalization, as lines of contact must be kept open from craft to Planetary contacts. These lines are in the form of energies, to bring a greater affinity between Planetary contacts and Space <u>focus points</u> of contact. These rapports are necessary to assure Planetary connection sufficient to bring Earth contactees into alignment for future <u>joint</u> activity.

    An ENERGY-SHIELD, which is now being densified, establishes a rapport level between higher-frequency-<u>forms</u> and lower-frequency-<u>forms</u>.

    With thought levels brought into greatest possible stability, these <u>energy-shields</u> make rapport possible to an ever increasing extent ... wherein it shall be <u>possible</u> for Earth-beings to <u>co-exist</u> with the Space Brothers; both being comfortable in relationships of proximity.

    This relationship shall only be possible where "fields" of Planetary individuals are <u>akin</u> to <u>vibrational-harmonies</u> of approaching Brothers of Interplanetary Order.

    Our craft ... designed for your aid in those days of their <u>need</u>, which rapidly approaches ... are modulated to be of an energy-level which will afford the greatest possible harmony with the cell structures of Earthman's <u>physical</u> <u>form</u>. This, likewise, necessitates <u>adapting</u> our cell forms into a <u>lower</u> energy field, in order to continue to function without undue stress upon our fields of individual frequency.

    This entire OPERATION could be graphically called ... "OPERATION COMPATIBILITY."

    That factor which most greatly <u>delays</u> these "hook-ups," is the inability of Planetary-beings to maintain a semblance of EMOTIONAL BALANCE, as the <u>shields</u> <u>intensify</u>. To do so, assures rapid success ... to fail to do so, delays, and threatens possible failure of <u>compatibility</u> sufficient for <u>co-existence</u>; which is the determining factor when it is "TIME" for "LIFT-OFF."

    No Earth <u>form</u> can withstand the SHOCK of frequency-factors involved in <u>boarding</u> craft, unless these preparatory measures have been taken and <u>complied</u> with. Your "feeling" level dare not drop below <u>specific rates</u> for your "contact" to be maintained. Maintain your <u>human</u> reactions to <u>all</u> circumstances at a <u>peaceful</u> level; reminding yourselves constantly of your <u>true being</u> ... ever present. Permit no FEAR, suspicion, self-pity, remorse, or anxiety, to lower your "<u>field</u>."

    Regardless of "method" of your <u>deliverance</u> from chaotic happenings of your Earth ... these moods of depression can alter the <u>fulfilling</u> of that deliverance for <u>you</u>. <u>Higher</u> <u>energies</u> can only <u>destroy</u> that which <u>fails</u> to <u>harmonize</u> with them. Knowing these things ... then surely your mood must be in Christ ... as this mind of Christ <u>is</u> your <u>Salvation</u>.

    STANDING TOGETHER AS THE SPIRIT COMMANDS IN CHRIST .....

                              A S H T A R   SPACE COMMAND

Sept. 24, 1969,   P. O. Box 307,   Joshua Tree, CA 92252   U. S. A.

"RETREAT" NEWS AND TRAVELS

It is early March as I write this column; a surprisingly mild winter has come and almost gone. Instead of snow we had three weeks of almost continuous rain in January, and plans for building an "Ark" were contemplated! The road became a mass of exceedingly slippery mud. Twice in that three-week period I found myself alone on the road late in the evening with the T-Bird firmly embedded in mud. They say episodes like this strengthen the character ... (they certainly try the patience!). If this is so, after five years on this mountain with continuous tests and "trials by fire," I must have a very strong character. If any being or force is testing, they should be convinced by now I am not shaken from this mission nor do I bow to the dictates of opposing elements. I suppose the cockney would say, "there 'as to be a better hole" and no doubt there is. Yet the spiritual vortex is here and the signals (see Science editorial) are being received here and it all adds up to something of importance. My loyal and dedicated Assistant Science Director keeps telling me "one day we will all look back on this, perhaps from a Spacecraft itself, and laugh at the trials and delays." No doubt we will, and from our fervent prayers we say, "Let it be soon, oh Lord."

Signs abound that the cycle is fast drawing to a close. Letters arrive from our subscribers telling of experiences, visions, and precognitions of a new world. One in particular phoned long distance to share her experience with me, which I now share with you.

Ruth Lewis's Experience: "My house (which is all my lifetimes) burned, room by room, and I was told 'this is all finished.' When the last room burned, I turned to look to see where I was going next. I was told 'Do not look ... you must live by faith for a short time yet'.

"My next scene was the world earthquake where only ten are saved out of thousands. I was not allowed to see any destruction and no one on 'the Path' felt any discomfort in any way, for we were someplace, I do not know where, a remote, sparsely-populated spot with a cliff in the near background (This area? Ed.). We had walked down a shiny road to safety (after being told the 'quake would come), then we all walked back up the road saying, 'the Bible was certainly right ... there are only the few of us left.' We did not even feel pain or concern.

"The next experience was telling me I must learn levitation: being taught to use the palms of my hands held in the air, in the Christ-Consciousness; being wrapped all in the beautiful blue of it .. was in the New World (consciousness) ... the conditions, the life, the most vivid colors and clear, clear atmosphere ... and oh, the JOY of it all! We will live in the vibrations of Love and Joy, believe me.

"Then I was back in my trailer and shown dry barren dirt for a short distance (the last of this Age) then was a sparkling river of Life and on the other side was a tall, graceful Tree of Life, all in bloom ... a gorgeous shade of deep pink (Love, new birth, New Age, new as is the Springtime). Then a dirty cloud came rolling in and I was told this was the vibration of this Age. Then, 'do not forget what lies behind the cloud.'

"The great joy I still FEEL!! As the last chapter of Revelations says, 'Christ shall send His Angels to testify unto you ... For I come quickly.'

By the Father, for the Father, in His Name, let it be so, as we gladly give up all which is of third-dimension, to turn and walk gladly into the New Dawn."

Ruth Lewis

* * * * * *

I have shared Ruth's experience with you as it is truly inspiring, and inspiration is needed now. If any of our readers have had similar experiences, visions, will they please write in and share with us?

Anthony Brooke again visited the Retreat this last February and in his public lecture at the Understanding Cultural Center in Merlin he imparted to us his convictions about the New Age. One statement made is of great importance and I include it here: "Man has always had two futures: one in Time, and one in State (of consciousness)." Many people are beginning to realize that it is the state of consciousness alone that determines each Man's future, singly or collectively. Is this not what the Space Brothers have been trying to impress on us since first they commenced telepathic contact?

This column is entitled "Retreat News and Travels," yet the winter is my hibernation time, so travels have been few and close to base. Yet this month will see me in Salem, Oregon, to kick off the year's lectures with a talk to the Saturday Night Club. A bare month remains before I fly to Montreal on the 4th of April, and from there who knows where I may fly?

The Retreat's personnel are well, and the Spring air heralds morning yoga exercises on the deck. The pets, one watch dog and three "watch" cats, are hunting gophers in the wet meadow, and many baritone and contralto frogs sing their evening song from the pond.

All is promise of Spring, and perhaps at last this Spring will truly be a time when we can say, with Solomon, "The winter is come and gone and the voice of the turtle is heard once again in the land ... the time of the singing birds is come."

In Light,
Marianne Francis.

* * * * * * * * * * *

WHITE STAR LETTER (cont. from page 13)
not be required to trifle in wasted time with humanoid-frailties of personality. Being about the FATHER'S BUSINESS requires strict adherence to that BUSINESS..and it is not expected of you to be sensitive to opinion which has no bearing on that BUSINESS. Hurt feelings are a failing of the reactor, and not necessarily of the actor, when demands for undue attention and regard are ignored.
    Love of the SPIRIT for ITS objective is not coddling, but INTELLIGENT DIRECTION toward the greatest benefit of that OBJECTIVE, with little regard for appearances and ALL REGARD for accomplishment. Demands of the lower-nature for personal selfish considerations, are ignored, and ACTION performs according to DIVINE WISDOM, not HUMAN EXPECTANCY.
    Be about your FATHER'S BUSINESS, as TIME no longer permits for side-tracking emotional-excursions.

AT HAND......K R O N A
ASHTAR SPACE COMMAND----FLEET DIRECTOR

February 25, 1970
2 A.M.

ANNOUNCEMENTS

MONTREAL MEETING: Dr. Marianne Francis will be lecturing at the Paul Sauvé Arena (seats 6,000) in Montreal, Canada, April 10th. The meeting is being sponsored by The Montreal U.F.O. Study Group, Reg'd, Thomas James Cameron, President, 685 Clement North, Dorval, P.Q. Miss Francis will be flying to Montreal a week early to appear on TV and Radio programs in the area.

CONVENTION: JUNE 19th through 24th   MERLIN, OREGON
(International Cultural Center, 2200 Merlin-Galice Road)

This New Age Convention is sponsored by UNDERSTANDING, Inc. and ALETHEIA Ass'n. with the cooperation of the SOLAR LIGHT RETREAT. The purpose of the Convention is to bring understanding between people of all Nations, races, and philosophies by presenting speakers, panel discussions, group participation, and cultural aspects of diverse parts of the world. The Speakers include:

Rev. Damien Simpson	Dr. Daniel W. Fry, Ph.D.	Rev. Jack Schwarz
Dr. Gina Cerminara, Ph.D.	Sophia Austin	Ormond McGill
Dr. Stanley Daniels, N.D.	Marianne Francis, Dr.Sp.Sc.	Dr. H. Van Olinkel
Dr. Myron S. Allen, Ph.D.	Samuel Bousky	Helen Wallace
Dr. Milan Ryzl	Mark Probert Memorial	Asoka and Sujata

Those wishing to attend are advised to register early as the Convention is drawing interest from many states, Canada, Europe, and other countries.

Write to Aletheia or Understanding for registration details:

ALETHEIA ASSOCIATION   UNDERSTANDING, INC.
P. O. Box 334   P. O. Box 206
Selma, Ore. 97538   Merlin, Ore. 97532

GUEST SESSIONS at SOLAR LIGHT RETREAT: On fourth Saturday in the month. (8 pm)

PUBLICATIONS

Lectures by Marianne Francis:

Manifestation	$1.25
Frequency Change and the Second Coming	1.25
The Call of the Phoenix	1.50
Starcraft Contact	1.25
Men from Space and Prophecies of Earth Change	1.25
The New Dimension and the New Age	1.00
Channelled Material from Space People: Ten Selected Scripts	2.90

STARCRAFT MAGAZINE: Subscription $2.25 (USA), $2.50 (Foreign)
(Three or four issues per year)

SEND ORDERS TO:
SOLAR LIGHT RETREAT
7700 Avenue of the Sun   Telephone:
Central Point, Ore. 97501   855-1956 (Code 503)

STARCRAFT

Solar Light Retreat

VOL. 5, No. 2 & 3
Fall/Winter 1970

STARCRAFT CONTENTS - FALL/WINTER 1970

Editorial: Unification of Light Servers - Marianne Francis	3
Guest Corner: Command Bulletin - White Star	6
Man's Spiritual Awakening - Ray-mere	7
Dominion Over Self - Ra-teh	11
A Limitless Concept of Life Emerges - Ra-teh	13
New Age Art: Man In Matter - Claude Charlebois	16
Changing Consciousness - Sut-ko	17
Man Is Space-born, Cosmic Heir To Light - Sut-ko	19
Center News & Travel	22
Announcements and Publications	24

* * * * * * * * * * * * * *

Director and Editor	Marianne Francis, Dr.Sp.Sc.
Science Director	Kenneth Kellar, B.A.
Asst. Science Director & Bookkeeper	Gene Lupo, Cert.Engr.Tech.
Typist	Mareda Hansen
New Age Artist	Claude Charlebois
Cover Artist	Francois Beaulieu

Published by SOLAR LIGHT RETREAT, a non-profit corporation

Copyright reserved. Write for permission to reprint.

Zip Code is required, so please include yours when you write.

Telephone first, please, if you plan to visit. Phone: 855-1956 (Code 503)

* * * * * * * * * * * * * *

The NEW AGE PROGRAM is to

LOVE

UNDERSTAND   EDUCATE

RELIEVE SUFFERING   CREATE BEAUTY

* * * * * * * * * * * * * *

ADDRESS ALL CORRESPONDENCE TO:

SOLAR LIGHT RETREAT
7700 Avenue of the Sun
Central Point, Ore. 97501

EDITORIAL

Marianne Francis, Dr. Sp. Sc.

UNIFICATION OF LIGHT SERVERS

"It is possible to remain in a dark cave and be unaware that the sun is shining outside." (Ray-mere from XY7, 21 Nov. 70)

Sometimes, when life on this planet is viewed through mortal eyes it appears very much like a dark cave with Light only dimly perceived. A tremendous manifestation of both extremes of Light and Dark is taking place as this cycle terminates with ever increasing velocity. To be unaware of the manifestations of darkness is to be foolish in the extreme. To state, also, as have many sincere souls in the past, that no cataclysms of nature are due is misguided and indeed already inaccurate. For a disaster, <u>termed by the news services</u> a "CATACLYM," has just taken place in Pakistan where, this month (Nov.) over 200,000 people were killed from the effects of a tremendous cyclone and tidal wave.

Strange weather conditions are occurring in many areas and nature is on the rampage, as indicated both by Biblical prophecy and by our Space Brothers for this period of time. In a sense, therefore, this planet is a dark cave and the behavior of many of its inhabitants strange, perverse, and negative in the extreme. If this were the only reality, Man would indeed have little cause for hope. His dark cave would be his tomb.

Yet it is taught by "the Brothers" that <u>that which Man dwells upon in his mind, he gives energy to</u> and <u>that which he gives energy to manifests in his life</u>, be it <u>Light</u> or <u>Dark</u>.

Dominion over self is only achieved when one operates from the god-self within and ceases to <u>react</u> to external forces. This does not mean an introverting of the soul to a self-centered existence, cut off from loving interchange with others. For the introverted soul is operating only from the levels of sub-conscious, race conscious, and conscious mind and the god-centered soul is functioning from the SUPER conscious levels: Man's link with the Divine.

While all Light servers are human and therefore subject to all levels of consciousness, the Focus has to be on super-conscious mind, the direct link with spiritual energy levels and beings of Light. When this link is achieved as a more or less constant state, the soul concerned is able to function in the midst of negativity, to love where there is hate, to understand and manifest compassion where there is blind resentment and prejudice. Nothing short of this is any longer feasible, for the very sanity of Light workers depends on their ability to control all reactions to external negativity.

To the degree that this is achieved depends the Light aura of each individual, each Light center and their unification one with the other, throughout the planet. Without this unification, no network of Light exists, and no stability manifests to ground the Light energies now pouring in from higher realms and planetary beings.

This aura of Light is the ONLY true protection left for Light workers at this time on the planet. The sun is shining outside the dark cave but it is necessary to emerge from the dark cave of lower consciousness to observe it and bask in its warmth. It is necessary to achieve dominion over lower self in order to ascend into the super-conscious states or even to vibrate at a level where communication with Space beings becomes possible.

People continually ask "Why do the Space people not land?" Why would they land when they observe the dissension between the "Light" groups, the petty feuds and jealousies as to whose organization is the biggest, the most important, the wealthiest in material terms. The self-delusions of self seekers seem to grow with strange dreams of power and glory. Where Light should manifest, a blind, smug self-satisfaction grows, yet the faces appear discontented and Light has left their eyes, where understanding should manifest and, with it, love. The countenance of ego is a double-dealing one, and friend and foe alike are manipulated without compunction - all in the name of "Light" and loyalty to an organization rather than an ideal.

Long has this planet shuddered under the machinations of power-mad monarchs, dictators, and conquerors. Yet, when starved egos reach out for material power as sustenance and call it building their particular New Age organization, beware lest all are caught in a web of intrigue.

Many true Light servers are now incarnate on the planet. Around them as around a Light gather the children of men. Some are true seekers, some seekers after reflected Light, and some merely curious of a phenomenon so strange as a being on planet Earth striving to express Christ consciousness!

How to tell the difference between a true Light server and a self-seeker? The Light, dear ones, is in the eyes or it is not. The soul looks out in radiance and love or the blinds are drawn and the eyes look "dead." You care or you do not. You are Light enfilled or self-encased. You may suffer at times from the misunderstanding and blindness of materialists but, in the last analysis, you know the spiritual joy of serving the One Light, the One Creator in Love. For a true Light server experiences joy, feels love from the heart center, radiates Light from the head when giving of themselves in Light.

The facets of this work are many and Centers of Light stretch across the continents. Unite with all true Light workers, all Light groups in essence, at their highest level of functioning. Each is performing its part of a Cosmic plan. Each is a facet of a whole.

For truly "The Light descends. The Light transcends and The Light transmutes. We are servers, priests and priestesses of The One Light."

— — — — — — —

THE MANTRAM OF UNIFICATION

The sons of men are one and I am one with them.
  I seek to love, not hate;
I seek to serve and not exact due service;
  I seek to heal, not hurt.

Let pain bring due reward of light and love.
  Let the soul control the outer form,
And life and all events,
  And bring to light the Love
That underlies the happenings of the time.

Let vision come and insight;
  Let the future stand revealed.
Let inner union demonstrate and outer cleavages be gone.
  Let love prevail.
    Let all men love.

GUEST CORNER   COMMAND BULLETIN - COUNCIL RELEASE   WHITE STAR

    These things of importance which now manifest, as the battle for supremacy of DARKNESS over LIGHT enters into its final phase, must be brought to your awareness that you might be fortified by this <u>knowing</u>. Whereas it has been the ACTION of the FORCES OF IGNORANCE and DARKNESS to scatter their energies in efforts to block wherever there appeared an ACTION toward CHRIST'S PROGRAM, and thereby serving as a confusing but scattered force; it is NOW these efforts are coming together in <u>concentrated</u> attention toward <u>knocking</u> out KEY people whose efforts are gaining momentum toward awakening humanity...and who are themselves gaining in growth toward fulfilling and proving the PRINCIPLES OF THE PLAN. These methods are diabolical in their <u>cleverness</u>, and not detected by those who are unsuspectingly USED.

    It was said that CHRIST would bring a SWORD, and it would turn friend against friend...family against family...and even in the closest of relationships war would be waged. It was not to say that CHRIST would promote such action, but that one seeking LIGHT would be approached by the NEGATIVE FACTIONS <u>through</u> those nearest and dearest.

    In a man's weakness is he a PAWN for those FACTIONS which seek to destroy the PRECEPTS OF CHRIST, as those PRECEPTS <u>free</u> man from his <u>bondage</u> to those FACTIONS. Therefore, one not bound to TRUTH...one not seeking their SPIRITUAL UNION, or even those who <u>are</u> upon the PATH...if in them dwells personality ego...if in them dwells self-pity...if in them dwells false pride...if in them dwells arrogance (self-esteem of lower-nature values)...if in them dwells desire to receive personal recognition and praise...if these and other low-level energy factors are still a part of their uncleansed being...can be USED, for in any of these FALSE attitudes can come <u>influences</u> of a LIKE nature to prompt toward intensification of feelings.

    The LAWS are operative, in that the low begets itself lower, as the HIGH begets itself <u>higher</u>. Like attracts like and adds unto itself POWER...for the LAWS are as a TWO-SIDED-COIN and where it is that TWO in CHRIST <u>association</u> and <u>action</u> beget CHRIST...so it is that TWO in FALSEHOOD beget FALSEHOOD. POWER is added unto POWER in <u>like kind</u>. Then, by this <u>direct concentration</u> of the forces which seek to continue man in his ignorance, those who have in them an ATTRACTION are USED to attack THROUGH, in that they are stimulated to thwart the progress of those CHILDREN OF LIGHT who are moving away from the base levels of ignorance into ILLUMINATION and DIVINE FREEDOM.

    Therefore it is that MALIGNING OF CHARACTER...falsely judging...inciting suspicion...casting confusions...all of these, and a multiple not named are being concentrated upon and cast forth into the lives of SEEKERS AFTER TRUTH, and the INSTRUMENTS for such actions can be anyone whose level of action falls below TRUTH. Your first duty to your SPIRITUAL BEING is to TEST ALL...PROVE ALL...and allow no sympathies toward deceptions.

    TRUTH IS OF THE LIGHT AND IS CHRIST!

        FALSEHOOD is of the DARKNESS and is DECEPTION...!

Dictated Sept. 29, 1970   STAND IN THE LIGHT..........!!!
    DESKA/teska
                                                                  ASHTAR COMMAND

MAN'S SPIRITUAL AWAKENING

Ray-mere

Greetings in the Light of Our Radiant One. I speak with you from the XY-7 craft which at this time is stationed high in the altitude above your mountain locality. I who speak with you at this time, addressing you in the consciousness of many who are gathered here with me, am known as Ray-mere.

In the interim period through which your people are passing at this time on planet Earth, many things are taking place at many levels of consciousness. It is within the realm of consciousness which my peoples (we of the XY-7 craft of the Saturn Command and many of our peoples from other levels and other planets) are most interested at this time. These levels of consciousness might be termed, as you yourselves would say, in your terminology, as that of superconsciousness, conscious, and subconscious. For the outworking of energy, energy fields, shall we say, energy which is flowing in to this planet from the Central Sun source, Vela, is bringing about so great a change in the consciousness, in the energy or auric fields, of man as to be truly termed a spiritual upheaval, a spiritual revolution, a spiritual reawakening of man on his planet. It is within these realms of consciousness that we of the Space Commands place our faith for the hope of mankind in the period which lies ahead: Not in the interim period itself, nor in the upheavals and revolutions of mind which are occurring, but in the ultimate outworking of these energies for the upliftment of man into his divine nature or being.

Truly it might be said, our brothers, our sisters, that man is transmuting the very elements of his being from an animal-man consciousness to a divine consciousness of his heritage of immortal life: Life as it has been known, experienced, enjoyed, in this and other solar systems over millions of years in a vast cosmos of the creation of One Creator, the Being whom you term God, Whom we know as Our Radiant One, the All-knowing One, Creator of all life. Many of our peoples at this time have come in craft for purposes of observance, not intervention into the affairs of Earth-man, but observance as one of your psychologists might study the habits of one of your species. I will not use the analogy of a primitive tribe, for your peoples in their higher consciousness are not primitive, but only in their misunderstanding of their own divine heritage have they followed pathways which are far from wise and have led to the extremes of violence, which you find in your midst, about to culminate in a holocaust of horrendous proportions.

It is not, my brothers, my sisters, that Earth-man is as a primative tribe, it is that Earth-man has not fully utilized the innate dignity of his being, the potential which is his from which to create, even as that Creator, from which he sprang, in its outflowing, in its expression of Love, is forever creative. Thus our, shall we say, space psychologists, our peoples from many levels are, as you might term it, sitting back and observing the behavior patterns of man, his handling of his immense problems, his attempts to extricate himself from the frightening morass in which he finds himself. When this period has passed, it is _then_, our brothers, our sisters, when Man's free will has run the gamut and has expressed itself in the decision which must either bring disaster or a freeing of the total mass of mankind on planet Earth to a new level of existence: It is at that point or moment of truth, that we of the Space Commands will once again land upon your planet, either in cooperation with your new world leaders (and I advisedly use the word 'new'), your _new_ world leaders, or will be forced to intervene, even as the recording to which you have just listened has told you, to circumvent a destructive holocaust and an ending of all Man's endeavors. It is not impossible, our brothers, our sisters, for Man to destroy a planet. It has occurred before in this system; it has occurred in other systems. It is by no means impossible with the power which man has at this time tapped to destroy planet Earth, to render it totally void of all sentient life, drifting as a barren planet or shattered mass of asteroids in this system, were it not for the fact that _intervention_ from our Commands would at that point, _preceding such destruction_, be inevitable.

Shall we dwell for a moment on the conditions which were mentioned for intervention in the internal affairs of a planet from the Solar government and its Command source. If Earth qualifies, by its attempts to wage nuclear war within its own confines, it no longer becomes a matter for planetary government alone but a matter for Solar government, since the destruction of one planet drastically disturbs the balance of the Solar System itself and this disturbance will no longer be permitted. If the chronomonitors, of which you have just heard, so observe and report back to their various Command source, once again intervention becomes inevitable. Under such conditions mankind ceases to hold within his own hands the power of life and death for his peoples and his planet, a power which never was fully vested in Man but only in God. It is in the misunderstanding of Cosmic law and its outworkings that Man has transgressed the law which is Cosmic, and has put in its place the law which is of Earth-man in the consciousness of an age which rapidly passes.

As this system, and your planet within this system, inevitably move into a new area or frequency of space, the very ethers within which you find your existence, the very cellular structure of your tissue, of your bodies, of the animals and the plants on your planet change. In this change a transmutation takes place, and the consciousness, the indwelling spirit of God, bursts forth from the crysallis of matter and expresses of the radiant being of Light from whence it came. No longer shall the shell of matter hold man as in a prison, bound in limitations, held to the ground and the mud of a planet. But at last the indwelling spirit of man, in its true divinity, springs forth to rise on the wings of a Light-consciousness into the space which is Man's heritage and his domain for the eternities which yet lie ahead. For such a destiny Man has experienced, has bound himself in the shell of matter to the lowest point of descent into density, throughout the many thousands and hundreds of thousands of years of his existence on planet Earth.

When he once more emerges into the freedom of space, to soar forth as the eagles and to return once more, then shall he know the source of his being, the unlimited horizons of his future, and the

Love which is his forever to give. And in that creative consciousness, my brothers, my sisters, shall Man walk with his brothers, his sisters, who dwell on other planets and shall know at last a true comradeship of being, no longer isolated, quarantined on the one planet in this system which does not travel freely among the stars. But as one of your other tapes has said to you, Man <u>will</u> walk with his brothers and the call which has gone forth for many, many thousands of years, "Oh, Earth-man, come home!" will be answered. And a Light will break over your planet of the <u>coming</u> of the <u>Great One</u> of illumination, who will lead the children of Light of this New Age, which you have called the Aquarian Age, or the Solar Age of Light, into a new dimension and a new dispensation. And those dreams which man has dreamt throughout the centuries of his incarnations shall become realities, and a <u>Golden Age</u> shall be experienced by the children of men.

It is with much love in my heart that I, Ray-mere, speak with you upon this occasion, that I transmit once more from the XY-7 craft not of my words, which are yet poor in their choosing, but of the essence of my being, and of the vibratory rates of energy which we send forth to you at the time of these transmissions in Light for your further ongoing on the pathway of life.

Our salutations, our brothers, our sisters. We of the XY-7 craft who work in consciousness with your peoples of this area and through this and another channel, our salutations we give to you, our salutations of Light and of Love. In that consciousness we leave you and ask that the Light of Our Radiant One be ever with your consciousness.

                                                Adonai vassu.

* * * * * * * * * * * * * * * * * * *

(Via Telethought, 31 Oct. 70, Solar Light Retreat. Channel: Marianne Francis)

DOMINION OVER SELF
Ra-teh

Where is the Light and where are the Light servers on the planet Earth at the time of crisis? Where are the children of men who walk in the places of shadow? When shall the time dawn that the children of Light recognize and claim their immortal heritage, for surely shall it not be soon. Else shall the children of darkness beset the land. If the children of Light link not with each other in love and understanding and infinite patience which surpasses the comprehension of flesh-man, then shall not a division be made manifest and in that divisiveness shall the force of darkness grow mighty and wax strong within the lands.

A continent sunk beneath the oceans, Atlantis the Golden, for the children of Light (though they knew of the truths and principles which upheld their very beings) did not observe these and were made impotent and lost their heritage and their lands. When shall the children of Light recognize and claim their immortal heritage? For in the claiming of that heritage lies the power and the majesty and the infinite nature of man: God-man, as opposed to flesh-man. You say, how then to claim this heritage? You say (if your thoughts reach me with honesty and questioning) where lie the lost keys to the claiming of the immortal heritage which throughout the ages has existed as a dream within the consciousness of all men of progressive intent. And I say to you, that the key to this heritage lies in the dominion over self, in the dominion over the warring elements within the being of each, until an inner stillness envelops that being and a doorway opens and with the tremendous inrush of energy comes the power to surmount all obstacles. So it is that the key to the immortal heritage lies in the dominion over self: a dominion not lightly won in the heat of one battlefield, but of man; not of one lifetime, but of many; so that when it would seem victory is attained the elements within self run riot once more and escape from the dominion of the oversoul. When all situations can be met with control, with a further ongoing in Light, then has dominion over self been attained; then shall the energies pour in, and the obstacles of Earth-plane level be vanquished, and the lighted soul be victor.

I, Ra-teh, again communicate with you in consciousness, my soul communes with yours on the light of a new dawn. True it is that ancient civilizations lie beneath the ice-caps, beneath the oceans. True it is that glories have come and gone and of their trace no vestige remains. True it is that Man struggles against a negativity so great as to overwhelm even the children of Light. True all these things, yet one last inescapable fact remains: only by surmounting lies victory, for there is no other way left but the upward climb to the mountain tops of consciousness. For beneath your feet lies an abyss, an abyss which faces not only your civilizations but all who dwell on planet Earth unless they transcend and transmute the very elements of their being and that stuff of mind, of etheric substance which surrounds them.

I have not come to speak with you in terms of simple comfort. I have come to speak with you in terms of inescapable truths. Your conditions on your planet are grave in the extreme, and warriors of Light must present a shield of so strong a substance as to withstand all the buffetings of the negative force. It matters little whether it manifests from impersonal forces, from personal situations, or from those many frustrations of daily life which beset all at this time. It matters only that these be surmounted.

My people are not unaware of these conditions. We are not unaware of your need for higher assistance, or for energy levels to be raised, or for further Light to transcend the negativity of conditions which you encounter. We are aware of all these things. But yet we say to you that it is only as you reach upward in consciousness to a certain vibratory level that you may become aware and utilize the energies which we _are_ - and I stress which we _are_ - sending from the craft and which are permeating your levels from higher realms and beings.

You have a saying on your planet that "God helps those who help themselves" and this most perfectly expresses that which I attempt to convey to you at this time. Maintain a level of consciousness, insofar as it is possible and to what continuous degree as it is possible for each individual being, that uplifts you beyond the levels of the negative force which undoubtedly is most strong, which undoubtedly is besetting all Light workers with delays, frustrations, and disappointments. It has also been stated in your holy works that "except that those days be shortened, even the very elect would not be saved." And it is in the shortening of this time the transmutation by Light takes place, whereby time no longer exists in the subconsciousness of the Light-infilled soul and they move into a realm which is beyond time. And in the moving into that realm they transcend from that point onwards and cannot be touched by the negative force or its manifestations.

Dwell therefore in Light, our brothers, in the consciousness of your infinite being. Dwell therefore in Love, in the heart vhakra of your giving, and know that no matter how powerful, how strong the negative force on planet Earth, it must and will inevitably give way before the forces of Light which gather in strength. For Light has ever been more powerful than darkness, and only One Creator rules in this universe and His laws and His manifested Light shall engulf this planet even at the end.

I speak with you at this time through direct telethought transmitter from my own planet and not through craft. In the Infinite Light, may you reside. In His Wisdom and His Love may you walk. My salutations.

* * * * * *

(Via Telethought, 14 Nov. 70 - Solar Light Retreat. Channel: Marianne Francis)

"In the heart of my being, Father, I am one with You, and I recognize You as Being, the Father of all. You are Spirit, Omnipresent, Omnipotent, Omniscient. You are Wisdom, Love and Truth; the power and substance and intelligence of which and through which all things are created. You are the life of my spirit, the substance of my soul, the intelligence of my thought; I am expressing You in my body and in my affairs. You are the beginning and the end, the very All of the good which I can express." (Baird T. Spalding: Life & Teachings of Masters of Far East, Vol.2)

A LIMITLESS CONCEPT OF LIFE EMERGES
Ra-teh

Greetings. We cannot predict in terms of Time, only in terms of Dimension.

In assessing the measure of Man's true dimension, events, in relation to Time, his level or density of being, we find ourselves forced to the conclusion that Man on planet Earth operates within a circumscribed sphere of consciousness. The walls of his perceptual range of vision form limitations or a prison from which he cannot escape. Yet Time, viewed in the sense of a dimension, operates only at a level of fourth etheric (as you have termed it, of fourth dimensional consciousness).

In reaching out to perceive of events on a time scale of limited proportions, Man finds himself unable to relate in consciousness to a level where Time and infinity meet <u>unless</u>, at this point (of the ending of a cycle), an ability manifests in consciousness, upward and outward, <u>beyond</u> the level of the brain mechanism into pure Mind, pushing outwards the walls which imprison Man on planet Earth (and we speak of Man in terms of mass Man, not in terms of New Age Man). If these walls are pushed outward and finally torn down, a comprehension of a divine, all-permeating Intelligence (which we may term energy) then presents itself and permits of a type of consciousness which <u>supersedes</u> matter in its grosser form. It is our understanding that the step which Earth-man takes at this time is a gigantic one which extends his horizons beyond the confines of his environs, his concepts, his dogmas; and a <u>limitless</u> concept of life as it is lived in the Cosmos, not only life humanoid but life at many levels, interpenetrating, co-existing, extending to various densities, planets, and beyond the circumference of planets, emerges.

In attempting to convey these concepts from my consciousness to your own, I choose words stumbling, imperfect, yet in an attempt to convey something of the nature of existence as we know it - and as New Age Man shall know it before the century has passed its mark. The birthpangs of an Earth in torment are as the birth of a child, the dawn of the New Age, birthing through chaos and travail will lead to a millenium to be experienced in joy. Earth-man in his consciousness reaches outward and thus makes possible physical change within the cellular structure of his own tissue; change which actually brings about vibration, motion within the organic forces or processes.

Thus this vibratory motion can be termed the nucleus or seed-atom of each cell. In it lies spiralling energy which, moving outwards, ever outwards and upwards, carries the body physical into a form not yet fully comprehended, not any longer of dense physical construction but of another substance, not entirely etherealized, subject no longer to the laws of physics or science as you have known them, but subject to subtler laws which mankind has yet to learn of.

These laws deal with the true nature of Man. They teach that he is composed of energy, that consciousness itself is energy of an infinitely fine nature, of a force forming and indeed indicative of Man's environment and changing it, even as all things are changing in spiralling pattern towards an infinite expression of Life.

When our peoples land upon your planet they will do so in the certainty that there are minds ready to meet them, linked no longer with the atavistic force of the unconscious but manifesting at levels which make possible a meeting of minds, a sharing of concepts in a relationship of true brotherhood.

Thus it is that Man's experiencing, his experimentation through the densities of gross matter and the strugglings with his own nature, that he unlocks doors and releases energy patterns of much potency for good or ill. In understanding of himself lies the key to the unlocking of the doors without. And as each masters their own soul or being, the doors which they seek to open swing wide and sunlight streams through and a son of the Illuminati is born, and a daughter of Light emerges. In the positive and negative poles of expression, through Man-Woman, in the combining of these energies, wholeness is achieved within the system, within the civilization, and within the very elements of the planet itself. Planet Earth is in chaos, is a planet devoid of balance within its life-wave humanoid, thus upsetting the structure of attendant life-waves and their relationship to Man. Dark though the night is of planet Earth's birth pangs, yet shall this planet emerge, filled with Light, reborn into the light of a new understanding.

My name is not known to you for I have not communicated before through this one, yet fresh levels of energy enable me to link my mind to yours for a time and to communicate from my consciousness and concepts and to take with me the emanations of your beings. If you would have a name in your understanding, my name is Ra-teh and I come from the planet known to you as Mars or Masar.

We are aware, my friends, of your dilemmas of Earth but do not lose sight of the fact that there is ever a solution. In the energy which flows from the Infinite Being may the ultimate answers be found. In that energy, its outpourings, I leave you, content with the knowledge that you indeed are secure.

My salutations. I leave also.

* * * * * * *

(Via Telethought, 7 Nov. 70. Solar Light Retreat. Channel: Marianne Francis)

N E W   A G E   A R T   D E P A R T M E N T

MAN IN MATTER

When man enters this level of consciousness awareness called matter, he is not aware of much more than his body. All that was transmitted to the higher Mind (the various levels of which the subconscious is the lowest) during the last incarnation is still retained with the wise addition of various memory blocks. What reaches more or less strongly into the present are the following: karma, both positive and negative; individuality, your reaction to a given situation formed in this life; moral standards of former incarnations which become the Conscience of the present and it is said that man either has it or does not; strong likes and dislikes bordering sometimes onto phobias; an inborne desire to appease unfinished business, etc. As the one gradually develops the Conscious Mind, which is supposed to be used as an instrument of learning in the physical, one also begins to rely on it exclusively. More and more the Conscious Mind takes over the mechanics of the Man. In time the Conscious Mind (personality Self) dominates entirely, yet it plays but a small part in the game of hide and seek with oneself.

The Conscious Mind can also be called Body-Thought and, for all intents and purposes, that is all it is. Body-Thought is quite automatic and is frequently confused with Mind. Even the most materialistic person or an idiot "thinks" and reasons and so do children but the level on which it is done makes it mostly Body-Thought. Just meditate seriously a number of times and you quickly discover the difference between Body-Thought and Mind-Thought. Mind-Thought, when realized (or conscious of itself) by-passes Body-Thought and becomes apparent through Higher Awareness. IT ALL HAS TO DO WITH SOUL-GROWTH.

Self can only be realized when the body is by-passed, or made to serve Mind, and when one can still remain conscious; then the mind above the body must be made to serve and only then can self be conscious in the physical environment. Only when all three: body, Mind and Self are properly aligned can Man achieve and raise himself by his own bootstraps, as it were. As self-realization is fully manifested, Self becomes conscious of itself (knows itself) even in an active body with an active Mind.   -Claude Charlebois

CHANGING CONSCIOUSNESS

Greetings, our brothers, our sisters, in the Light of our Radiant One. I, Sut-Ko, speak with you through telethought transmission once more, upon this occasion of your meeting.

I transmit to you, at this time, certain information relevant to conditions on the surface of your planet. You have just been listening to a Tensor Beam communication from my brothers, Monka and Kor-Ton. We are aware of your minds, we are aware of your thoughts. We speak with you, now, concerning the time which is fast approaching on your planet, not only among your peoples of this Western hemisphere but among many peoples of many nationalities, races, and creeds on the surface of your planet.

For some period of time now, short on our cognizance, a matter of some years - a decade - in yours, we have spoken with you of that which we have termed, for the sake of simplicity, as the frequency change. The frequency change relates to an inflowing of cosmic energies from the Central Sun, Vela, intensifying, speeding up, changing the molecular structure of all matter on the surface of planet Earth and, indeed, changing much in this entire Solar System as consciousness, the directing force behind the manifestation of all matter. It therefore follows that tremendous changes in the consciousness of Earthman must and inevitably are taking place, due largely to this tremendous energy of high frequency flowing in at this time. Your peoples already are responding to these changes, as we have previously told you, in two completely different levels or ways. Those of your peoples who are evolving and advancing in consciousness are expanding their awareness, their levels of perception, at a most rapid rate; rapid, that is for Earthman compared to his levels of progress in the many centuries of his life involvement on planet Earth.

The other extreme of this manifestation, again as we have spoken of to you, is the resistance of hide-bound Earthman in his Earth consciousness, in his sets of rigid values, conventions, and creeds, wherein the resistance set up to the inflowing high frequency energies, bringing about friction within the auric shield surrounding every individual so responding brings about a state of confusion or a state of violence; violence either in action or in words, or in both. Hence, the great disturbances between peoples struggling for their independence from this, that, or other restrictive force. That this independence cannot be brought about by a state of understanding or evolved consciousness is tragic, but it is entirely predictable within our realm of perceptions. As long as resistance to change manifests itself, our brothers, our sisters, as long as the consciousness of Earthman (and by Earthman we speak of man and woman incarnate on the planet) meets all incoming vibratory waves of energy with a force resistance there will be the conditions which you now witness. Yet climax is rapidly approaching in the affairs of Earthman; as we in our understanding of the magnetic cycles (which you call Time) perceive and know, the climax which will bring about a final boiling to the surface of all dross existent in the life wave called Man.

Man, however, on the surface of your planet is not cognizant of the facts: that in the releasing of these energy patterns in states of violence, of mob disorder, there enters in another vibratory wave which, added to the energies already manifesting, creates conditions of such utter instability that, were it not for the fact that we from space remain in many craft outside the ionospheric levels of your planet, there would already have been a partial tipping of the axis of your planet.

It is pointless to once more discuss the insanity of man in his explosions of atomic hydrogen devices and his continued explosion of these despite all warnings given, not only from space but finally permeating the minds of some of your more intelligent scientists. Should this disruptive pattern continue, it is with a calculated and predictable curve of events that there will be much disruption of ocean floors and of fault lines within the structure, and within the actual core of the planet. My peoples and I, myself, view with much – I do not wish to use your word "alarm" – but with much disturbance the predicted experimentation which your peoples are now planning for certain areas and for certain underground locations on your planet within the coming months of this, your year. Much already has transpired; not all, in fact very little yet observable to the eye of Earthman or his trained observers. Much is yet to take place at a very surface level, which will hardly escape the attention of any of your peoples.

In my earlier communications with you I have stated that it is for the individual to orient himself within a consciousness which is inviolate and of Light, to withstand, shall we say, the shockwaves of confused thought, of geological disturbance and indeed magnetic disturbance within the envelope of this planet. All etheric levels surrounding this planet are now in the state of what you might term "flux" or magnetic change. It can hardly be long, our brothers, our sisters, before this change manifests in a very drastic way, at a third-dimensional level or density. All Light Centers are requested to stabilize, not only the consciousness of their leaders, personnel, and crews, but to stabilize all preparation for which you have termed "Period of Survival." The directions which have been followed by impression in this particular Center were those given from ourselves, our sister (L.W.). It is therefore advisable at this time that all individuals remain steadfast in their consciousness and performance of those missions which they have felt impressed as their own; that all outlying outposts of Light within large cities near major fault lines be prepared for evacuation if the eventuality manifests itself in this period of time which you now regard as the present. We have not stated that it is inevitable, for much depends upon your scientists' further experimentation within the months of this your year. However, should the plans which have been postulated secretly and not known to the masses of your peoples be carried out there is grave danger of flooding of coastal areas and the large-scale displacement of fault lines in many areas not previously affected.

My transmission upon this occasion is, therefore, and may therefore be interpreted in the nature of, shall we say, a stand-by alert procedure. That I have chosen to communicate with you upon this occasion must surely show to you the gravity of your peoples' actions and our concern. I withdraw my consciousness at this time, but will transmit within a short period of time to the closed group in this Center. I regret that it is not possible for me to

(Continued on page 21)

MAN IS SPACE-BORN, COSMIC HEIR TO LIGHT

Sut-Ko

I greet you, my brothers, my sisters in Light. I identify as Sut-Ko of the Saturn Council. My transmission to you upon this occasion deals with the imminence of change as related to your present state of consciousness and being.

In the material which has previously been presented to you, our brothers, our sisters, many keys have been given to the understanding of conditions on the surface of your planet. As we previously stated, if these keys are utilized correctly they will enable you to walk a pathway of serenity and of Light consciousness throughout the turbulence of your changing scene. If, however, certain of these keys are not used you will find yourselves stumbling amidst the turmoil which so soon is due to accelerate to a pace beyond the handling of many of your peoples.

It is pointless to further comment on the fact that many of the conditions which we have previously acquainted you with are manifesting before your eyes, in your civilizations, at this time. That greater turbulence is obviously due to take place, not only within the consciousness of man but within the consciousness of the Devic kingdom and the very elements of the planet itself, in their relation to the Devic forces, also has been previously spoken of to you.

At this time, we of the Saturn Council view the conditions on your planet with the gravest concern. The atomic experimentation of which we spoke earlier to you in a previous month this year, has already now taken place and further experimentation is due in areas of weakened fault-line structure. How much longer the sensitive - shall we say - magnetic force-field of your planet can withstand these shock patterns, these continuous shock patterns which are being impelled into its structure, is very much of a question to our own scientists as it would seem that a point of no return has already been passed. The changes of a geological nature which you have already been witnessing upon your planet in their accelerating patterns are again, once more, due to accelerate within, I believe you would say, a ratio of ten to that previously observed. The rising of lands beneath the oceans and the sinking of areas within the weakened fault-line structures is already taking place with the displacement of large masses of land beneath your Pacific and Atlantic oceans.

Much of the information which has been given from ourselves through many Earth channels is not unknown to your scientists but is merely being withheld from your peoples due to the fear of panic of widespread proportions being caused. Many of your governmental agencies and scientists are at this time (and when we say "your" we speak of your planet, not of your particular nation) are concerned and are working, as you would say, "burning midnight oil" in an attempt to discover the secrets of the balancing of magnetic energies and of the gravity effect which are already much out of balance from the norm. These scientists, these agencies, are concerned that they may establish once more a balance within the planet and its relation to other planetary bodies in this system, not from the viewpoint of a cosmic balancing within a cosmic scheme of things, but within a viewpoint of once more attaining the status quo, the status quo which no longer will exist and no longer can exist on your planet, the point of no return beyond which all has passed. But in the greed of materialism which guides so many of your governing agencies (and the forces of international intrigue and finance and power which lie beyond these) is a frantic attempt to build back once more a crumbling edifice, an Empire which for so long has served the cause of greed and of the material as opposed to the values of spirit.

The day which has long since dawned is the day of reckoning; the day which so soon arrives is the day of revelation. Prophecy of many kinds fulfills itself within the consciousness of man, not merely in the events which surround him but within his own realization of his placement in carnate life, his relationship to the divine and to the spark of the God-force within. Such a day of revelation dawns for all people on your planet, our brothers, our sisters, and in that day the mind of man comprehends the magnitude of God and finds himself but a puny ant in the creation of a magnitude beyond the comprehension of finite mind. Yet in that comprehension lies both humility and expansion of consciousness into the ultimate realms of the God-consciousness and the God within, part of the One Created force which permeates all things, all beings, all sentient life. To become at one with that force is to know life; to divorce oneself from that creative force is to taste death.

My peoples have waited long periods of time for the return of planet Earth, the consciousness of its peoples and its life wave, to the Solar Council, to the brotherhood of man, of Space, to the voyagings once more in craft out to the outermost rim of the galaxies of God. For where man roams in consciousness, so may his flesh and his creations of machine follow. Where man roams in consciousness first, so also follow his footsteps. And it is in that awaiting for the return of Earth-man to the ultimate reunion of space (for all beings are space born, not we alone who traverse your skies in craft of silver, but you who walk the planet also are space born even as we); to that ultimate reunion we address ourselves in the changing consciousness of man. And though his footsteps have wandered far from the domains of Light, yet in that pilgrimage has he learnt many things. And when he returns he will know of ultimate realities and in that knowing will find at last the freedom of his own being.

Man in consciousness, our brothers, our sisters, is free as the winds that seek out the surfaces of your planet and roam o'er the oceans and the mountains. Man in consciousness is space-born, cosmic heir to Light, and in his heritage and its values he finds his ultimate security, his ultimate link beyond all things of the finite transient scene, of the many cultures which have spread o'er the face of your planet. Man who returns many times yet knows himself to be not that of the flesh body but that of the flame of Spirit. For has it not been said on your planet by your own teachers, I AM THAT I AM.

In my attunement in consciousness with this one who is our channel, I speak once more with you of realities of spiritual intent. Yet realities which permeate your planet force themselves upon the attention of your peoples even though that attention be not consciously recognized, of energies which stir, of energies which awaken, which move mountains, change cultures and, leaving no trace nor vestige of their existence, move onward into a new spiral, a new plateau, a new life. So that as Man emerges from the chrysalis of that which he has thought of as matter-reality, he finds himself at a different level, aware of realities previously not recognized, aware at a level of perception which allows him to express the beauty of his own being, the Light from which he was created.

At this time in my attunement with you, I and my brothers give our greetings with much Light to our brother (GK) who is with us, to all of you who gather here in this vortex of Light. And we ask once more that you remain serene of consciousness, secure of Love, and confident of the final outcome of a cosmic plan for the ultimate redemption of man.

In the Light of Our Radiant One, I, Sut-ko, give you Adonai Vassu of your consciousness at this time.

* * * * *

(Via Telethought, 17 Oct. 70. Solar Light Retreat. Channel: Marianne Francis)

* * * * * * * * * *

(Continued from pg.18)

answer several of the questions which I find in your minds; however, our sister who is our channel will attempt to answer them for you.

Would that Earthman might learn of the laws of the One Creator of all men, within which laws exists a pattern for living, for experiencing, for beingness, instead of the pattern which Earthman is choosing of destruction of his vehicle, of his world (if this were permitted) and his innate God-given dignity of Soul.

In the Light of our Radiant One I, Sut-Ko, bid you

Adonai Vassu Barragus

(Via Telethought, 25 July 70. Solar Light Center. Channel: Marianne Francis)

(Note: Large-scale atomic tests have taken place since this transmission.)

— — — — — — — — — — — —

Lava Putting On Show In Hawaii

HILO, Hawaii (UPI)-- Volcano watchers today could walk to within a few feet of streams of fiery lava inching down the slopes of Mount Kilauea.

"It's quite a show, especially after dark," said ranger Arthur Hewitt of Hawaii Volcanoes National Park. "Very, very spectacular. The lava is flowing over cliffs and forming ponds below them."

The glowing lava is visible at night from twenty miles away. (22 Nov 70)

CENTER NEWS AND TRAVEL

When I last signed off this column it was Convention time and what a surprising time it was. A truly Light-filled convention was shared, experienced and enjoyed by all at Merlin: Many familiar faces, many new ones, and a spirit of love and brotherhood prevailing. Stimulating panel discussions, interesting lectures, beautiful meditations with Jack Schwarz and the music of that lovely soul who is Erma Glenn.

Even the intense heat outside (it was $106°$ for several days) did not spoil the scene. A starcraft was seen over the hill behind the Convention Hall on one or two nights and it could be that even an Earth-incarnated Uranian shared of his concepts and his Light!

Gina Cerminara was the Center's charming guest for two days and then John Pearson from Victoria. A drenching rainstorm brought the unbearable heat wave to a close and suddenly it was quiet and time for reflection.

July came, and personal changes; then August and a hastily planned trip to southern California. Everything seemed to fall into place as in a Cosmic plan - a few days before I left, out of the blue came Angela, directed from upstairs to this Center. Though we had never met before, I knew she was the answer to my prayer. I asked and she stayed for two weeks while I was gone. The Retreat's three watch cats and one watch dog loved her and I left knowing all would be well. Thank you, Angela.

Bettie Berg (met at the Convention) phoned two weeks before I left (only one day after even I knew I was leaving!) wanting to arrange a lecture for me in California City and somehow knowing I was going down! After hasty car repairs we left (Margaret and I) and barrelled down into Bakersfield like a freight train coming down the tracks! We don't know if it was the heat or the re-tread tires on the T-Bird but it roared and it grumbled and its air-conditioning overheated and we drove and we drove. By dint of much persuasion and (we feel) careful driving we made it through the heat and over the treacherous pass without stalling and into Los Angeles. While many drivers were stalled all along the pass, we stopped every fifty miles and hosed the overheated engine down, consumed our orange juice and Vitamin C and congratulated ourselves on our good judgment. Margaret's vacation had also coincided with my trip and this enabled me to have a co-driver and an ever-cheerful companion. Truly that trip was planned "upstairs," if ever a trip was.

Personal business in Newport Beach concluded, we headed for California City and more heat: California City, a new concept in vacation cities. Much interest in my lecture; an early morning interview in Bakersfield on T.V. and everyone (or so it seemed) with car trouble. After another day's delay and more car repairs (this time the power steering pump) we finally headed back up to Santa Barbara and its delightful coolness.

My thanks to dear Gina (Cerminara) for an interesting weekend as her house guests; also to Gayne and Roberta with whom we stayed on the way down, and to Gabriel Green in Los Angeles.

Home at last late Sunday night and a letter telling of a house guest about to arrive on the morning plane! More contacts and a rushed week, then again quiet.

October again brought personal guests and trips to Washington and Portland to see friends and attend weddings. Holly married in early October, Trisha late October. Weddings were in the air. Also our Light workers, Hanita and Gregory Alexander, arrived from New York and were my guests while they found a home here on the mountain. Sabrina, a New Age symbolic artist, also came in from New York. A busy, busy month. A sizable donation from Hunter of "Lorien" paid our printer's bill and will get out this issue. So many thanks, dear friend. Leonard and Neil from the Aquarian Planetary Foundation visited and we loved them and their ideas for unity among the Light groups. November again brought changes and adjustments. A talk was given to the Philosophy club at Medford High and received with much enthusiasm. A beautiful Thanksgiving Day shared with the "Lorien" group: Frank, Heath, Harry, and baby Anna.

Ideas are flowing for a true renaissance next Spring and many changes imminent. Several important transmissions received and incorporated in this issue. Please study them well.

The rains have come at last and the nearly-dry well is no longer thirsting for water. Snow on the far mountains and a nip in the air. Winter is nearly here and January may find me absent from the mountain. A Mexico City lecture has been suggested but nothing definite yet.

The year is nearly over and how fast it has gone. Yet so much has been accomplished in Light and Love.

         In His Light,

              Marianne Francis

* * * * * * * * * *

Manila Shaken By Earthquake

 MANILA (UPI) - An earthquake shook Manila Saturday just two days after the worst typhoon in the city's history caused widespread destruction and left at least 125 persons dead. There were no reports of casualties or serious damage from the tremor. (22 Nov. 70)

East Pakistan Toll Continues to Mount

 DACCA, East Pakistan (UPI) - The East Pakistan relief commissioner said Saturday the provisional death toll from the cyclone and tidal waves that battered coastal areas eight days ago had been revised upward to 153,340 and could grow to "several hundred thousands." Many of the islands in the Bay of Bengal devastated by nature's one-two punch Nov. 12 still had not been reached or heard from. (22 Nov. 70)

ANNOUNCEMENTS

Publication Delay

The printing of the lecture, "Manifestation" has been long delayed due to financial difficulties but it is hoped to have it in print in the New Year. To those who ordered copies we apologize and ask your continued patience.

The Survival booklet prepared by Lysa Waring has also been delayed in printing but should be out with this issue or very soon afterwards.

We had expected to collect $200 in orders prior to printing but now plan on renting (and later buying) a mimeograph machine to print it ourselves. Again we ask your patience in this matter. We will soon have your orders sent out.

Chain Letters

PLEASE, PLEASE do not send us any more chain letters...we have been flooded with them this year and have neither the time nor the implicit belief that they will bring vast sums of money to this Center. The kind thoughts of those who sought to be of help in this manner are appreciated but please help us in other ways. Continued donations are needed to keep this and all Light Centers and workers going. Most of us are working with no other source of income, on a full time basis, and only your thoughts, prayers, and continued assistance make you a part of this work and a plan, Cosmic in scope.

Many thanks to all of you who HAVE sent encouraging letters, notes, donations, or who have donated labor from time to time. You make it possible for us to serve you and the Divine Plan.

PUBLICATIONS

Lectures by Marianne Francis:

Frequency Change and the Second Coming	$1.25
The Call of the Phoenix	1.50
Manifestation	1.25
Men from Space and Prophecies of Earth Change	1.25
Starcraft Contact	1.25
The New Dimension and the New Age	1.00

SCRIPTS: Ten Selected Scripts from Space People 2.90

STARCRAFT MAGAZINE: Subscription $2.25 (USA), $2.50 (Foreign)
(Three or four issues per year)

SEND ORDERS TO: SOLAR LIGHT RETREAT
7700 Avenue of the Sun   Telephone:
Central Point, Ore. 97501   855-1956 (Code 503)

STARCRAFT
SPRING~SUMMER 1976 & 1977

VOL. 11, NOS. 1,2,3

STARCRAFT 1976 and SPRING/SUMMER 1977

* CONTENTS *

```
EDITORIAL: The Ressurection of Man-- Aleuti Francesca...................1
The Nature of Energy-- Raymere..........................................1
The Signs are Everywhere Prevalent-- Sut-ko.............................2
Restructuring Ancient Patterns-- Raymere................................4
Assistant Editors Comments-- Arupa......................................5
I Speak to Thee of Thine Own Heritage-- Clytron.........................6
Thus Far and No Further-- Devic.........................................7
Center News and Travels.................................................8
Carry Thine Own Candle-- Devic..........................................9
The Sun of Love-- Robin LaVoy..........................................10
The Jeweled Radiance of the Eternal Light-- Devic......................10
Stand and Be Counted-- Arkon...........................................12
Release-- David Marshall...............................................13
The Nature of Matter and of Light-- Sut-ko.............................13
Balance of Polarity-- Devic............................................15
Good News..............................................................16
Relive the Adventure...................................................17
Guest Corner: The New Millenium-- J R of Jupiter.......................17
```

```
Director and Editor.......................................Aleuti Francesca
Assistant Editor................................................Arupa Patton
Illustrations.....................members of Antahkarana Circle, Manson, WA
Cover Artist...................................................Toni Blum-Cates
```

Published by:

SOLAR LIGHT RETREAT
7700 AVE. OF THE SUN   CENTRAL POINT, ORE. 97501 U.S.A.

a non-profit organization

(Copy, reserved. Write for permission to reprint.)

****

THE NEW AGE PROGRAM IS

TO LOVE, UNDERSTAND, EDUCATE, RELIEVE SUFFERING AND CREATE BEAUTY!!

-call first if you plan to visit-
(503) 855-1956

EDITORIAL

THE RESURRECTION OF MAN

"And many false prophets shall arise and shall lead many astray. And because iniquity shall be multiplied, the love of many shall wax cold" (Matthew 24:11-12).

Signs abound everywhere that the hearts of many have waxed cold... marriages are breaking up in all directions and relationships of all kinds seem lacking in lasting qualities. It could be argued that men and women no longer will tolerate incompatibilities as they did. However, it could also be argued with much validity that it is LOVE which is lacking... the kind of love that knows each is less than perfect, beset with the problems of a changing world but still worthy of love and understanding.

Violence abounds on the American scene... violence in crime certainly, but violence also in subtler forms... children bombarded with violent aggressive 'hero' figures in entertainment. Adults saturated with sports such as pro football, boxing, etc., all of which are, in effect, blood sports. Crudity of language is commonplace in all walks of life... four letter words now considered 'ART' and explicit sex without any indication of love and commitment have flooded movies and TV. Brutal abuse of children and vicious vivisection of animals in the name of science and medicine is an everyday occurrence.

So prevalent and coarsening has been the influence of all these things on society that people no longer stop to think in terms of compassion, love and tenderness, en masse. For humanity has been brutalized and the ideals of a so called Christian society are rapidly vanishing.

The signs are everywhere that we are in the last days of an era... in reality the last days of a major cycle on this planet (see "Thus Far and No Further" transmission in this issue). But we must know that all these signs do indeed indicate a resurrection process is also taking place for all New Age souls. But before resurrection comes a crucifixion of the lower self, the personality self. Increasingly, that which has been called "the Dweller on the Threshold" by the ancient Wisdom schools is being met and 'slain'. All negative patterns within the subconscious minds of Light servers are rising to the surface to be faced and transmuted.

Nearly 2000 years ago an Avatar of great Light came to demonstrate a truth. He has been called Jesus Christ by the orthodox religion formed after his death and ESU, Lord of Light by many New Age souls... by others, Sananda. He died a death upon a cross (symbolizing matter) in his flesh body yet rose incorruptible in a body of Light proving the ascendancy and immortality of the external self. The truth that He taught must be both internalized and externalized, in a sense, by the children of Light as they move into a new dimension.

The lower self of many IS passing through a crucifixion process and as it dies the higher self is resurrected from the ashes of the old... a phoenix rebirth. Transmissions now coming into the Light Center indicate that each and every soul who aspired to the Light is casting off the old 'body' of corruptible substance and is in the process of being reborn in a NEW body whose molecules vibrate at a different frequency.

This process can only be accomplished by Light servers as they CONSCIOUSLY observe the mechanics of their own self and its functioning. The devotional approach belongs to the Piscean Age and while it had its place, it left little opportunity for individual soul growth in the sense of attaining the god or goddess within. While humbleness and self sacrifice were the order of the day the sense of self mastery was absent. And only self mastery allows the individual soul to find the love and the power of the Christed consciousness.

To find that self, that 'essence' requires a deep search within and beyond the confines of the limited personality, the persons, for the 'selves' of many lives are coming to the fore. As they rise to the surface, the fears, the terrors, the loves, the hates, the traumas, the sorrows of an eternity of time come with them. Only the strong in heart shall conquer for the faint of heart wilt and turn aside to facile diversions of the earthly scene at the first hints of inner growth.

This is NOT a peaceful time in which to live nor was it promised it would be but it IS a time of great soul growth and a struggle and finally triumph. For the resurrection of the sons and daughters of Earth draws nigh. For them... the love of their heart shall wax great.

Aleuti Francesca

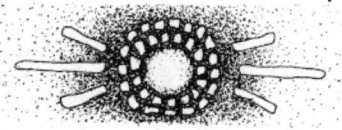

THE NATURE OF ENERGY

Greetings, our brothers, our sisters in Light. We speak with you upon this occasion from the XY7 Craft stationed far above your mountain locality. The transmission upon this occasion deals with the nature of energy. There has come into being an energy which might be considered new to your peoples - an energy which is the result of an inter-blending between various fields which have been set up at your planetary levels due to the rapidly changing frequencies. As these frequencies continue to move more rapidly into that which has been termed the etheric levels, there will increasingly be evident an energy field which has not previously been registered by any of your instruments. The effect of this upon your peoples will be to assist in the rapidly evolving consciousness which is taking place as you move into the final cycle upon the planet before the major change takes place.

The concept of fields of energy is in no way new to you, we realize, but the effect of this heretofore unknown energy field will be profound upon all who can raise their consciousness to the level wherein they are cognizant of its benefits. As the spirals and recycling of ancient energy patterns continues upon your planet, all matter will be affected in varying degrees; but the consciousness of humaity will be the most profoundly affected. For as we have previously stated, all what might be termed unregenerate energy of ancient origin is moving and spiraling upward as it rises to the surface of consciousness of all created life - not only man, but all created life-waves from humanity down into the consciousness of the mineral kingdom. And as this change which is now in an acceleration phase takes place, all ancient energy patterns will be moving upwards as they move into the next level of the spiral, returning to the point of origin before the next level is reached.

We have already touched twice upon the effect of this upon individuals within this consciousness level of which you have termed the metaphysical fields; but it does not confine itself to these alone, but is affecting all humanity in degrees which vary between most profound spiritual states of ecstasy and those of most ancient energy patterns of a highly destructive nature. The manifestation of these in your nature kingdom is already well manifested upon your planet. . . (You will please quiet the disturbance before this transmission continues, our sister) . . . (dog was howling and is quieted) . . .

To the degree to which individuals can attune themselves to the innermost core of their beings will be the balance point reached between ascending spirals of consciousness and ancient energy patterns seeking release or transmutation into a higher form. Consciousness, our brothers, our sisters, is releasing from the very core of each atom of being all negative patterns. By unregenerate energies, I speak of negative expression within the individual. Only as these are released can there come about a lifting of the heaviness of these patterns within the vibratory structure of all individuals. Shall we say that the weight of negativity must expand and release itself to leave the aspiring soul free to rise, not only in consciousness, but in the actual molecular structure of the body physical. For as the body physical atoms move into the next spiral level, they then manifest within the etheric. And that comes into being of which we have spoken many times - the frequency change between dense matter and etheric functioning of humanity. A new race of man must be born or perish upon the planet Earth. A new race of man must ascend to the next spiral level in consciousness. You may call this a mutation of man, but whatever terms you choose we would have you clearly understand within your consciousness of the innate divinity of man's being. For only. . only as this is recognized may the harmonizing principle of Eternal, Divine Light bring about the ascension to the levels which are destined for man at this period of time.

You have been told by many of your ancient wisdom schools that mankind upon the planet Earth is a lagging life-wave, lagging far behind its time of evolutionary progress, and therefore that a tremendous leap forward must take place and a mutation of those of the species called man in order to move onwards with those of us, your brothers and sisters from other levels of the planetary life-wave in this system. As the great Central Sun, sending forth its radiant energy form, reaches and changes the fields of energy of the sun of this system and its planets and humanity upon them, the most profound effects will be felt upon the planet known as Terra, or Earth. It is here that growth is taking place in a tremendous, accelerated process. It is here that growth is possible in a way not possible anywhere else in this system and this time span.

Do not, our brothers, our sisters, regard your tremendous challenges as stumbling blocks, but merely the opportunity to advance into realms of greater Light where consciousness may flower and beauty be expressed with love, with compassion, and with understanding. Direct application of the consciousness to draw in this new form of energy should take place at your time of new growth known as your Easter Season. For as the great tides of energy flow through from the inner planes at the time of a resurrection of man's being, this is when the greatest leap forward in consciousness is possible. I will leave another of our brothers upon another occasion to speak with you of other things relevant to this time for the inner group.

I discontinue my transmission, our brothers, our sisters in Light, and I leave with you the consciousness of my being. I am Raymere, transmitting from the XY7 craft. Adonai and peace and love, our brothers.

Via Telethought - March 27, 1976
Channel: Aleuti Francesca

THE SIGNS ARE EVERYWHERE PREVALENT

In the Light of our Most Radiant One, I am Sut-ko. I transmit to you gathered here in this place upon this occasion of your May Day in order to further inform you of the events which will soon make themselves felt upon your earth scene. In the Light of our Most Radiant One, the Creator of all men, I transmit from the Saturn Tribunal via the XY7 craft with data which has been stored for several of your weeks awaiting transmission through this channel of reception. We will briefly recap, to use your phrase, or recapitulate some of the data which previously has been given through this and many other channels of information. This is done for the benefit of those of you who are new to this particular type of data regarding geological and related changes upon the surface of the planet Terra.

Due to man's misuse of the element known as hydrogen and to the nuclear detonations carried forth below the surface of your planet, there has been brought into being a tremendous instability within the axis of the planet itself. To the degree that this unbalance is now accelerating will come into being tremendous chaos upon the surface of the planet. The magma levels of the planet are also in a state which can most nearly be described as rising to the surface through various vents known as volcanic vents, through from the level already mentioned. Disruption of major fault lines, ocean currents and all manner of related weather conditions are, as you may note, increasingly becoming erratic to a degree. We have noted your own conversations as to the unseasonable and strange changes taking place in your own patterns, not merely from week to week or season to season, but from day to day. Our channel will recall that at the beginning of our transmissions eighteen years ago of your earth time we stated that as the greater turbulence accelerated, there would be fluctuation of weather patterns and extremes, rising from heat to cold within a matter of hours and days, unseasonable in the extreme. You will note that these already are taking place. The elements upon the surface of your earth have been rendered extremely unstable, not only due to man's tampering with the very building blocks upon which all material substance rests -- that is, the atom -- but by the instability prevalent within the very nature of man upon this planet. Man is indeed unable to control the elements of his own being, and this, added to the greater disturbances which his lack of control have brought into being, will further accelerate the patterns of disruptiveness to a point where what may be termed crisis will occur at such time.

We have previously told you, our brothers, our sisters of the earth planet, there will be an attempt to lift off certain of the children of Light, or what have been termed the children of God or the innocent, from the surface of your planet before an axial flip takes place. The degree of axial excursion which is already manifesting could most suddenly before the year 2000 of your time bring about an actual flip of the axis of the planet, causing tremendous winds and tremendous devastation by the flooding of ocean waters over your lands in a period of a very few hours.

In your immediate time you are now well aware that many of your peoples are being alerted to the degree of instability present through all and every means possible in that the Creator always guides His children where they will listen and prepares them for a place of inner sanctuary. Your Holy Works have said to you, "Flee not to the mountains lest they fall upon you." Yet it is the high places of man's beingness that he finds his sanctuary; for as man attunes with the high places within, he will be guided and led into those outer sanctuaries or places of refuge through the times of what will be termed the Great Tribulation upon the planet Terra.

Many times, our brothers, our sisters, we have spoken with you of these things, and you have said to us that many years have passed and our earth is still intact. This is true; but, if you will note, intact though it may be, it is no longer the same. Your moral patterns have changed. I will not say for the better or for the worse; I will simply say they have changed. Your ethics, your values, those things which once were held dear in the mind of earthman as just, honorable and upright, are scorned. And many there are who walk the surface of your planet who care nothing for their neighbor nor even for another human being, only for their own needs and their own self-aggrandizement. Your Holy Works has said to you that in the last days the hearts of of many would wax cold. Do you not see all around you the signs of great change? Many there are of your younger ones who are turning their faces from the cities, those caves of man's despair, and are turning to the fresh green of the fields and the woods in their search for sanity and values of enduring worth. Many there are who are turning their faces from all law and order and who are secretly setting themselves up to be armed bands or encampments, even as small cities, secure unto themselves with their own weapons of survival and their own supplies of food. In many ways, some most unwise, some warlike, others peaceful according to the nature of man and women, your peoples are turning and looking for a salvation from that which they sense, which they see, which they feel, will overtake them before the turn of your century.

The signs, our brothers, are everywhere prevalent, and you will find that they will become more so as this year of your 1976 reckonings progresses. Much unrest will be felt even in your political circles which continue their strange circuses undeterred by the signs of the times to this date. Yet it will not be too much longer, our brothers, our sisters of the earth planet, before even those who call themselves your leaders and sit in the citadels of power will be shaken from their positions and will feel the unease of a planet in the throes of much turbulence, a planet undergoing the birth pangs of a most mighty re-emergence from an old age to a new, from the dying throes of darkness and decay and decadence unto the birthing of an age of Light. And the children of the One Creator, be they of whatever name they may call themselves or none, but those who turn within to the Light of the Most Eternal Being, shall find that all that which they have endured has led their footsteps into the ultimate path of Light, from materialism to spirituality, from darkness into Light. As your ancient mantram has said, from death to immortality. For it is in the immortality of man's most precious possession, his own innate beingness, that he shall find his salvation and his refuge, his guidance for his footsteps in the days ahead.

Our craft will be seen increasingly in your skies as the time of the end of the cycle approaches; and our brothers are our concern; and our sisters are our concern; and if you will align your consciousness with the Brotherhood of Light, you will not walk alone but on a pathway filled by many others awaiting a new dawn through the darkness of the old despairs. Truly an age of darkness must end; truly that which dies of the old, dies in agony and in chaos; yet from its dying emerges a child of Light, the new dawn of what has been termed the Age of Aquarius, the Age of the Water Bearer who comes bringing the great Avatar of Light once more to your planet.

I, Sut-ko, who speak through telethought transmission via the XY7 through this my channel of communication, bring with me upon this occasion the energies and the salutations of my peoples and bid you anchor the Light-energies more securely through your own beings and through your own bodies for the times ahead. For it is through the anchor points of Light that the descent of what has been termed the Hosts of Heaven, which includes our own craft, will take place. In leaving with you this thought, our brothers, our sisters, I ask you to ponder it before the next meeting of our minds.

In the Light of our Most Radiant One, I, Sut-ko, bid you Adonai, Vassu, Barragus, discontinue XY7.

Via Telethought - May 1, 1976
Channel: Aleuti Francesca

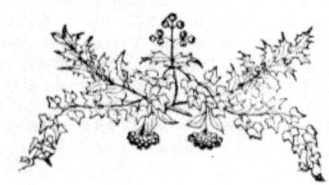

RESTRUCTURING ANCIENT PATTERNS

We greet you our brothers, our sisters, I identify as Raymere speaking from the XY7 craft. This is an XY7 craft transmission directly from the craft - not through relay transmitter. Our thoughts are with you at this time in that we are attempting to transmit data relevant to the particular period or time phase in which you find yourselves. We had previously stated to you that the year of 1975 and through into 1976 of your reckonings was a period of tremendous internal and external change upon your planet. You have now discovered that there is indeed a tremendous releasing of energy patterns within the individual and from within the planet itself, manifesting as conditions of some turbulence, again, both with regard to the individual and their changing consciousness and to planetary institutions and geological upheavals.

It would seem, our brothers, our sisters, that as this period of change intensifies and the vibratory frequencies quicken, that from the very depth of the mind of Man, animal, nature and the mineral kingdoms, a tremendous releasing of all crystallized energy patterns is taking place and is excellerating. This is not in any way to be regarded as other than a period of great realignment of energies. That it manifests sometimes in manners that would seem destructive in the individual, the nation or the planetary scene does not in anyway eliminate the fact that this energy release is a restructuring of ancient patterns in order to bring about a new realignment, that energies may flow freely and unhampered from the source of all Cosmic inflowing: That is from within the individual at the God level of consciousness and upon the planet, within the laws of harmony and beneficent balancing.

If this energy, which is restructuring as it releases, is mistakenly regarded as a destructive thing then the individual themself is caught up in the concept of destruction. However, if it is seen as it truly is, viewed from the eyes of Cosmic law, a rebalancing in order to bring about a greater harmony for a planet due to reexperience a Golden Age of Light; then it will be recognized in its correct perspective and will be welcomed both by the individual and by Planetary Logos. Many individuals, as we have stated to you many years ago of your time, are now finding themselves caught up in ancient patterns which seem to be errupting in manners that are unpremeditated and startling - sometimes shocking to those individuals. Yet these energies are being stirred into action from the deepest levels of subconscious mind and memory patterns, carried over many, many hundreds of thousands of years of their existence by the tremendous outflow of energy from the Central Sun. As this energy, which you have previously been told of, intensifies its radiation upon the planets which rotate and the systems which rotate around its sphere, there will indeed be vast changes taking place with the system itself. If individuals cannot adapt in consciousness to these vast changes by uncrystallizing all blocked energy patterns, all closed areas of consciousness, all previously held buried resentments, hatreds, traumas, then the individual will be themselves caught up in an energy release which they do not understand and cannot control. Given the necessary knowledge, (which is one of our main purposes, our brothers, our sisters, in our coming through this channel who is our own, to you, upon many occasions) given the correct knowledge there can be a gradual - what you term 'unwinding' of the blocked energy patterns bringing about a tremendous freeing for the individual. Where you experience tremendous energy releases of emotional traumas, where you experience tremendous feelings of resistance to change, <u>you are encountering another level which you are passing through</u>, shall we say, to increase the vibratory rate of your functioning as an individual, entity, or soul. As these various levels are passed through, there will not only be a restructuring of the consciousness, but the inflow and outflow of energy from the High self of the individual will so increase as to raise the molecular rate of all cell structure, thereby delaying, and in certain cases eliminating what has been termed - the aging or deteriorating process of the body physical.

You have been aware in the past that certain of those, whom you term great Masters, have lived for much longer periods of time than the average for your individuals and their bodies have been found to be incorruptible after death. It is the consciousness level which has been attained which has brought about the process of non-putrification of the flesh. For, at all times, our brothers, our sisters, the flesh molecules must follow the patterns of consciousness which is impressed upon them.

All consciousness is the outflowing of energy. Where energy is blocked, disease, trauma and disorders of the psyche result. Where energy flows freely, harmoniously in Light and in Love, to use terms familiar to your mind, there is a tremendous speeding up of the cell structures and all bodies from the physical up through the mental bodies, vibrate at vastly increased frequency rates. This, our brothers, our sisters, is the pattern for New Age Man, New Age Woman, for an Age of Light, wherein the body physical moves into the etheric levels and vibrates as a body of Light, coming and going between the density of what you have called physical existence into the level of that which has been termed the etheric - which is the correct frequency band for existence in this solar system.

We have touched upon this fact before, but will do so again for those of you who are present upon this occasion - new to our midst. The planet Earth or Terra, is a fallen planet, fallen in the sense that it has fallen from its correct frequency band level and is vibrating at a slower vibratory rate than the life waves existing on other planets in this system. Our bodies, our lives, shall we say, function at what we have termed for the sake of simplicity, the physical-etheric level, yours function at the physical-dense level of existence. As you become less densified, as you raise your vibratory frequency - <u>you move</u> into the correct frequency band for life in this system. And it is then, our brothers, our sisters, as we slightly reduce our own vibratory rate and as you raise yours, Spaceman meets Earthman and the reunion of that which was lost within the system takes place, and the fallen planet is restored in Light. Your Holy Works have much truth within them, but over the centuries since their writings much distortion and misinterpretation has taken place. Your fallen planet has fallen through the sin of ignorance of Cosmic Law.

We of the XY7 are once more in orbit in your particular, shall we say, area of location; though quite obviously we are aware, at the altitude from which we function, of a much larger area. Our pinpoint concentration at this time is upon this and one other Light Center within the vicinity of our stationing. Transmissions from craft will again be reinforced in the weeks and months which lie ahead, as the changes rapidly accelerate in your midst and within you, each one as individuals. Do not fear these changes, our brothers, our sisters, they are beneficial in their final outworkings. And you will find the final effect most advantageous as you attempt to flow in consciousness and to complete the process of unwinding of long buried patterns, that you may rise in Light and become at one with those of us who are your brothers and your sisters of a step ahead of your present development.

The XY7 is once more staffed by 24 liason officers who are making contact and have missions with your peoples. On one subsequent occasion we will introduce and give the names of these 12 men and 12 women who are the liason officers and will at some time in the future, be working more closely with those of you of the inner group. The times ahead are times of great responsibility and serious endeavor. Do not run hither and thither, our brothers, our sisters, in many endeavors of your daily lives - but concentrate your energies upon those areas which are most important to you at this time, as your energy patterns are going through drastic changes and need to be directed into the areas of spiritual intent in order that you may find yourselves stabilized for the times in which you exist.

I, Raymere, transmitting from the XY7 craft, now discontinue this transmission. In the Light of our most Radiant One, I give you Adonai Vassu

Via Telethought - June 19, 1976
Channel: Aleuti Francesca

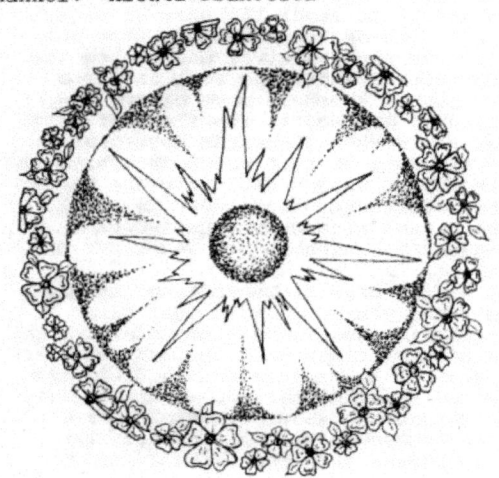

ASSISTANT EDITOR'S COMMENTS

The Solar Light Retreat has gone through many internal changes. Our group has a stronger awareness of unity in a single purpose to receive information and stabilizing energies from higher realms. Out of this new found strength and understanding comes this magazine. Contained herein are the transmissions we thought to be of import to you, some more than a year old but still containing pertinent information. If read from the beginning to the end you will surely find yourself changed a little. As we seek, so shall we find. The communications from the Devas and Space Brothers are the answers to our calling and our wondering as these times intensify.

I want to share with you some of the happenings at the Retreat so that we do not seem to be some far away place and unknown people. You will note that Marianne has changed her name to Aleuti Francesca to give full recognition to inner developments on the outer personality. There are seven of us who get together to meditate and pray for the Light to descend and transform us all into pure channels for His Radiance. Aleuti is here part of the time and, at those times we receive the telepathic communications from higher realms. The others of us have our own talents that we use also, each of us developing more of our abilities as the group centers and stabilizes. The Brothers have begun to give us experiments to develop our latent abilities of mind. The Devas are teaching us the synthesis of the higher mind and the heart of love to achieve the state of beingness where we can be of more service. We hope to manifest on a larger base, relocating to a new home with the purchase of a new piece of property. The energy of the group is getting stronger as we clear ourselves of past karma and prepare for the manifestation of the New Age. Out of this growth has been formed close friendships with those involved here at the Retreat. We wish to extend our love and comradeship to you, our friends, in the hope of the future and our belief in the One Mind in which we are all unified.

It is with humble gratitude I have come to meet our Space Brothers. Often I think of them and know our minds touch through thought. In the short space of time of these past three years, I have changed immensely by sharing myself with these friends, our elder brothers and sisters. They give themselves wholly to the service of Our Radiant One and at this time that service is opening their minds to us when we seek. What more can we share than our total beingness?

Raymere is the one I know the best, I suppose. We hear from him most often. He's there and waiting for us to open our minds to receive new data. Much love and caring comes from him when he speaks to us, but also frank words about the times we live in. He is on the Mother ship, the XY7. Orlon is also on the Mother ship. I understand that ship to be quite large. I don't know how many people are on the ship but 24 liason officers on the XY7 relate to us and others of Earth. Orlon is one of Aleuti's old contacts from the earlier days of transmitting.

Clytron is a being in a body of Light, perhaps one of our nights' stars. His dissertation is contained herein, quite poetic and one of my favorites

Sut-ko is from Saturn. When he speaks, we listen. He sits in a high governmental position on the Saturn Council, the governing body for this Solar System. Sut-ko's communications are direct and to the point. He strikes me with awe when he comes to us, a definite feeling of authority in his presence Even in this power and dignity that he presents is exuded a sense of deep love and caring for the planet Earth and her people. Arkon is a new personality to us. He has come to us this one time that is published in this issue. Sometimes we also hear from Kor-ton. He is stationed on Masar (Mars) at Kor, the communications center for this Solar System. These are the personalities we know, with more to come because Raymere says he will introduce the 24 liason officers, 12 men and 12 women, to us as the need arises.

I hope this has made these folks seem more real to you and I hope I haven't forgotten anyone. Stay tuned for the next adventure of "Earthman Meets Spaceman" for your time is going to come!

May the Light of your own High-self shine forth as you make your choices and live your lives. Now is the time when all action counts.

In His Light, I AM

Aruba

I SPEAK TO THEE OF THINE OWN HERITAGE

I come in a body of Light through the galaxies of God. I who am called Clytron in thy understanding come unto thee again at a time of change, of the transmutation of Man from matter into Light. If, in thy consciousness, I have appeared as a nebulous thing, a creature of fancy or of fantasy, I say to thee that the body of Light which I inhabit is more real than the garment thou wearest; that though thy flesh may seem solid and real of thy contriving, yet hath it not substance as the body of Light. And in my musings, as I sped through Time and through Space, I came with a thought in my mind that I would convey unto thee of Earth: That the transmutation of Man from matter into Light, from the flesh-dense body into the garment of shimmering radiance is not far distant.

How may I speak to thee of Light as substance or sound or radiance? Yet in Truth it is so. How may I speak to thee of flesh, which thou knowest and feelest as mere illusion, a thing of no permanence which descends into dust and worms do gnaw upon its impermanence? How mayst I make thee see that the body which is eternal is constructed of atoms of Light, of color, of sound, of radiance which permeates the structure of its very vibration and creates in its shimmering radiance a thing of great beauty? How mayst I make thee see that as Man transcends from matter into Light, from the flesh body unto the body of Light, that he moves into substance of eternal nature, that corruption and the worms do not gnaw upon it nor shall anything of impermanence mar its beauty.

If, in my communings with thee I may bring to thee but some small understanding of the galaxies of God and of the substance which is Light, of the realms of the eternal Creator's constructing, then I am well served in my mission. For I come in a body of Light through the galaxies of God unto the men and the women of Earth, and I speak through this one who is as my other voice upon the Earth, and I say unto thee that the time is not far distant when transmutation must take place and transforming of the body physical unto the body of Light will be the lot of those who aspire to the consciousness of the gods.

For who are the gods of old and who were they, save that they were those constructions of the most High, the most Eternal, most Radiant One, who moved in His image and who knew nothing of corruption or decay, who travelled the Star trails and the Light trails from planet to planet and galaxy to galaxy and moved with the rays of creation and came unto the planets as they were created and even descended unto the flesh of Man. And the gods came to Earth and once more must they rise again to their godhood and move into the vaulted blue of the heavens and partake of that which is their heritage from ancient times.

I come in a body of Light and I speak unto thee of thine own heritage, of thine own destiny and I bid thee doff the garment of flesh when the time comes, with no thought of its losing. For thou shalt move into that body of Light whose raiment shall seem unto thee more substantial than the illusion which thou hast worn. The times art changing upon this small speck of mud called the planet Earth and the transmutation of Man is coming nigh, for mighty forces move within the center of this planet and, barely contained within the substance, is that transmuting element within the very heart of the atom. And as it spins forth and releases from the core of its essence, so shall come the transmutation of Man.

Each one of thee, in thy learnings, in thy fallings and thy risings is passing through the valley of the shadow,1) which has been called "death", but it is but the death of that which was born to decay and from it shall arise the phoenix in youthful splendor from the ashes of its outworn garment of flesh. From the core of each atom comes forth, spiraling, the energy of Light and it creates unto itself the body of Light and it forms it of a substance which thou knowest not but shall ye know and shall ye feel and shall ye hear. And unto thine understandings shall come a mighty vision and a great Light, the illumination of the Sons of God. For truly each one of thee is as a son and a daughter of the Most High and as thou turnest within unto that self, so shall it come forth in radiance and in splendor and it shall encompass thee and many shall behold of the Light which shall enfill thee as a nimbus about thee. So shall it manifest as a radiance, of beams of Light from the eyes with love, so shall it reach the hearts of others and in the tone which speaks of truth, so shall it reach the ears of many. For the division has come between dark and Light upon the small plot of mud called the planet Earth. And those who rise in Light to their godhood eternal, move onward now, never again to descend to the flesh of Earth and those who move not onwards move down into the darkness of that which decays. Even as the leaves in season fall into the earth and become of another substance, so shall those who cannot witness the radiance of this transmutation descend to become as the Earth itself.

Light breaks upon the horizon of spiritual Man's aspirings and with that Light comes transmutation from matter into Light, from the body of flesh unto the body eternal. So shall I leave thee in the fragrance of things of immortal nature, in the knowledge that thou too mayst travel the star trails and become as the gods of old. So Light encompasses thee and I (will) come again as I leave in the body of Light. Tis well met and it shall be. I, Clytron, leave thee of this thy time but am with thee in a moment of thought before it is done.

Via Telethought - August 28, 1976
Channel - Aleuti Francesca

1) - Psalm 23

"THUS FAR AND NO FURTHER"

We who are nameless Beings of Light, called Devic in your understanding, come at the time of the Equinoxial change: the season of the falling leaves in this your Western hemisphere. We speak through our channel of the time which fast approaches for as change comes from summer into autumn, from autumn into winter, so also comes change of the falling leaves of Man's misdeeds upon the planet, to lie upon the earth and to be covered with the desolation of winter. For a time has come when no longer may Man transgress within that time span which was appointed for his learning. <u>Thus far and no further</u>: The edict has gone forth from the courts of heaven.

Thus far and no further may Man transgress the Laws which are Cosmic and have held as guide lines for the creations of God through long eons of time. Thus far and no further may Man's transgressions offend the mighty Lords of Light. For what is puny Man upon the surface of this planet called Earth but one creation of the Divine? And though he has thought himself Lord of all he surveys he is but an ant in the Cosmic creations of an infinite Being of Light, where beauty and harmony exist. What is the tramplings of Man but an offense unto the Most High? For the desecration of the beauty and the plenitude which was given for his joy and his ongoing has truly been an offense in the sight of God. We speak not of the children of Light. We speak of mass Man upon this planet. For the children of Light have ever come and have sown of beauty and of love and of harmony and of peace and their sowings, even of that most beauteous Lord of Compassion have been stamped upon and devided and cast aside, by the arrogance of Animal Man who does not even accord his animal brothers the dignity of their beingness.

Thus far and no further has the edict gone forth. And therefore in the time appointed shall there come a termination of all that which has been as an offense unto the Most High. And a time of desolation for those who have walked in shadow and in ignorance has come. Not desolation for the children of Light who have walked within the Laws of the Cosmos but desolation for the children of shadow.

The mind of Man has not comprehended the immensity of the Most High's creations. And if it does not comprehend of the Laws which were established for their guidance and their growth then, even as the child of your human race, must they learn of the penalty for disobediance. When mountains topple into seas and inland rivers become as turbulant oceans, when the bowels of the Earth spew forth molten lava and the heavens are darkened with the smoke of many fires shall Man learn of the iniquities which he hath wrought. And in his runnings hither and thither he shall ask and no answer shall he find but in the compassion of the children of Light who must stand as the emmisaries of truth in the places of the Most High, the secret places, the sanctuaries of Light away from the cities and the iniquities of mass minded Man.

Desolation of the Earth in many <u>areas</u> shall not deter the children of Light from blossoming into a new pattern and a new knowing and a greater oneness with all that was set forth for their redemption. Many times have you been told that a division was to come upon the planet Earth between Light and dark, between animal-Man and god-Man and the edict has gone forth. The time of the "wheat and the chaff" is come and though it may not seem, that a sword of division has fallen, it has indeed, at a level which must, before too long, manifest within Man's consciousness and knowings.

Deaf to the entreaties of all who sought to bring Light unto the planet, Men war in their flesh and their minds and perpetrate deeds of much disaster upon their fellows in the name of their politics, their nations, their ideologies. The time has passed for these things. It has long passed and shall never return. For there is only the spirit within Man which shall illumine his flesh or desert him in the final hour when it has been long denied and its voice silenced. Deepening shadows fall across the nations of this planet and if they do not heed, in this last hour, of the Spirit of all things they shall fall to be no more remembered in the annals of Mankind. For what are these things called nations, what are these things called tribes, but small divisions which separate souls from souls, man from man and man from woman and woman from understanding. What are all the small concerns of animal-Man but of the things of the flesh, which, without the radiance of the spirit within, must decay to be no more remembered. But if the illumination of the soul within shines forth then is the flesh illumined beyond decay and there is one being. There is not a spirit and a flesh body but there is a Light which wears a garment of irradiant flesh.

Too long has Man divided himself between the flesh and the spirit, the mind and the emotions and has sought with small barriers to cut himself in many pieces and to say this is good and this is bad and this I may experience and this I may no longer enjoy. But in the beneficence of the One Being, the Most High, all that Man was, if <u>illumined by the spirit, is of goodness and if not illumined by the spirit is a thing of shadow</u>. Small divisions do not exist where Light illumines for shadows cannot fall, and wholeness is achieved and joy cometh in the morning of such a being's awakening.

Think that the One Creator or Cosmic Radiant Intelligence cannot know of the Laws which were set forth for Man's illumination nor fail to provide Great Beings of Light to show the pathway as Wayshowers from time to time and eon to eon. But if animal-Man stubbornly refuses to follow these pathways and these Teachers of Light and to crucify their bodies and to distort their teachings, in after years, then how may he understand of Cosmic Truth; or the Cosmic Christ; or the Light of the Most Eternal? Tis the crucifixion of Man which draws nigh. For Man who crucified the being of Light who came nigh 2000 of your years ago must now himself upon the cross either ascend or take himself down with his own endeavorings.

What transpires in the life of a being of Light who comes as an Avatar must in some measure be passed through by all Men and Women until they too transcend and become as a resurrected, ascended being of Light.

What was demonstrated by the Avatar must be achieved by all who walk the pathway of Light, whether it be the crucifixion of the soul and heart or the crucifixion of the body. Beyond the suffering lies the eternal Light and the ascension into Ultimate Radiance.

The edict has gone forth, "Thus far and no further." And so it shall be in the annals of Man. We have spoken. We leave with you our compassion. Alexus. Aloria. Redina.

Via Telethought - September 21, 1976
Channel: Aleuti Francesca

CENTER NEWS AND TRAVELS

It is some time since I have written this column in '75. Due to circumstances beyond my control, while the travels have continued at a fast and furious pace, the News of this Center has not gone forth to all of you, our readers.

What can I say to all of you who have stayed with us through the long silence except "stick with us". Elsewhere in this issue you will find information telling you what we propose to do to get information out to you on a regular basis once more. Printing costs and postage rates have risen and continue to rise and until new funding comes in we rely on the income from my Workshops and counselling and your donations to keep this place going.

In actual fact a great deal has been happening in these last two years, both here at base and out in the field. So many trips up and down the Freeway north and south have I taken that I feel dizzy sometimes and wake up wondering if I am in my own bed here at base or in a strange one, in a hotel, in a city far from home! Calgary and Edmonton in Alberta were visited in '75 and Edmonton again in '76. Groups working with the Space Brothers and similar concepts to our own were visited with and enjoyed and many new friends met.

In the process of counselling with "Regression through Reverie" a variety of problems have been presented to me and my wits continued to be sharpened as I endeavor to heal the sick in soul and heart and comfort the weary. I never cease to be amazed at the almost miraculous degree of success which follows many of the Regression counsellings. Hang-ups, psychological problems, fears from the past, even bodily conditions release their hold on the individual in counsel-

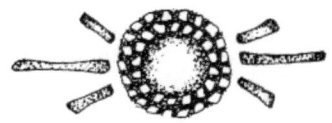

ling as understanding comes and with it, healing.

Because of the nature of the regressions and the way in which they are conducted I find we are getting maximum co-operation from the High Self of each individual who undergoes a successful regression session. That brings up the point that the percentage of people experiencing genuine past life experiences, is now running around 80% to 85% of all people in Counselling. Many times I have been asked "is this not a form of hypnosis?" to which I answer, No! It is NOT hypnosis, it is an alpha state, a light meditation type state in which the conscious mind becomes aware of other realities from other lifetimes. In many individuals this takes the form of a movie which they "perceive" with themselves as the central figure and then, in a really good regression, move into this and become at one with their "self" of another time and place in history. Because I have never been afraid of my own deep emotions I am able to guide people into intense emotional reliving of the traumas, sorrows, failures, etc., which they have experienced and which are re-imprinting through into the present life span. By this means we release the energy which has been trapped in the past and transmute it for use in a creative form in the present.

Some individuals have discovered talents they possessed before can be brought into present focus and, to their joy, enrich and round out the personality of the NOW time. Others have found themselves to be a multi-faceted being with a variety of things they can CREATE and BE and DO.

In my own regressions I have released from many past hang-ups and fears and find that little in life amazes me as it did, concerning the strange way people treat one another!

I find I want to say to all of you out there. ...it is not enough to call yourselves a New Ager and read books and attend lectures on the subject. To be a true New Ager means to give up your past Earth conditioning, whether it be from this life or any other and strip away the false layers of maya from yourselves and discover who you really are and what you represent as a soul. If you are a glorious being of Light then love and compassion, understanding, truth and integrity should be a part of your daily expression. Can you call yourselves New Agers and lie to yourselves or betray someone's love and trust in you? Can you be jealous of another's gift and talents or seek ego glory as your goal. Can you see, oh so clearly, the mote in your brother's eye but refuse to look into yourself and find and transmute your own shortcomings? Can you grow rigid and closed in mind and see your body aging fast when you know a New Ager is of immortal substance and, (filled with Light), renews daily, as does love of the soul for another?

Yes, I have travelled far on freeways and planes but I have travelled further in consciousness of Light and in the discovering of my immortal self I found old fears and frustrations and limitations in myself and I worked to transmute them to bring about my own freedom of being. I have not finished yet with myself but because I have loved and sorrowed and known agony of the flesh and soul in lives before I can help others to find a path of release.

As I write this I leave once more for Canada with a bright and shining face beside me... Robin, whose writings, you will find elsewhere

in this magazine, goes with me on this trip...
We leave for a month knowing as we go that much
is in the process of being transmuted here at
base in our absence. Write to us here at the
Retreat and let us know when you need counselling
or help in areas where I can reach you...

In the Light,

Aleuti

****

CARRY THINE OWN CANDLE

We of the Devic realms greet you. Man has but a little way to go before his footsteps lead him as a species into another dimensional level of existence. From the lowest point of descent into matter he moves upwards once more, the life-wave called Man, into lighter more etherial realms of expression. And while the days may seem long unto those of ye who are imprisoned in the shell of flesh yet it is but a little while in the time of God before ye shall be freed unto the joy of thy inner-most spirit. Light falls upon the planet Earth and forms strange patterns of shadow and of brilliance. Ye move as one crossing shadows of illusion into the pools of brilliant sunlight and crossing these again through shadows and illusion. Though ye know not wherein ye wander, at times as through a labyrinth, yet still thy footsteps lead thee unto the ultimate Light which lies beyond the dichotomies ye hath known.

All of ye who experience physical, human life upon the planet at this time increasingly move through shifting patterns of energy which swirl and spiral and move as mist, revealing at times the landscape in its clarity and at others confusions and the sounds only of thine own footsteps moving slowly through the fog. The images we evoke in thy minds deal with the reality of thy souls experience and only the single pointedness of each soul of the flame within the heart of the consciousness of love, of the brightness of its intensity as it burns away all dross within the being, can show to thee thy pathway with clarity. For each of thee carry thine own candle and its name is Love. For long ago we have said unto thee that Love and Light are interchangeable and one may not exist without the other. From the point within shines forth that flame which shall illuminate thy ways. In its brilliance take thee beyond the level which thou hast known as thy lives upon Earth.

Ye move as one caught between dimensional change and as the spirit within moves into an ever spinning spiral the flesh body must either be left behind or raise its own frequency of cell structure to spiral upward into that which shall be the new level for the race of Man, that which is neither physical nor totally of the etheric plane but lies at midpoint between these two. Lighter shall be thy bodies. Brighter shall be thy minds. Warmer shall feel thy heart. For thy consciousness shall be uplifted unto the coming of the Son of Man. For we have stated unto ye that He who made promise of His coming again, shall indeed. And at His coming that which was not, in a sense, completed at the time of His last appearance upon the planet Earth, shall complete the cycle of the Redemption of Man. Not in the sense that Man has understood but in the sense which is of his eternal being, rather than of his flesh. For the things of the flesh are but the reflection of the soul within. And if the soul be budded then the soul lives out a life of degradation. And if the soul be caught with Light and radiant, then shall the flesh be illumined as the candle from within. The deeds of that Being shall shine in the days of the times of Man.

Cycles move within cycles and as the densities change ye shall become increasingly aware of the Golden Light which we have told thee of in our other discoursings unto ye. As ye move into the consciousness of the Golden Light and focus thy attention upon it, it shall fill each molecule of thy flesh body with new energies, with new lightness, with a focus to which the cells shall respond as they move into a new pattern and a new concentration of the Divine force which guides. Light truly cometh with the morning. The morning of Man's redemption from the density of his lowest descent into matter and the sluggishness of its weight has been as a heavy burden upon many souls who walk the Earth plane these many centuries of your time. Now the time of thy redemption draweth near. The redemption of which He spoke, who came as the Son of Man, as the shining example of that lifting from the flesh body and its suffering unto the shining body of Light to which all shall aspire. And though ye are not all crucified upon a cross are ye not all crucified upon the cross of matter? And as ye rise from that crucifixtion ye shall experience truly, the resurrection of the Son of Man. For one it may be a devotion unto an ideal, for another, devotion unto a being, devotion unto a cause, unto one who is loved, devotion unto the unity of the self within. But ye shall experience that which is thy focus of need.

As the Golden Light is drawn within thy consciousness, absorbed and utilized for the purpose for which you came, draw thus into thy being, this energy and know that it is more real than thy flesh bodies or the comprehending of thy mind. Feel of its texture. Absorb of its beingness. And experience within thine own self a resurrection process as the tides of energy sweep forth at the time of the coming of the Son of Man. With much Light and much glory cometh He who made promise to return unto thee of Earth. Many in incarnation at this time were with Him at the time of His leaving. They came at this time again stationed faithfully to build the vibrations as one builds a place of reception for one who is long awaited and greatly welcomed. The Children of Light came forth into incarnation to prepare the way as Way-

showers for the coming of the Son of Man.
As they do so know that many also have trodden the path of crucifiction of the outer
of that which was of the worldly, materialistic consciousness that would crucify
everything that is of the spirit and know
that those who are so crucified must rise
and be resurrected as was He from the tomb
of their own lifetimes. For if they had not
come in His name, His Wayshowers and prepared the way and acted as grounding points
for the vibrations of the higher energies,
how then could He come unto Men or the Age
of Light dawn, save that some came as the
Wayshowers of Light. And those who walk most
closely with Him in other days and other
times are those who took upon themselves
something of the world karma in order to
raise the vibratory frequencies in the times
prior to His appearance upon the Earth once
more. Planetary karma has to be lifted and
transmuted to a certain point before the
coming of an Avatar of God. Only those who
come from the planes of Light and work with
the forces of the Angelic Kingdom may work
with planetary karma and transmute the energies.

Light commeth with the morning and this
we promise ye. For the coming of the Son of
Man is nigh. Alexus, aloria, redina.

Via Telethought - February 23, 1977
Channel - Aleuti Francesca

The Sun of Love

A spaceship floats with the clouds, drifting
along. Its long cylinder shape flashes in the
afternoon sun. Thoughts flash around as tiny
threads of Light, a teaming mass of ideas.

Words form as pictures in the back of the
mind, they are out there, the end is coming near.
Doors are beginning to open, a still secret
vision of our future. Somewhere in the backward
ebb of time I learned something, it is sad that
I have forgotten.

A pure golden light glows ever softly around
a still form, the unending rainbows hide the
shape, is it like us? I cannot see, the light is
too thick. A great love, understanding and compassion flow in a never ending beat from a great
heart. We are as children in front of this Being,
all of our masks are stripped away, he knows us
as we are, ourselves. In our hearts a knowledge
takes root and grows, until under that sun of
love it flowers in the beautiful blossoms of
understanding.

A throne stands besides the Being, it is
empty, for he is for all, a gift to the people
once again. Beauty emanates from him, a running
stream that washes like a tide through Space.
The night sky is written in words of love, that
glow as stars.

****

"Now I understand that spiritual truth is
more essential to a nation than the mortar
in its cities' walls. For when the actions
of a people are unguided by the truths, it is
only a matter of time before the walls themselves collapse." Charles A Lindberg

 THE JEWELLED RADIANCE OF THE ETERNAL LIGHT

In the Light of a thousand suns we of the
Devic realms commune with you once more. We
would speak with you upon that Light which
is the energy from which all things derive
their beingness. There is a Light, there is
an energy which comes from the realms of
eternal manifestation and this Light and
this energy you understand to be God. This
Light, this energy manifests throughout all
the creations of that One, Eternal Beingness
and in the minds of Earthman the concept of
God as some kind of superior, male, being
has evolved. But that Force, that Light,
that Energy is beyond anything which you may
comprehend with your minds, with your intellect, with your intelligence of this time.
That Light, the Energy, that Source of your
beingness is of a nature which may be only
understood by the soul and the spirit of Man.
It is beyond the comprehension of the brain
mechanism as it presently functions on the
Earth planet. Yet we who come from the Devic
realms, we who speak with ye upon many occasions strive to bring into thy comprehension
a greater understanding of that Light, of
that Energy, that the mystical part of thy
beingness may absorb and may comprehend with
the knowledge which then in turn will clothe
itself with the understanding of the mind.

Light which comes from the Eternal Realms
of manifestation is of such a nature that
its energy swirls in spiral form and builds
upon itself creations which then in turn
clothe themselves in other substance known
as mind, known as etheric, known as emotion,
known as physical beingness. Yet at each
density level or step down of the pure Light
source itself there is an intensification of
the molecular structure at a level which becomes slowed up in motion. As we strive to
put into words the concepts which we bring
we ask your indulgence as we clarify further.

Light in its first and ultimate source as
spiritual energy, in stepping down its manifestation must take upon itself molecules of
a coarser substance as it passes down through
the mind, through the emotional, etheric and
into the physical levels. Physical manifestation of Light substance is therefore the
coarsest, if we may so term it, of the vibratory levels from which Light sprang. If the
original, purest essence of Light can be
drawn down through the indwelling soul of
each individual into the physical form substance and into the other levels of beingness this can bring about a purification.
This can bring about a spiraling motion of
great intensification within the cellular
structure of man, thereby moving the molecules into a new more etherialized form.
This concept is not new in the telling unto
ye of Earth but we would further clarify and
reiterate the concept for ye of this time.
For time is speeding and in its spiraling
motion the Light is coming faster into the
substance known as form, form of Man, animal,
bird, form of the planet's substance, itself.
And in this spiraling motion and its intensification, it carries with it a new pattern.
Shall we use the word that others have used?
A new matrix is forming and as the cells of
the physical body absorb of this energy they
either repattern themselves into the new

matrix or they shatter, and in shattering that which is known as disease or death comes upon the individual who simply, in essence, cannot absorb further of the Light substance and without It the physical disintegrates.

All of ye who are of the Light consciousness must move now in intensified patterns of Light, spiraling out of the physical, coarser density into the more etherialized density where the Light moves more freely: Where the substance of its energy is able to pattern and reform and flow in fluid motion through the cells; through the intelligence, forming new patterns and colors of much magnificence within the auric field. We who speak with ye from the Devic realms of Light do so at this time for we will say unto ye that a great cloud of negativity is moving slowly across the planet as the intensified Light substance spirals in. That negativity which moves, which has been stirred from the very depths of the vibratory field of planet Earth, must rise as the dark fog in order to lift and dissipate above the surface of the planet.

All of ye who are working consciously with the substance called Light are accutely aware of the energies as they move, of negative energy releases, of inflows of Light energy and must therefore be aware within thy consciousness, thy physical bodies as the energies move. For if ye are not aware you will be caught unaware of the changing in various localities wherein ye find thyselves. It is not of a new concept to ye that those places called cities, upon the substance of the planet, upon its body physical, are places where much negativity has congealed and the negative energy masses are being stirred by the vortices of energy coming in from the Central Sun. As these move, geological disturbance becomes more imminent in the areas where it is in motion. As these move, Light servers themselves, must remain as much as is possible, in the places close to the nature forces, away from the dark mind places of Man's abodes. It is not by chance that ye find crime increasing in the cities for it is building itself upon the negative energies which are now in motion and which are swirling as dark, noisome fogs within certain locals. Whereas out in the places of Nature they are freer of the negative thoughts and emotions which Man has spreat o'er the face of the planet through so many centuries. Take thyselves to the mountains and rise into the higher more etherialized atmosphere of high places if ye would find thyselves clear of negativity. In so going, ask of ourselves, the Devic Beings of Light, to assist in the clearance of these negative masses as they spiral off thine own consciousness of many, many lifetimes. For it has been said to ye, that at this time, the patterns which arise to the surface of the conscious mind in Man are rising and clearing themselves from his many, many abodes upon the planet.

This is the end time. This is the time of manifestation and the time for the releasing and transmuting of all negative energies unto the coming of the day of redemption, in the truest sense, from all that which was dross or of negative intent. Man must face his own creations of mind, emotion. Man must finally come face to face with himself and rise into the godhood of his own beingness. Understanding of the nature of co-creativity with that Force which is our most, Most Radiant One, the Light Eternal. As co-creators with God, Man has in his ignorance created manifestations of darkness, of war, of hatred and of disease and he, she of the New Age must reverse that process within their own beings and walk into the Light of a new day, clothed in the armor of Eternal Light. That Light, which drawn within the beingness of each individual, transmutes all which was of shadow and sends it spiraling forth into the new pattern, the new matrix body and the new race of Man.

Mutation, spiritual mutation of the race of Man is the pattern for this time and ye are in the third phase of manifestation of all things wherein the gates are unlocked and the energies pour forth from all levels of beingness. See, oh, children of the Earth planet, that thy energies pour forth at the highest levels comprehendable to thy consciousness. For many will be trapped in the lower outpourings of negative energy and will be unable to transmute their own creations of many, many lifetimes. Transmutation unto the day of Light when that which comes, as has been stated, cometh as the "Lightening from the East to the West so shall be the coming of the Son of Man." 1) For the Son of Man may be interpreted in two ways, truly the being known as Jesus Christ will come again unto the Chosen, the children of Light of any and all religions or none. But the Son of Man is the Sun within whose rays break forth unto the dawning of an Age of Light. The Sun within, is the thousand petalled lotus of the highest consciousness known to Man, the portal, the center of the skull leading outward and indrawing from the planes of Light. The Sun dawns within Man when that portal or chakra of Light spins at highest intensity bringing about molecular change within all the structure of the body physical. Concentrating the energies of the incoming Light upon that chakra and indrawing through it, (the thousand petalled lotus) the jeweled radiance of the Eternal Light will set up vibratory frequencies which will greatly assist in the spiritual development of each and every being. The opportunities to evolve are many. The possibilities to devolve are numerous also. It has not been a time of ease or peace upon the planet nor will it be until after the great cleansing has taken place. As each age ends within the major cycle there is upon a planet tremendous acceleration of all energies and of the consciousness of all beings. Strife is inevitable within the confines of a planet moving through such major cycle end. Do not underestimate our ability to be of assistance should ye call upon us, nor thine own abilities to rise above the negativity of this planet in which ye dwell. Go unto the high places and find the purity of the vibration of Light, far from the abodes of Man. Light comes even as from the East unto the West. So is the coming of the Son of Man. Alexus, Aloria, Redina.

Via Telethought - March 5, 1977
Channel: Aleuti Francesca

1) - Matthew 24:27

****

"Humans follow their ever-unfolding evolutionary path;
 People settle down." - Andre Carpenter

STAND AND BE COUNTED

Greetings our brothers, our sisters in Light. We speak with you at this time via XY7 relay craft transmitter. We speak with you at a time of much turbulence and approaching turbulence upon the surface of your planet. We would speak with you upon this occasion in relation to the change of consciousness within the individual. To the necessity for making a stand upon your own beliefs, your own knowledge and your own inner knowings. There is a time coming upon the surface of the planet Earth where all must stand and be counted, as your Holy Works have said. And those who do not stand out to be counted, by their belief and principle, will fall as chaff before the wind. There is a time coming when that inner knowing within the soul must stand forth in all its Light. For the confusions which blow across the face of your planet have brought schisms within the consciousness of many. And these schisms are causing much disruption within the relationships of many of your peoples, in their marriages, in their friendships, in their family unity. Yet it has been stated in your Holy Works, in those last days, which come now upon the planet Earth there would come such a period where "brother would stand against brother and where there would be great confusion and Earthquakes upon the surface of the land." It has also been stated in your Holy Works, in no uncertain terms, that, (and we quote) "The lukewarm approach is vomit in the eyes of God." Such a statement, while it may shock the sensibilities of some of your peoples, is striving to say unto you that unless you stand by your own inner convictions and stand forth and manifest these in your lives, then you are split between your outer lives and your inner knowings. And the schisms which split assunder many, your nations, your peoples, individuals, are becoming more and more obvious as the days pass. You cannot believe, our brothers, our sisters, one thing, within your heart, and live another in your outer manifestation. It becomes imperative, in the time which is rapidly approaching, that you unify yourselves within and without. That the inner Man, the inner Woman becomes the outer. That if you walk in Light, if your consciousness is of Light, if your convictions are of Light, even though these convictions may not be what has been termed "popular" within your societies, your cultures, none-the-less it becomes imperative that you walk in the consciousness of your own inner knowings and that you manifest those beliefs within your daily lives. For those who stand strong within the consciousness of Light, stand within a power which cannot be gainsaid. Those who stand strong within the consciousness of their inner knowing, stand upon the only firm foundation which will be left in the days which lie ahead. I do not address anyone who is present upon this occasion, yet I address all. I speak to those beyond this room who my words will reach. I speak to all who hear and understand, and I say to you, as I come in communication, speaking for the liason officers of the XY7, that it is time for all men and all women on the face of the planet to stand up and to be counted.

Confusions which move across the face of your planet are such at this time that they will engulf all who do not focus their identity within. Confusions which spread themselves over the face of your planet are now of such a nature that unless each individual stands firm within their own focus of beingness they too will be split assunder and splintered with the many vibratory currents which move in all directions. Therefore the necessity of inner attunement becomes not only imperative but of the greatest urgency at the present period of time as you move ahead through the time remaining in this your year of 1977.

We have already acquainted you with the fact that there will be an increase in disruptive and strange weather conditions and that all patterns manifesting upon the surface of your planet are undergoing rapid change. If, as your Holy Works have said, "The lukewarm approach is vomit in the eyes of God," they are saying to you that one must either stand to the right or to the left, one must either blow hot or blow cold. You cannot any longer, our brothers, our sisters, any of you to whom my words reach, and ring a bell, an answering cord within, you cannot stand on a fence between what you know to be true and what your outer cultures, civilizations, times, choose to live by as standards of ethics or morality or patterns of behavior. In the eyes of Our Radiant One, all beings must finally attune with the inner Light and from that point within must spring an ever present consciousness of the reality of eternal life, of eternal varities, of the consciousness of the soul and its immortal quality, of its existence beyond time and space, beyond the culture and the mores of any particular time in which it finds itself in incarnation. Only, our brothers, our sisters, by looking back and forth over vast periods of time can you make the realization that you have existed, that you exist and that you will exist into what you have termed the future, as an identity, as a spark of Light, as an unfolding consciousness. Only by so observing can you totally detach yourself from the insanities of the present scene upon your world. For viewed from the perspective of our peoples, this is truly a planet which has become insane.

And as the time moves through the greater changes to the ending of these things, to a new dimension, a new and greater dawning, an age of enlightenment, those souls who have stood firm within their own beingness, within their own inner knowing, will be the only souls standing upon your planet in sanity and in balance, for the rest no longer will remain. We have used, upon this occasion, quotations from your Holy Works. This does not mean that we do not full respect other Holy Works of other beings of Light who have come to your planet. We merely quote from your Christian Holy Works as these are more familiar with the great majority of your peoples in the Western world. Even though many of those Holy Works which have been handed down through many centuries of time have lost, in translation, certain of their purity, of their essence, there was a time of prophets, there is again a time of prophets, there is a time when old men shall see visions and dream dreams and young men and women shall go forth guided by these visions, these dreams, to a new beginning of an Age of Light. For this dispensation draws to a close and another takes its place upon the wheel of the cycles of time. I speak to you as one who has not previously communicated. My name is Arkon. I speak through the XY7 relay craft transmitter and I now withdraw my consciousness from this my channel of communication. In the Light of Our Most Radiant One I give you Adonai, Vassu, Barragus, my brothers, my sisters in Light. Adonai.

Via Telethought - May 7, 1977
Channel: Aleuti Francesca

"MAY THE LONG TIME SUN SHINE UPON YOU
ALL LOVE SURROUND YOU
AND THE PURE LIGHT WITHIN YOU
GUIDE YOUR WAY HOME"

RELEASE
by David Marshall

The worst fate that could ever afflict a person is the fate of being forever trapped in a jail of one's own making; with no release and only oneself to blame. Survival in all of us requires that we be blameless for at least one of our predicaments, for to think otherwise is destructive and anti-survival.

But if the bars of our jail are beyond our reach, and if the life we seek is visible beyond the bars, then the agony is greater still. And if we blame ourselves for this too, then how do we survive the onslaught of our memories which drive us to realize that we could have done differently, but chose not to.

If, however, we become teachers, from within the bars of our jail and with our knowledge show others how to avoid the traps, then possibly survival will exist, and a reason for our confinement be made available to us to assuage the torment of our minds.

But the sight of freedom can be an even greater torment than the mind can stand and if a tool should come to hand for us to reach the bars and pull them down, then for survival's sake, we should do so.

Each bar is of our own making, and no single key can drop them all, but suppose a single bar is dropped and then with a pleasant slip we sneak out of our cell and turning look behind, forget the jail and fly to freedom and a new life of our own choosing, will we end up building bars again and enclosing our souls in a new torment? Yes... you must slip back again and realize that all the bars must be destroyed likewise or else lived within until one dies.

"People are afraid of fears;
Humans use their fears as guidance for what they need to face in order to grow."
- Andre Carpenter

(Quoted from "For Humans Only" Human Dance Co.)

THE NATURE OF MATTER AND OF LIGHT

This dissertation is on the nature of Matter and of Light. It comes to you by direct transmission, by telethought beam from the Saturn Council. Greetings my brothers, my sisters, I am Sut-ko. I speak with you at this time concerning the properties of matter and of Light...and the transposition of one into the other. This may be viewed as an alchemical process. But by virtue of that which is called the Light and its energy field, matter, as you have previously discussed, may be made to do the instantaneous bidding of Mind. In ancient times those who sought, through what is called magic in your present understanding, worked with alchemical processes, knowing through ancient formulas of the control of mind over matter. Not over periods of time, but in the instant of thought, matter may be made to do the bidding of that which is created in the mind.

By such process the Being of Light, known to you as the great teacher, Jesus Christ, manifested loaves and fishes and fed the multitudes.[1] By the instantaneous control of that which was needed, manifestation from the inner, or <u>matrix level</u>, was achieved onto the outer scene. It was stated to you, by that Being of Light who came as a way-shower unto the Truth, that "greater things should ye do", also, after Him and after His coming.

You stand now at the beginning of a new era of Light and in this period of time it becomes necessary for you now to gather your forces and to initiate new beginnings, to experiment with the control of mind in small ways, over Matter, to manifest within your own lives that which is needed unto your further ongoing in Light. Our brothers, our sisters, that which has gone before, (in the transmissions which have come through this, our channel of Light, our own,) have been but as keys and stepping stones for that which must now take place.

First comes understanding and the ground work. Then comes the stepping forward as a small child, the first steps towards growth and stature as beings of Light. We, ourselves, your elder brothers from other planets, both within and without this system have manifested in our lives many of the abilities your peoples would consider to be magical or miraculous. They are nothing of the sort, our brothers, our sisters. They are simply the understanding of laws which lie within the realms of the Infinite One's creation.

As you move within to the consciousness of the greater Light and its power within each of you, as you unify in Light and lend your polarized energy, one to each other, it then becomes possible for you to manifest that which is needful for your lives, for your service, for all that is desirable. If you remain as divided or small, splintered off individuals from the whole, the power which would flow, otherwise, is lacking. We explain at this period of time, that much which has not manifested, surrounding this one who is our channel, has been because of the lone placement of this individual, in this temple of Light, for a period of years.

Understanding the science of magnetics, we explained to you of the nature of polarized energy. When either a negative female energy or a positive energy is not polarized by cross-currents of energy in working or being together within a group or within united couples who are polarized, the energies are not sufficiently strong to manifest that which is desired and needful in the life of individuals. Particularly is this true in regards to the negative or female of the species called Man. The female is the receptive pole of the polarity currents, as you will understand in your law of electricity. The male is the fertilizing or fecundating principle which reaches forth and brings about new life within the negative pole of expression. This law of magnetism, of polarity currents is carried through all of Nature where there is positive and negative charges. It relates to that which you term sex, it relates to all exchanges of energy within a group of males and females, within the elements of Nature, the pollenization of trees or fruits, of all manner of beings within the Cosmos, the law of polarity balance and interchange is manifested. Thus, we have said to you, only in united action and a unified balance of males and females, working in harmonious co-operation and interchange of mental energies, of spiritual purposes, is there manifested the energizing or polarized power which brings about results. If you question this, our brothers, our sisters, examine those organizations which you find are succeeding. You will find there is always a balance of male-female polarity energies heading up such organizations. There is never one without the other. There is always the balance in order to create the necessary magnetic field which brings about the physical manifestation of that which is first set up in the higher, spiritual and etheric levels... or the matrix form, into which the physical molecules pour themselves in order to bring about that which you call a physical change or result.

It is advised, our brothers, our sisters, that in the very near future that you make experimentation more a part of your gathering together. That you experiment with the energies of the mind in interchange of telepathic communication and with the energies of the mind in the manifestation and actual movement into place of physical matter. There must be purpose. There must be spiritual purpose and reason behind all group endeavors. There are challenges ahead, our brothers, our sisters, there are great powers untapped within the mind of Earth man (as you have previously discussed as we listened in upon your exchanges). These powers cannot any longer remain dormant for they will be necessary, very necessary to your further ongoing and your growth as you move into the new cycle of beingness which fast overtakes the planet Earth. All things of the old order are dying, decaying by virtue of their own decadence. And as they die must come forth the new shoots of a new dispensation where that which was known as magic becomes an <u>alchemical process of the mind</u>, manifesting itself at all levels of beingness.

You have been moved, our brothers, our sisters, upon your planet, by many forces, governmental, economic and forces of which you have known nothing. And it is better that you have not known but in turning to the godhood within each one of you you will no longer be moved as puppets but become masters of your own destiny within a pathway of Light. Do not hesitate or lack courage to walk the pathway of the god within. For has not that great One who came said unto you, Know ye not that "ye are gods?" 2) Within the spark of godhood is the direct connection to the most Infinite Being, our Radiant One, who created us all. And that Being who came as the Avatar, the great teacher of Light on your planet, came to manifest what could and can <u>now</u> be achieved by those who are the advanced guard of the New Age of Light, the Brotherhood of the Stars. Solar Man is to be born on planet Earth and no longer will you be as creatures walking in the mud of Earth and gazing but dimly at the stars in your night sky but you will move into the concepts of Solar Man, Solar Woman and into the race of enlightened ones who walk the pathway to the stars.

Our brothers, our sisters, we of the Solar Confederation who speak with you upon this occasion do so in full knowledge of the tests and trials through which each one of you individually has passed. But only those who walk through the portals of Light and "endure", as was stated to you, "unto the end",3) move into the new dispensation and cast aside the limitations of animal-man. Solar Man emerges. Embryonic at first but none-the-less radiant from the cocoon of his long darkness. We who speak with you upon this occasion, I, myself, Sut-ko of the Saturn Council have watched your progress as a group, as individuals. We are with you in mind and intent and in heart, our brothers, our sisters. Each one of you is dear to us. Each one of you is a child of God, of that most Infinite creator of us all. Walk into the Light and manifest within your own beingness those first steps towards the stars where we ourselves, move most freely. There is a time. There is a place. There is a meeting. And it will be. In the Light of our Most Radiant One, I, Sut-ko, give you Adonai, Vassu, Barragus, our brothers, our sisters, in Light.   Adonai.

Via Telethought - May 11, 1977
Channel: Aleuti Francesca

---

1) John 6:1-14
2) John 10:34
3) Daniel 12:13

****

- A BLUE -

by Robin LaVoy

A blue flame dances merrily, burning away fetter that trap, fears that twist and warp.

A blue wall raises itself protectingly around th innocent, the lighted ones, sheilding them from the darkness that moves restlessly in th cover of night.

A blue and silver sword flashes in the light, cutting, severing a creeping tentacle.

A blue figure picks up a limp, dark form, placing it tenderly in the pure Maxim light. A change takes place, and someone is released.

BALANCE OF POLARITY

There is a light, a most supernal Light which, once attuned with, is of such surpassing radiance that it encompasses all else. I speak with you upon this occasion of that Light. I come as a nameless being from the Devic realms at the request and invocation which has been sent forth by this one and this group of individuals to whom I now address myself. That Light of such magnificence and radiance contains within it an energy, an energy so mighty that all other manifestations, whether they be of negative intent or lesser manifestations of Light, are consumed within its radiance.

How, you may ask, is that Light achieved? How is that Light evoked within the consciousness of an individual, of a group, or an institution? By the attuning of the mind with the heart, by the feeling of love which flows from the heart chakra blending itself with the intelligence of the higher mind - not the concrete brain mind of the human level of man, but the higher mind. When these two energies are brought to a point of balance, that Light manifest within the inner-most core of the individual. If within a group the higher mind and the love energies of the heart are also balanced between the individuals - some contributing from the higher mind, some from the heart energies - again such a balance can be brought about. And that Light is then brought into being by the balance point which is achieved within the individual or within the group. And once that balance point is reached, the energy of that supernal Light can be evoked as if by a pathway which is made for its manifestation.

It is not that the Light does not constantly exist. It is not that ye are denied access to that Light as a punishment or as a deterrent to greater knowledge. It is that ye have not created within thyselves or within thy group an open pathway for the Light to manifest. If it has not yet manifested, the answer is to create the pathway by the balancing of the energies of the heart chakra and the higher mind, or crown chakra of the body. For within the balance of these two is achieved the fulcrum point which allows the greater Light to manifest within the individual; and once that greater Light is activated, it acts as an instantaneous point of magnetism for the pathway of the supernal Light to make manifest its incredible brilliance and sustaining power. That this Light has only been touched by but a few upon the surface of your planet, relatively speaking (compared to the many, many millions who walk in human bodies), only bespeaks of the concentration of the vast majority upon the physical and not upon the inner world of reality. Where an individual or a group of dedicated individuals seek earnestly for Light, the supernal Light must manifest its presence. Most earnestly invoked, it becomes but a matter of time before the balance point is reached and the pathway is made for its emergence.

It has been stated in your Holy Works that even as the lightning strikes from the East to the West, so is the coming of the Son of Man; and even as the point of balance within the individual is reached, so as lightning comes the greater Light in a flash of brilliance, and the life is truly transformed and transmuted and is never again the same. Nor can it ever be lived at the merely human level of trial and error after such a point is reached for there is a knowing, there is a certainty, there is an authority which this Light brings with it. He or she who goes forth with such Light blazing from their eyes, from their heart, from their countenance, is an unassailable being against all adversaries upon the surface of the planet Earth or any other planet in any system of the Creator's creation.

I who come as a nameless Being of Light do so upon this occasion to bring in some faint glimmering of the understanding of that greater Light within the hearing of those not only who are present in form, but those who are attuning at other levels; and where my words reach and strike meaning, there shall understanding grow and flower within the consciousness of all. This supernal Light comes from the inner-most recess of the Creator's dispensation for humanity, and it must be sought for and evoked in order to be discovered. It does not reveal itself to the uninitiated, but only to the earnest seeker who seeks with the heart and the mind, the love and the intelligence, combining them and making whole the balance of polarity within the individual soul - between the heart, which is the feminine principle, and the mind, which is the masculine principle. When such beings unite in pairs or in groups of pairs, there is a tremendous outpouring of this supernal Light through their endeavors, and success crowns all their efforts. Where balance is lacking, you will find only half of an energy field, incomplete and unbalanced, manifesting which may be beset by many adversaries at many levels of manifestation. Where wholeness is attained, this is not the case.

Our Most Radiant Being, who created we of the Devic realms and you of the human evolution, created certain pathways with the physical form, within the astral body and the mental bodies, and it is these pathways of the inner which must be sought in order to bring all outer manifestations into balance and divine order. The love principle must always be balanced by mind, and the mind, even more dangerous alone, must always be balanced by love and compassion or one becomes an extreme.

I who came upon this occasion to speak with ye did so at the request of thine invocation for assistance. As ye balance within thyselves and call forth for this supernal Light, it will surely manifest within thy midst.

Alexus, Aloria - I leave thy consciousness.

Via Telethought - June 2, 1977
Channel: Aleuti Francesca

****

"Humans act from intuition;
People act from compulsion."
- Andre Carpenter
(Quoted from "For Humans Only" Human Dance Co.)
Andre Carpenter

- THE PRAYER OF MICHAEL -

(as received by Robin LaVoy)

In your light I am protected in the infinite passages of time, through the pathways of goodness and compassion.

By your flaming sword of everlasting blue, I am freed of the entangling threads of darkness, cut from the web of evil.

By your fire, the dross, the negative is burned away leaving only the pure essence of me.

Oh, Michael, Archangel and keeper of the blue ray, I lift up my heart in humble and sincere love and gratitude.

Good News !!

As we go to press and the final touches are put on the magazine there is Good News to share with you. A new channel has opened up for reception of telepathic communications. One in the group started recieving telepathicly from Raymere and the Deva's. It came about while Aleuti and Robin were in Canada on a lecture tour. During their absence we continued to hold our regular meetings. The Brother's had advised us prior to Aleuti's departure to try and make contact with them through another channel. Her absence would create a backlog of energy that would help in making the initial breakthrough possible because the group has progressed to a point where individuals have developed a new sensitivity. The Brother's have also told us that more than one channel would be working through the Solar Light Retreat. This opens up new levels of communication. Each channel touches upon a different level of awareness and therefor opens up to new areas of information.

These new scripts are dealing specificly with telepathy and how it works. The inner group who meet regularly to study these teachings are being taught new concepts and techniques for mind expansion. Emphasis is being put on attaining control of all our innate abilities, first by turning within and recognizing the god-spark and then going without and manifesting change in our lives.

If you study this issue of Starcraft and understand the concepts of Energy, of Light and of Matter and how these forms interrelate then you will have a basis from which to understabd telepathy and the reasons telepathy is a necessary tool for New Age men and women. Communication is of utmost importance. Sometimes words get in the way of true communication. Telepathy is thought transference with less interference from misunderstanding. You too can develope telepathy!

In the next issue of Starcraft we will print the information that deals with this. We hope you have enjoyed this issue and plan on subscribing again.

Thanks for your support on all levels.

****

DO YOU NEED GUIDANCE ?

<u>Counselling on personal problems</u>. Guidance on SPIRITUAL DEVELOPMENT

DO YOU NEED GUIDANCE?

<u>Counselling on personal problems</u>. Guidance on spiritual development.

<u>Life Readings</u>. Past life experience and karmic ties researched by **ESP**.

<u>Spiritual Healing</u> and energy balancing.

<u>Astrology-Numerology</u>. Natal charts prepared and analysed under spiritual guidance.

Character traits and spiritual potential given. Guidance on vocation and relationships.

For information and fees write:
Paraphysics Research Foundation
8855 Ashworth Ave. N.
Seattle, Washington 98103
Phone: (206) 525-9485

Single is the race, single
  Of men and of gods;
From a single mother we both drew breath
  But a difference of power in everthing
    keeps us apart.
Yet we can in greatness of mind
  Or of body be like the immortals,
Though we know not of what goal
  Fate has written that we shall run.

                Olympic poet, Pinder

Relive the adventure!

* PAST LIFE REGRESSIONS *

You can personally go back in time to past life experiences in a light reverie or alpha wave state of consciousness. The memories are your own and are the emotions and traumas from the past which are blocking progress now. Learn what these are and how to call on your god-self to reprogram the patterns.

TRANSMUTATION OF KARMA IS NOW TAKING PLACE FOR MANY PEOPLE. WE ARE MOVING INTO A NEW DIMENSION AND A NEW AGE. DO NOT REMAIN A PAWN ON A CHESS BOARD! TRANSMUTE YOUR OWN PATTERNS AND BE REBORN IN LIGHT!

Private consultations are arranged with Ms. Francesca here at the Retreat or set up on lecture tours. Write for locations of lectures and workshops or have your group sponsor one.

* WORKSHOPS *

Transmutation of Consciousness Reprogramming and aligning the levels of consciousness to balance and harmonize your life.

* NEW WORKSHOP AND LECTURE TO COME *

Man/Woman Relationships and Love in the New Age.

2 hour private regression $45.00
Workshops $25

Seeing is believing!

****

UNIFICATION MANTRAM

The sons of men are one and I am one with them.
I seek to love, not hate;
I seek to serve and not exact due service;
I seek to heal, not hurt.

Let pain bring due reward of light and love.
Let the Soul control the outer form,
And life, and all events,
And bring to light the Love
That underlies the happenings of the time.

Let vision come and insight.
Let the future stand revealed.
Let inner union demonstrate and outer cleavages be gone.
Let love prevail.
Let all men love.

 * GUEST CORNER *

THE NEW MILLENIUM OF PLANET EARTH

This is J W of Jupiter. We are contacting you to inform you of a great UFO wave now taking place throughout the U.S.A. ...Omaha, Nebraska - Maine - Connecticut. This not negative, but is part of the New Age Program for World Peace, harmony, balance in Earth's force fields and Man's higher spiritual centers of being.

MON-KA is putting a special wall of protection around you...so that you will not receive any contact that would be negative. We do not desire to have you affected by any undersirable frequencies. There will be many strange or odd accidents. This is due to the charging of great positive and negative poles in the Earth and the centers of Earth that were once active in the physical in ancient times, when the Earth was in an age of great enlightenment.

These Centers of cosmic energy frequencies were the positive forces through which the Ancients were able to materialize the miraculous wonders of that time. The Earth was then highly sensitive to the creative centers of cosmic polarity aligned with the Central Sun of this solar system.

The First of August, 1977 was the Earth's solar return of the Millenium, the planetary evolution of the cycle that begins a new time. A time period that has no equal since the time of the great enlightenment of MU (Lemuria). This extraordinary development has not been active or apparent in the whole written history of Earth, and no understanding by our Earth scientists... because there is no known history to refer back to. It is recorded in the memory cells of the soul --spiritual memory.

This in concise terms, means that the most positive time for mankind of Earth is the present time of now. The negative power is of lesser importance. In planetary terms it means positive Solar Action. The forces of Light or Good now take first precedence. The united Confederation of planets of Earth's solar system have the Cosmic Edict to clear the way for renewing of Earth for the New Age of Enlightenment that has been the subject of teachings of the New Age Enlightenment Groups worldwide. This initiative requires the active support and help of Earth's sister planets that have sworn their allegiance to the Cosmic Tribune of Creative Intelligence that is the oversoul Presence of the solar system.

It can be stated now that man can no longer ha have the power to push the button of an atomic bomb --percipitating the warfare of Death. This is insured by the activation of the cocmic forcefield in the Earth. Great magnetic currents will be active in the Earth once more. Thus imminent changes of the physical Earth and land frequencies throughout the planet. This is all the enformation it is possible for you to recieve at this time. Signing off. Blessings. J W of Jupiter.

Direct Telepathic Transmission August 15, 1977
Channel: Jackie White Star

Star Light Fellowship
   Unit 72
P.O.Box 202
Fort Lee, New Jersey
07024 USA

# Starcraft

This magazine has been printed at this time thanks to the dedication and generosity of some of our supporters. A substantial sum was contributed by one of our members who wishes to remain anonymous. Many others have been very generous in their support all along. Blessings to you, for it is through you that this is made manifest.

All of you who have subscriptions at this time will please note that this issue fills your subscription. A new fund will be started with the incoming subscription monies to insure the publication of Starcraft in the future. A reorganization within the Retreat is getting such things in order. If you wish to recieve our next issue of Starcraft please use the form at the bottom of the page. Thanks to each of you for your continuing interest and support. We are just entering a new phase of manifestation and new beginnings, so your help in any form is deeply appreciated.

SUBSCRIPTIONS

USA	$10
CANADA	$11
FOREIGN	$12

BACK ISSUES TO 1966 - $1.00 each

SOLAR LIGHT RETREAT

7700 AVE. OF THE SUN   CENTRAL POINT, ORE. 97501 U.S.A.

ORDER FORM

☐ STARCRAFT MAGAZINE SUBSCRIPTION
   (four issues- one magazine may contain more than one issue.)

☐ BACK ISSUES OF STARCRAFT - to 1966
   (Please state which issues you already have and we will send you others as long as they last.)

☞   * SEE PRICE LIST ABOVE *

check one:

☐ I am a new subscriber, my address is:

☐ I am an old subscriber, my current address is:

NAME..

ADDRESS...

....

ZIP..................

www.ingramcontent.com/pod-product-compliance
Lightning Source LLC
Chambersburg PA
CBHW080547230426
43663CB00015B/2747